THE
PASSION
TRANSLATION

THE BOOK OF
GENESIS

BroadStreet
PUBLISHING

The Passion Translation®
Genesis: Firstfruits

Published by BroadStreet Publishing® Group, LLC
BroadStreetPublishing.com
ThePassionTranslation.com

ABOUT THE PASSION TRANSLATION

The message of God's story is timeless; the Word of God doesn't change. But the methods by which that story is communicated should be timely; the vessels that steward God's Word can and should change. One of those timely methods is Bible translation. Bible translations are both a gift and a problem. They give us the words God spoke through his servants, but words can be poor containers for revelation because they leak! The meanings of words change from one generation to the next. Meaning is influenced by culture, background, and many other details. Just imagine how differently the Hebrew authors of the Old Testament saw the world three thousand years ago from the way we see it today!

There is no such thing as a truly literal translation of the Bible, for there is not an equivalent language that perfectly conveys the meaning of the biblical text. It must be understood in its original cultural and linguistic settings. This problem is best addressed when we seek to transfer meaning, not merely words, from the original text to the receptor language.

The purpose of The Passion Translation is to reintroduce the passion and fire of the Bible to the English reader. It doesn't merely convey the literal meaning of words. It expresses God's passion for people and his world by translating the original, life-changing message of God's Word for modern readers.

You will notice at times we've italicized certain words or phrases. These highlighted portions are not in the original Hebrew, Greek, or Aramaic manuscripts but are implied from the context. We've made these implications explicit for the sake of narrative clarity and to better convey the meaning of God's Word. This is a common practice by mainstream translations.

We've also chosen to translate certain names in their original Hebrew or Greek form to better convey their cultural meaning and significance. For instance, some translations of the Bible have substituted Jacob with James and Judah with Jude. Both Greek and Aramaic leave these Hebrew names in their original form. Therefore, this translation uses those cultural names.

God longs to have his Word expressed in every language in a way that would unlock the passion of his heart. Our goal is to trigger inside every English-speaking reader an overwhelming response to the truth of the Bible. This is a heart-level translation, from the passion of God's heart to the passion of your heart.

We pray this version of God's Word will kindle in you a burning desire for him and his heart, while impacting the church for years to come.

Please visit ThePassionTranslation.com for more information about The Passion Translation.

ABOUT THE TRANSLATOR

Dr. Brian Simmons is known as a passionate lover of God. After a dramatic conversion to Christ, Brian knew that God was calling him to go to the unreached people of the world and present the gospel of God's grace to all who would listen. With his wife, Candice, and their three children, he spent nearly eight years in the tropical rain forest of the Darien Province of Panama as a church planter, translator, and consultant. He assisted in the Paya-Kuna New Testament translation project, and after their ministry in the jungle, Brian was instrumental in planting a thriving church in New England (U.S.). He is the lead translator for The Passion Translation Project and travels full time as a speaker and Bible teacher. He has been happily married to Candice since 1971 and boasts regularly of his three children and nine grandchildren.

Follow The Passion Translation at:

Facebook.com/passiontranslation

Twitter.com/tPtBible

Instagram.com/passiontranslation

For more information about the translation project please visit:

ThePassionTranslation.com

GENESIS

Introduction

AT A GLANCE

Author: Moses the seer-prophet
Audience: Originally Israel, but this theological history speaks to everyone
Date: Sometime between 1520 and 1400 BC
Type of Literature: Theological history
Major Themes: Cosmic origins, God's blessing, the people of God, faith, and redemptive history
Outline: There are ten sections in the book of Genesis after its prologue, and each one begins with the Hebrew word for "Generation," or "The Family History":
Prologue — 1:1–2:3
Generations of Heaven and Earth — 2:4–4:26
Generations of Adam — 5:1–6:8
Generations of Noah — 6:9–9:29
Generations of Noah's Sons — 10:1–11:9
Generations of Shem — 11:10–26
Generations of Terah — 11:27–25:11
Generations of Ishmael — 25:12–18
Generations of Isaac — 25:19–35:29
Generations of Esau — 36:1–37:1
Generations of Jacob — 37:2–50:26

ABOUT GENESIS

Genesis is God's autobiography. The seal of perfection is stamped upon everything written in his Word. The combined skill of all the greatest literary minds could never design a composition that equals the splendor of the first chapter of Genesis. It stands in a class all by itself.

We see God at the very beginning as powerful, purposeful, wise, and full of glory. Speaking the word of creation from his eternal dwelling place of light, he created everything from nothing (Heb. 11:3). Creation takes us into the mystery of worship—we have no answers to our curiosity; we can only worship. Man was made by God not simply to analyze God as a scientist, astronomer, or philosopher. First and foremost, man was created to be a worshiper (John 4:24). We will never be able to take the mystery out of creation, for a God who is incomprehensible in his greatness accomplished it.

The purpose of creation is to display the glory of God. We are able to see in the created order of our universe the awesome wonder of the Maker of the heavens. The universe is God's advertisement—the display of his glory (Psalm 19:1). The earth is not "mother earth"; it is his footstool, and heaven is his throne. All of creation is for his pleasure.

But it is not the earth or the cosmos that is God's highest order; it is man and woman made after his image—creations in the likeness of God. God has created mankind to become a container for his glory. He longs to have the worship of those who love him, freely and with all their hearts!

PURPOSE

The purpose of Genesis is to give the origin of all things, both the cosmic order of the universe and the covenant relationship of God's people—demonstrating that God is the Creator and Originator of redemption. Not only do we find the beginning of the heavens and the earth, but we also see that Genesis provides the origin of nations, with God's choice of the Hebrews as the people through whom the Redeemer will come to the world.

Many have noted that Genesis is the "seed-plot" of the whole Bible, since every truth can be traced back to its source in this first book of God's Word. Genesis is the foundation upon which all revelation rests. It is quoted over sixty times in the New Testament. One of the over-arching themes of Genesis is God's blessing. We see the word "blessing" or "bless" eighty-eight times in this first book of the Bible. Does that not tell us that our Father God wants to bless us? If God blesses the fish and birds, how much more will he bless his beloved sons and daughters?

The primary way in which the Creator blessed created humanity was by bringing order to this disordered relationship. Through covenant, Yahweh lovingly sought after his beloved by choosing a people to be his very own, to steward and showcase his redemptive heart toward the world—a theme begun in Genesis and traced throughout the rest of the Hebrew Scriptures.

AUTHOR AND AUDIENCE

The book of Genesis is set within the larger collection of books known as the Pentateuch. Moses is traditionally attributed as the author of the first five books of the Bible, called the Torah or "the law of Moses" (Luke 24:27, 44; Acts 28:23) and the "Book of Moses" (Mark 12:26). Moses was a seer and a prophet who wrote his inspired account of creation and the days of the patriarchs for God's people between their leaving Egypt and reaching the promised land. Only God could have brought this level of revelation to Moses in order to offer revelation-insight into the formation and continuation of Israel's covenant relationship with Yahweh.

MAJOR THEMES

Origin of God's Creation. The first word of Genesis in Hebrew is *beresheet* and means "first," "chief," or "firstfruits." While the New Testament takes us into the new creation life of Christ until all things are made new, Genesis gives us the first-fruits of God's creation—from the heavens and the earth to the land and the seas;

from stars, planets, and plants to birds, sea creatures, and land animals; and finally God's crowning creative achievement, man and woman.

Many have noted how Genesis 1 is poetic in nature, showcasing the progress of creation from the lower to the higher, from the darker to the brighter, from the evening to the morning, from vessels to forms. Note that the Hebrew word for day is *yom* and can be translated in English into over fifty different words, such as "a twenty-four-hour day," "today," "time," "forever," "continually," "age," "life," "season," "perpetually," or "a period of time." The Hebraic mindset does not necessarily view *yom* as a twenty-four-hour period. The Scriptures speak frequently of the day of the Lord, which points to a time period of God's divine activity, not a day with a sunrise and sunset. Both Moses and Peter spoke of a thousand years being like one day.

The opening chapters of Genesis make it clear *who* created the heavens and the earth and everything in it: the God of Abraham, Isaac, and Jacob—Yahweh. Not only that, we also see the origin of the God-man relationship: a bliss-filled paradise became the home of Adam and Eve, Eden, whose very name reveals God's nature of love and grace. Humanity was created to experience the pleasure of being loved by God and relating to his heart. However, all is not as it was intended. For we witness in this first book of the Bible the origins of sin and all of the ensuing fallout.

Because Adam and Eve ate what was forbidden, pain entered the world: there is conflict in the home; the man produces food to eat through painful toil and the woman endures painful childbirth; all creation now labors with painful contractions; and we seek to make a name for ourselves through self-worship. Yet all is not lost! From the very beginning, God had a plan to rescue humanity and put this world back together, promising the famous Head-crusher of Gen. 3:15. This is the Protoevangelium, God's first announcement of a Savior, and presents a preview of Jesus Christ who would be wounded by the snake/sin on his heel but bring a death-blow to Satan by the power of his cross and resurrection— eventually restoring God's creation to the way he intended it to be.

Blessed to Be a Blessing. Blessing is perhaps the most important theological "glue" that holds Genesis together and connects it to the rest of the Hebrew Scriptures. In Gen. 1, God blesses humans (1:22, 28), and then they lose that blessing (ch. 3). God returns to this theme again in Gen. 12, where he seeks to restore this blessing to humanity once more through choosing a couple, Abraham and Sarah, and their *zera*—their seed, their offspring, their "nation." And this blessing is manifested in several lives, like Abraham's and Joseph's.

But what is this blessing? What does it mean to be "blessed" by Yahweh? A working definition is to "empower for abundant living in every sphere of life." This abundant-life empowerment flows from a vibrant relationship with God. When God blesses you, your life will soar into his abundance! This blessed, abundant life includes being fruitful (reproduction) and multiplying (increasing in number) (1:25); equal empowerment for both men and women to live on this planet (1:28); an infusion of power and favor to succeed in life (5:1–2); a relationship with the God of the universe (17:6); prosperity, abundance, and success (39:2). And yet, Yahweh's blessing was never an end in and of itself. We were always meant to leverage our abundant life for the sake of the world—we truly are blessed to be a blessing!

One of the clearest pictures Genesis offers of not only the meaning of blessing, but also the means of God's blessing through his people, is Joseph's story. Chapter 39 reveals "Yahweh's presence was with Joseph and he became successful while living in the house of his Egyptian master" (39:2). The implication is that Joseph excelled in everything, which carried over into Potiphar's household as well. And of course this blessing eventually flowed to Egypt and the surrounding nations when he assumed the role of second-in-command over Egypt. God blessed Joseph and in turn blessed the nations through him, opening the door for others to be fed. Joseph knew that God was in control and that he had been raised up by God to wear a yoke—the yoke of serving the will of God and nothing else, resulting in blessing over his life, the lives of his family, and the lives of the nations. As you read through Genesis, be sure to note every time you find the words "bless" and "blessing."

Origin of God's People. Coinciding with this renewed desire for God-empowered abundant living through an intimate, vibrant relationship with the Lord is his calling of a people to himself. One Old Testament scholar suggests this calling in Gen. 12 is a sort of second creation account, in which God's holy people are "created" through an act of grace, inviting Abram, who became Abraham, into a loving covenant relationship in order to birth a nation. Abram means "exalted father." Abraham means "father of a multitude." A generational transfer is in the heart of God and is here revealed to Abraham. Yahweh confirmed this covenant relationship between not only him and Abraham but also with all of his descendants throughout their generations.

Later in the New Testament, we see that this nation of descendants extends not only to Abraham's physical offspring, Israel and the Jewish people, but also to his spiritual "seed," the church. As the apostle Paul wrote to the Ephesians: "Our reconciling 'Peace' is Jesus! He has made Jew and non-Jew one in Christ. By dying as our sacrifice, he has broken down every wall of prejudice that separated us." (Eph. 2:14). He continues in Galatians: "And since you've been united to Jesus the Messiah, you are now Abraham's 'child' and inherit all the promises of the kingdom realm!" (Gal. 3:29). Non-Jewish believers are to be grateful for the Jewish roots of our faith. Our Messiah is Jewish and the Scriptures we read were given to the beloved Jewish people. We feast on the new-covenant riches, promises, and blessings that have been handed down to us through the "olive tree" of Judaism—the roots of which extend all the way back to Genesis!

Faith in God's Promises. Nearly half of the names listed in the famous Hall of Faith chapter in the book of Hebrews (ch. 11) are drawn from the book of Genesis. Abel had his heart set on the coming Sacrifice, confessed his sin, and brought the first and best of his flock as a sacrifice in faith, and God was pleased. Enoch was a man who walked in faith and was translated from earth to heaven without dying (*apotheosis*). Noah was moved with faith and acted on the revelation given to him. Leaving all that is familiar would display an incredible act of faith on Abraham's part, not to mention believing that barren Sarah would bear him a son that would multiply to descendants as numerous as the stars! Prompted by faith and contrary to his natural inclination, Isaac acted by faith in imparting his blessing to Jacob instead of Esau. In faith, Jacob asked to be buried near the spot where the Messiah would be crucified, knowing the fulfillment of the promise would be in Canaan, not Egypt. And Joseph's faith in God and the fulfillment of his dreams kept him faithfully waiting for his day of promotion, believing and trusting in God's perfect plans. We learn from these forebears of our faith that God really can be trusted, for he makes good on his promises!

Perhaps the greatest of all of these heroes of faith is Abraham, whom the apostle Paul offered as an example in explaining our own justification. Quoting Gen. 15:6, he wrote, "Because Abraham believed God's words, his faith transferred God's righteousness into his account" (Rom. 4:3). Abraham trusted every single word that Yahweh had spoken over his life. Paul goes on, extolling the virtues of Abraham's example, especially in offering up his son Isaac: "Against all odds, when it looked hopeless, Abraham believed the promise and expected God to fulfill it. . . . He never stopped believing God's promise, for he was made strong in his faith to father a child. And because he was mighty in faith and convinced that God had all the power needed to fulfill his promises, Abraham glorified God!" (Rom. 4:18, 20–21). Oh that we would follow in the footsteps of Abraham, truly the father of faith!

History of God's Redemption. From the beginning, the Lord God wanted nothing more than to plant himself in the dust of Adam and become life within him. Both a tree planted in a garden and God planted in man are the pictures we see in Gen. 2. As the tree was to receive nourishment from the soil, so Adam was to draw life and sustenance from his Maker, as one "planted" by the Lord. Obviously, things didn't turn out that way—and yet God didn't give up on his beloved! Genesis launches Yahweh's redemptive history.

The first question God asks in the Bible appears after our ancestors first sinned: "Adam, where are you?" (3:9). The question clearly shows that we belong to God, and that he longs for each of us to examine our own lives, be honest with him, and come out of hiding. It also launched God's redemptive movement to rescue us and restore our world—beginning with Yahweh-God making garments from animal skins to clothe Adam and Eve. Father God did what any good father would do when a child fails. He wrapped his love around them and did not degrade them. Moved by love, he clothed them to cover their shame. For God to use blood-stained animal skins as royal robes to clothe his beloved meant that animals had to be sacrificed to provide their covering. These themes continue throughout the book of Genesis, foreshadowing God's ultimate redemption in Jesus.

Noah's ark is a beautiful picture of Christ: it was made from sturdy wood (the humanity of Christ, Isa. 53:2; Dan. 9:26) and is sealed with tar (blood atonement); it was a place of salvation and preservation (Jesus our Savior); humanity is invited into this ark to find a place of security from judgment, and so we are hidden in Christ (Col. 3:3). When Abraham sacrifices his only son, there is a hint that one day God would require a human sacrifice to take away the sin of the world. On Yahweh's mountain, Moriah, where Abraham offered up Isaac, we see clearly the vision of God placing our sins upon his Son. Solomon's Temple was later built on Moriah (2 Chron. 3:1), where Israel offered sacrifices of atonement for their sins. The book ends with the death of Jacob, who longed to be buried in the cave of Machpelah purchased by Abraham from the Hittites in Gen. 23. Abraham, Isaac, and Jacob were all buried near the ancient site of Jerusalem, where, many centuries later, Jesus would be crucified, buried, and raised from the dead.

Many have noted how Jesus Christ is seen in Genesis in different pictures:

The Creator (Gen. 1:1; Col. 1:16)
The Beginning (Rev. 1:8)
The Light (Gen. 1:3, 16; John 8:12)
The Tree of Life (Gen. 2:9; John 15:1–5)
The Seed of the Woman (Gen. 3:15; Matt. 1:23)
The Clothing for Adam and Eve (Gen. 2:21; Rom. 13:11–14)
The Fire-Sword (Gen. 3:24; Heb. 4:12)
The Sacrifice of Isaac (Gen. 22; John 3:16)
The Heavenly Stairway (Gen. 28:12; John 1:51; 1 Tim. 2:5)
The Anointed Stone (Gen. 28:18–19; Acts 10:38; 1 Peter 2:1–5)
The Midnight Wrestling Man (Gen. 32:24–32; Gal. 5:17)
The Savior, Joseph (Gen. 37–50; Matt. 3:17)

GENESIS

Firstfruits

In the Beginning

1 When[a] God[b] created[c] the heavens and the earth,[d] [2]the earth was *completely* formless and empty, with nothing but darkness draped over the deep.[e] God's Spirit hovered[f] over the face of the waters.

---

a 1:1 Although most translations view verse 1 as an independent sentence serving as a general heading, it is likely that the first phrase serves as a subordinate time clause, such as "At the beginning (of time), God created" or "When God began the creation of heaven and the earth." The first word in Hebrew is *re'shiyth* and means "first," "chief," or "firstfruits." Genesis gives us *the firstfruits* of God's creation. The New Testament takes us into the new creation life of Christ until all things are made new.

b 1:1 This is *Elohim*, the commonly used Hebrew term for God. It stresses his sovereignty and power and could be translated "Mighty God." *Elohim* is the plural of *Eloah* and occurs nearly two thousand six hundred times in the Bible. *Eloah* is derived from the word *ahlah*, which means "to worship" or "to adore" and presents God as the One worthy of worship and adoration. After the word *Elohim*, there is an untranslatable marking, which most scholars believe is a direct object marker with the first and last of the Hebrew alphabet. However, it is seen by some as the word known as *Aleph-Tav*, which occurs over seven thousand times in the Hebrew text of the Old Testament. Some believe that this could be pointing to Jesus Christ who declared himself to be the "Aleph-Tav," or the "Beginning and the Ending." See Rev. 1:8, 17; 2:8; 22:13.

c 1:1 This is the word *bara'* and is used exclusively in the Old Testament for God's creativity, things which only God can do.

d 1:1 Or "the sky and the land." This is a merism (a figure of speech using two contrasting words to refer to an entirety) for the entire universe. See Ps. 33:6, 9. The Hebrew word for heaven appears seven times in this chapter (vv. 1, 8, 9, 14, 15, 17, 20). The first verse of the Bible shouts out: "God is all powerful!" Creating is an integral part of God's nature.

e 1:2 See Jer. 4:23–27. Darkness is a frequent Biblical metaphor for evil, misfortune, and death. It appears here as something more than an absence of light—a distinct entity. See Isa. 45:7.

f 1:2 Or "God's Spirit gently vibrated." The Syriac cognate word can mean "to incubate" or "to brood." The Hebrew verb *rachaph* means "to flutter," "to gently move," "to hover over with gentle wavering," or "to be relaxed (grow soft)" and describes the utmost care and affection of a mother eagle caring for her young (Deut. 32:11). This word is also used for a bridegroom hovering over his bride. This same Holy Spirit overshadowed (brooded over) a virgin named Mary to bring his perfect man into the world (Luke 1:35). God's Spirit danced over the waters on creation's morning.

³And then God announced:ᵃ

"Let there be light," and light burst forth!ᵇ

⁴And God saw the light as pleasing and beautiful;ᶜ he used the light to dispel the darkness. ⁵God called the light "Day," and the darkness "Night." And so, evening gave way to morning—the first day.ᵈ
⁶And God said: "Let there be a domeᵉ between the waters to separate the water *above* from the water *below*." ⁷⁻⁸He made the dome and called it "Sky," and separated the water above the dome from the water below the dome. Evening gave way to morning—day two.
⁹And God said: "Let the water beneath the sky be gathered into one place, and let the dry ground appear."ᶠ And so it happened. ¹⁰God called the dry ground "Land," and the gathered waters he called "Seas." And God saw *the beauty of* his creation, and he was very pleased.
¹¹Then God said, "Let the land burst forth with growth: plants that bear seeds of their own kind, and every

---

a 1:3 This is the Hebrew word *'amar*, which is most often translated "said," but it can also mean "to think," "to imagine," or "to speak inside your heart." God imagined light and there was light. God spoke and shattered the cosmic silence to give birth to creation. God spoke ten times in the creation account—the Ten Commandments of creation. See also Ps. 33:9; John 1:1–3. God's thoughts had already imagined and shaped the largest galaxy and the smallest atom before he created them. With exquisite skill and creativity, God shaped all things by his word and spoke them into being with intricate detail and skill (Heb. 11:3). A dimension separate from the Being of God was birthed. No detail was too small for God as he prepared to unveil his masterpiece of wisdom, his dream come true. God speaks order and goodness into his creation.

b 1:3 Or "and there was light." God created light but did not create the sun until the fourth day. It was God himself filling the universe with the light of his presence and glory. The Hebrew verbs used with the phrases "Let there be" and "and there was" are both related to the holy name Yahweh: *Yehi* (Let there be) and *Wayhi* (and there was). As he released this word of power, the universe began to expand and has been expanding ever since (Heb. 1:3). God's kingdom operates according to the principle of an endless increase (Isa. 9:6–7), not by a power that diminishes over time.

c 1:4 The Hebrew word *tov* can be translated "pleasing" or "good (beautiful)" and is used seven times in this chapter (vv. 4, 10, 12, 18, 21, 25, 31). God is mentioned 35 times (7 × 5) and earth 21 times (7 × 3) in the creation account. God's goodness is his intention in creation and embeds beauty within all he makes.

d 1:5 God begins in darkness and brings forth a new day. Chaos never hinders God from bringing forth light and order. It is not difficult for God to work where there is darkness, chaos, and confusion. See Ps. 139:12.

e 1:6 Or "vault, expanse (atmosphere)." See Ezek. 1:22.

f 1:9 On the third day, the dry ground was raised up out of the waters (Ps. 104:6–9), then God clothed it with vegetation. This can be compared to the new birth that comes to a believer, who is risen and clothed with the virtues of Christ. See Rom. 6:1–11; Eph. 2:1–10. The progress of creation moves from the lower to the higher, from the darker to the brighter, from the evening to the morning. The Word of God puts light into darkness, land in the midst of sea, air in the midst of water, and life in the midst of the uninhabited earth. In creation, God starts with form and fills it with fullness. In nature, the seed sprouts: first the bud, then the blossom, and then the fruit. In human life it is the baby, the child, and then the mature adult. So, it is also in grace.

variety of fruit tree, each with power to multiply[a] from its own seed."[b] And so it happened. [12]The land flourished with grasses, Every variety of seed-bearing plant, and trees bearing fruit with their seeds in them. And God loved what he saw, *for it was beautiful.* [13]Evening gave way to morning—day three.

[14-15]And God said: "Let there be *bright* lights to shine in space *to bathe the earth with their light.* Let them serve as signs[c] to separate the day from night, and signify the days, seasons,[d] and years." And so, it happened. [16]God made two great lights: the brighter light to rule the day and the lesser light to rule the night. He also spread *the tapestry of* shining stars[e] [17]and set them all in the sky to illuminate the earth, [18]to rule over the day and to rule over the night, and to separate the light from darkness. God *loved* what he saw, *for it was beautiful.* [19]Evening gave way to morning—day four.

[20]God said: "*Let there be life!* Let the waters swarm with sea life, and let the sky be filled with soaring birds *of every kind.*"

[21]God created huge sea creatures[f] and every living creature that moves of every kind—swarming in the water and flying in the sky, according to their species. God loved what he saw, *for it was beautiful.* [22]God blessed[g] them, saying: "Reproduce and be fruitful! Fill the waters of the sea with life, and the earth with flying birds!" [23]Evening gave way to morning—day five.

[24]God said: "Let the earth produce every class and kind of living creature: livestock, crawling things, wild animals, each after its kind." And so it happened. [25]God made the wild animals according to their species, livestock

---

a 1:11 Or "with seed within itself," or "seeding seed." The work of God at creation involved three separations. (1) God separated the light from darkness (v. 4). (2) God separated the waters above from the waters beneath (vv. 6–8). (3) God divided the water from the land (v. 9). Out of this separated, resurrected land, God brought a variety of life.

b 1:11 Everything with life produces life after its own kind. Each species is able to reproduce itself (Matt. 7:16–19; John 3:6; 2 Cor. 5:17; James 1:18; 1 Peter 1:23; 2 Peter 1:4). The Lord Jesus was the firstfruit of a new species of humanity.

c 1:14–15 The heavens contain the embedded codes of God's glory (Ps. 19) full of symbolic signs that testify to his greatness and wisdom. They are like huge billboards and advertisements in the sky telling people how good and great our Creator is. See also Psalm 19:1–6; Rom. 10:18.

d 1:14–15 Or "appointed times (feasts)." See Lev. 23:4. The stars are for signs, signals, and seasons.

e 1:16 Scripture often used stars as a picture of believers or ministries who shine with supernatural light (Dan. 12:3; 1 Cor. 15:40–44; Phil. 2:15). We see from Psalm 147:4 that as God named the "sun" and "moon," he also gave names to each of the stars. It is noted by numerous scholars that Genesis 1 never uses the names for sun (*shemesh*) or moon (*yareach*) which were also Canaanite names of deities. This was for polemical purposes against the stories of the gods and other creation narratives in the ancient Near East.

f 1:21 Or "sea monsters, dragons, dinosaurs."

g 1:22 This is the first mention in the Bible of God's blessing. On this day, God created life— birds and sea life—and blessed them. This blessing included being fruitful (reproduction) and multiplying (increasing in number).

according to their species,[a] and all the creatures that creep along the ground according to their species. And God loved what he saw, *for it was beautiful.*

Shaped by Love

[26]Then God said: "Let us[b] make a man and a woman[c] in our image[d] to be like us.[e] Let them reign over the fish of the sea, the birds of the air, the livestock, over the creatures that creep along the ground,[f] and over the wild animals."

[27]So God created man *and woman* and shaped them with his image inside them.
In his own *beautiful* image, he created *his masterpiece.*
Yes, male and female he created them.

[28]And God blessed them *in his love,*[g] saying: "Reproduce and be fruitful! Populate the earth and subdue it![h] Reign over the fish of the sea, the

---

a 1:25 God had a lamb before he had a man. Metaphorically, Jesus (God's Lamb) was slain before the foundation of the world (Rev. 13:8). The print of the nails was upon him even as his hands formed the world. As the Creator shaped Adam from dust, redeeming mercy was stamped upon him.

b 1:26 The plural form of the verb indicates there were more being(s) than Father God in the activities of creation. When taken as a whole, the Bible also points to the Holy Spirit and God the Son as participators in the glory of creation. See John 1:1–3; Heb. 1:1–3.

c 1:26 That is, humanity. The Hebrew word is simply *'adam,* which can be "man," but without a definite article it is here used as a collective term for man and woman. The definite article *the* does not occur before the word *man* until after God made woman, and together, they are *'adam.* According to the Talmud, the three Hebrew letters of Adam's name represent the initials of three men: Adam, David, and Messiah. The Hebrew word *'adam* means "to show (blood) red," and *adamu* means "to make." The statement to "make (*adamu*) Adam (ruddy) from (red) soil (*adamah*)" is full of Hebrew puns that are lost in translation.

d 1:26 Or "as our image." Image can also be translated "representation" or "resemblance." God created someone like himself to reflect who he is into all his creation. He created trees after their kind, birds after their kind, fish after their kind, and animals after their kind, but now he creates a God-kind of being. Man and woman will resemble him and bring his image into the created order. Christ is the image of God (Rom. 8:29; 1 Cor. 11:7; 2 Cor. 3:18; 4:4; Col. 1:15; 3:10; Heb. 1:3). The first man, Adam, was a type or figure of the Last Adam, Christ. See Rom. 5:14; 1 Cor. 15:40–58.

e 1:26 Or "according to our likeness," or "to be like us (comparable to us)." God is neither male nor female (John 4:23–24), but he has both male and female dimension to his nature. What is this image given to each of us? It includes personality, the capacity for worship, and the ability to make moral decisions (our conscience), and the ability to reflect God. Created as his image-bearers, all human beings bear the expression or image of God. As "photographs" of God, our characteristics are copies of his. Because he desires to "give" himself for you and to you, he took his own nature and likeness and fashioned a creature just like him—one he could love with unlimited passion.

f 1:26 Man was meant to rule over all the things that creep along the ground, including the "serpent and scorpion," which represent the powers of darkness (Luke 10:18–20; James 3:7–8).

g 1:28 God's blessing upon the human family implies love. God blesses both men and women, empowering them to live on this planet, infusing them with power and favor to succeed in life.

h 1:28 The word subdue means "to take dominion" or "control." This would imply harnessing of natural resources in an appropriate fashion, caring for the earth, cultivating and harvesting its fields, mining its resources, and releasing its potential to benefit God's highest creation, humankind. See Ps. 8:6–8.

birds of the air, and every creature that lives on earth."[a]

²⁹And God said: "I give you every seed-bearing plant growing throughout the earth, vegetables, and every fruit-bearing tree with its seed within itself. They will be your food.[b] ³⁰They will also be food for every animal and bird, and every creature that moves on the ground—every creature with the breath of life."[c] And so it happened.

³¹God surveyed all he had made and said, "I love it!" For it pleased him greatly. Evening gave way to morning—day six.[d]

Creation Details

2 And so the creation of the heavens and the earth were completed in all their vast array.[e] ²By the seventh day,[f] God had completed creating his masterpiece, so on the seventh day, he rested from all his work. ³So God blessed the seventh day and made it sacred, because on it, he paused to rest from all his work of creation.[g]

---

a 1:28 Man and woman were both given the command to care for the earth and subdue all things. Man and woman, blessed by their Creator, with authority to rule with him as co-regents. God's *image* is reflected in both men and women and so is rulership.

b 1:29 After the fall of Adam and Eve, meat was likely included in their diet. See also Gen. 9:3; 1 Tim. 4:4–5.

c 1:30 A day will come when the carnivorous animals will become herbivorous again. See Isa. 11:7; 65:25.

d 1:31 Because God created man on the sixth day, the number six is the Biblical number of man.

e 2:1 The seven days of creation hint at the seven stages through which one passes to become fully mature in Christ, complete in his image. Once we lived our sinful, empty lives in spiritual darkness (Eph. 2:1–3), the Holy Spirit brooded over our soul to draw us to salvation (John 6:44). Then God spoke his word of power, cascading revelation-light into our being (2 Cor. 4:6). The Savior, Jesus the Word, is the Light of salvation (John 8:12). Until finally, we cease from our own striving and enter into the Sabbath rest of completion and maturity (Heb. 4:11).

f 2:2 The Hebrew word for day is *yom* and can be translated in English into over fifty different words, such as "a twenty-four-hour day," "today," "time," "forever," "continually," "age," "life," "season," "perpetually," or "a period of time." The Hebraic mindset does not necessarily view *yom* as a twenty-four-hour period. For example, the Scriptures speak frequently of the day of the Lord, which again, points to a time period of God's divine activity, not a day with a sunrise and sunset.

g 2:3 God was not weary; he simply rejoiced in his masterpiece. God's work in us, for us, and through us, continues through time. God's last day of creating (6th) is man's first day. As soon as man was created, he rested with God. In this way, he became one with God, dwelling with him and resting in his accomplishments. There is no mention of evening and morning completing the seventh day, for God's Sabbath rest endures forever, and there is no night there. Our true Sabbath rest is found in the finished work of Christ (Matt. 11:28–30; Col. 2:16–17; Heb. 3:17–4:9; Rev. 21:25).

⁴This is the account[a] of the heavens and the earth after they were created.[b]

At the time[c] Yahweh-God[d] created earth and heaven, ⁵there was yet no vegetation, grains of the field, or shrubs sprouting on the earth, for there was no one to cultivate the land,[e] and Yahweh-God had not yet sent rain. ⁶In those days a mist[f] arose from the soil and watered the whole face of the ground.

⁷Yahweh-God scooped up a lump of soil,[g] sculpted a man, and blew into his nostrils the breath of life.[h] The man came alive—a living soul![i]

---

a 2:4 Or "These are the generations (genealogies)." This phrase is used numerous times to begin a new section in the story line of Genesis.

b 2:4 This is the word *bara'* and is used exclusively in the Old Testament for God's creativity, things which only God can do. However, there is the Hebrew letter *hei* inserted into the word, which is incorrect grammatically. The letter *hei* is the fifth letter in the Hebrew alphabet and is recognized by Jewish sages as the "divine breath of God." Its occurrence here signifies that it was God's breath that gave birth to all that is created. See Ps. 33:6.

c 2:4 See footnote 2:2 on the Hebrew word *yom*.

d 2:4 The Hebrew is *Yahweh-Elohim*, or "the God who is Yahweh," the God of mercy and power.

e 2:5 Before the earth could flourish under God's blessing, there needed to be a man and woman to take dominion. The Lord created them to walk with him and to cultivate a garden. God made the earth to need a human touch. God and man were to work together to subdue, cultivate, and take dominion of the earth. See Ps. 115:16.

f 2:6 Or "vapor," "mist," or "subterranean spring."

g 2:7 Or "clay" or "dust." The Hebrew contains an obvious play on words, a paronomasia, for the word for man is *'adam*, and the Hebrew word for soil (dust) is *'adamah*. See Job 10:9. Everything else was formed by an act of speech—only man was sculpted by the hands of God (Isa. 29:16). One day, Jesus picked up some earth, spat on it, and made mud; he touched the eyes of a blind man with it, and the blind man saw.

h 2:7 Or "the breath of lives." To breathe into someone's nostrils is what happens when two people kiss. God kissed life into Adam. God's Word likewise is "God-breathed" (2 Tim. 3:16). Jesus also blew his breath upon his beloved disciples (John 20:21–22). The lovers of God long for this "kiss" (Song. 1:2). See also Ezek. 37:9. Instantly, every portion of Adam's being was filled with life as Spirit-Wind poured into the man of clay lying in his Creator's arms. Adam's first sight was looking into the eyes of the Image-Maker. The dust of earth and the breath of Deity mingled as one, so that Adam could interact in both realms (physical and spiritual). This breath or "Spirit of life" was more than air; it brought intelligence, spirit, wisdom, light, and the image of God into Adam (Job 32:8).

i 2:7 The Mishnah (a collection of rabbinical teachings) uses a synonym for nephesh (soul). The word is *mav'eh*, derived from the root *ba'ah*, a verb that means "to ask," "to seek," or "to request—as in prayer." In other words, the Talmud defines man as "the creature that prays." Furthermore, the Talmud teaches that even nephesh, the life-sustaining soul, is synonymous with prayer. A nuanced translation could be "and man was manifested as a praying being (one who could commune with God)." In a sense, being human means moving in the direction of the divine design that God embedded within us. See Ps. 109:4.

⁸Then Yahweh-God planted*a* a lush garden paradise*b* in the East,*c* in the Land of Delight;*d* and there he placed the man he had formed. ⁹Yahweh-God made all kinds of beautiful trees to grow there—fruitful trees to satisfy the taste. In the middle of the garden*e* he planted the Tree of Life*f* and the Tree of the Knowledge of Good and Evil.*g*

¹⁰Flowing from the Land of Delight was a river*h* to water the garden, and from there, it divided into four branches.*i* ¹¹The first river, Overflowing Increase,*j* encircles the gold-laden land of Havilah.*k* ¹²The gold of that

---

a 2:8 The Lord wanted to plant himself in the dust of Adam and become life within him. Both a tree planted in a garden and God planted in man are the pictures we see in Genesis 2. As the tree was to receive nourishment from the soil, so Adam was to draw life and sustenance from his Maker. Life for Adam depended on what he did with the "Tree." Life for you and me depends on what we do with the Tree on which Jesus died. Jesus Christ is now to us the Tree of Life and is accessible to all who come by faith (John 15:1–8; Heb. 10:19–20; Rev. 2:7; 22:2).

b 2:8 Man began in a garden, sinned in a garden, and was driven out of a garden (Gen. 3:23). Then Jesus came. He went into a garden called Gethsemane as the Perfect Man and tasted the fruits of our suffering and pain (Matt. 26:39). He was then laid in a garden tomb that we might become the garden of his delight (Song. 6:2–3). God set man in a garden, not in a factory to toil, nor in a school to study, but in a garden—a place where life grows.

c 2:8 That is, east of the land of Israel.

d 2:8 Or "Eden," a homonym that can mean "a plain (steppe)," or "enjoyment," "bliss," "pleasure," or "delight." A bliss-filled paradise became the home of Adam and Eve. Eden's very name reveals God's nature of love and grace. See also Song. 4:12–15; 6:2; Isa. 51:3. Eden is the realm of glory and bliss that God wants to unveil to the believer. Ezekiel called it both the garden of God and the Mountain of God (Ezek. 28:13–16).

e 2:9 Metaphorically, the garden of God is within the believer. In the middle of our "garden," we are feeding on one of these two trees. See Song. 4:12–15; Jer. 31:12; Joel 2:3; Rom. 8:6; Gal. 5:16–17; Col. 1:26–27.

f 2:9 That is, the Tree of Life, or the Life-Giving Tree. The Tree of Life for the believer is Jesus Christ, the Wisdom of God. See Ps. 1:3; Prov. 3:18; 11:30; 13:12; Song. 2:3; Jer. 17:8.

g 2:9 That is, the tree that gives the knowledge of good and evil, a possible merism for "the knowledge of everything." The great need of the human heart is life (relationship), not knowledge. God never intended for man to covet knowledge apart from a relationship to God. In the beginning, God didn't give Adam a list of commandments but offered him living food to sustain him. Jesus Christ is that Living Tree. He is meant to be the life and sustenance of all whom God has formed (John 6:57). By eating of the Tree, Adam would daily show his dependence on God. See John 6:53–54; Rev. 2:7.

h 2:10 Eden is a preview of the New Jerusalem. See Rev. 22:1–2.

i 2:10 Or "four heads (headstreams)." As the one river (God is the one River) went from the garden, it separated into four heads. Four is the number of universality (four winds, four corners of the earth). These rivers refresh and water the whole world. Rivers are frequent metaphors for the Holy Spirit that Jesus gives us and the life-giving presence of God. See Ps. 46:4; Ezek. 47; John 7:37–39; Rev. 22:1–2. The Hebrew word for river (*nahar*) comes from a root word that means "sparkle," or "to be cheerful." The River of God will truly make his people sparkle with cheer!

j 2:11 Or "Pishon," which means "overflowing increase," "to leap forth," or "to spread out."

k 2:11 Havilah has a number of possible meanings: "to cause to grow," "to give birth out of pain," "a stretch of sandy land," "mud," "to twist or whirl in a circular or spiral manner (to writhe or fall grievously in pain or fear)," "to grieve," "be sore pained," "be sorrowful," "tremble," or "be wounded." All of the possible meanings seem to point to our human nature. The overflowing increase of God's river within us uncovers the gold hidden in the mud.

land is pure, with many pearls and onyx[a] found there.[b] [13]The second river, Gushing,[c] flows through the entire land of Cush.[d] [14]The third river, Swift Flowing,[e] flows east of Assyria.[f] And the fourth is the river Fruitfulness.[g]

[15]Yahweh-God took[h] the man and placed him in the garden of Eden to work[i] and watch over it.[j] [16]And Yahweh-God commanded him: "You may freely eat of every fruit[k] of the garden. [17]But you must not eat of the Tree that gives the knowledge of good and evil, for when you eat from it you will most certainly die."[l]

Creation of Adam and Eve

[18]Then Yahweh-God said, "It is not good[m] for the man to be alone. Therefore, I will fashion a suitable partner

---

a 2:12 Onyx were mounted to the breastplate of the High Priest and adorn the gates to the New Jerusalem. See Ex. 25:7; Rev. 21:19–20.

b 2:12 The flowing river with its gold and precious stones points to finding treasure in the river of life, a beautiful metaphor for the life of Jesus, flowing within us. God's loving generosity provided man with these garden treasures. See 1 Cor. 3:1–15; Rev. 21:11–21.

c 2:13 Or *Gihon*, which means "to gush (as a geyser)" or "to give birth."

d 2:13 Cush means "darkened" and refers to Nubia, one of the earliest civilizations of ancient Africa (present day Ethiopia).

e 2:14 Or *Hiddekel* (Tigris), which means "swift (flowing)" or "like a swift arrow in flight."

f 2:14 Or "Asshur," comes from the Hebrew word for "successful."

g 2:14 Or "Euphrates" which means "fruitfulness." When we interpret together the names of the four rivers we read: "The River of God will bring overflowing increase, gush like a geyser, to swiftly bring God's people to success and fruitfulness." See John 7:37–39. It was a limitless land of freedom. God gave the entire paradise of Eden to earth's first pair—a realm of endless pleasure without sin.

h 2:15 The Hebrew word for "took" (*laqach*) can also mean "to marry" or "take a wife."

i 2:15 Or "serve." The Hebrew word for "work" (*'abad*) can also mean "worship." Our work is to be of service to God and as an act of worship (Col. 3:23–24). God validates working for him, as Adam did, to steward and tend the garden.

j 2:15 The Hebrew word is often used in the Old Testament for "watchman." Adam's role as the watchman over God's creation was to keep the garden (within him, Song. 1:6) and watch over it to keep the serpent out. Man's created role is protector, keeper, and watchman! God wants to redeem what was lost and nurture his sons and daughters making them into strong "keepers" and "watchmen" over his work on earth.

k 2:16 Or "tree."

l 2:17 Or "dying you will die." God is neither unkind nor harsh; our tender Father God is gracious and generous to humanity. God alone knows what is good for us. To enjoy the good, we must trust and obey him. He knows that true freedom is in the loving shade of Eden. God knows that if we disobey, we will have decided for ourselves what is good and what is not good. We will have eaten the forbidden fruit and made ourselves our own gods. Death came into the world through Adam's sin (1 Cor. 15:22).

m 2:18 Or "good," "pleasant," "cheerful," or "beautiful." God's loving gifts can be seen in giving man his life-breath, a beautiful place of bliss (Eden) to work in, and now, a life-partner.

to be his help and strength."*a* ¹⁹For Yahweh-God had formed from the soil every animal of the field and every bird of the air and brought them before the man to see what he would call them. So, whatever the man called the living creature, that was its name.*b* ²⁰He gave names to all the various cattle, birds, and wild animals, but Adam could not find a fitting companion *that corresponded to him.* ²¹So Yahweh-God caused Adam to fall into a deep trance, and while he slept, he took a portion of Adam's side*c* and closed its place with flesh. ²²Then Yahweh-God used the portion of Adam's side and skillfully crafted*d* a woman*e* and presented her to him.*f* ²³Then Adam said,

"At last! *One like me!*
Her bones were formed from my
    bones,

---

a 2:18 This is the Hebrew word *'ezer*, frequently used for military help and a term ascribed to God himself fourteen times (e.g. Psalm 33:20; 54:4). It could be translated "strong rescuer." We would never say that God is inferior to man, nor should we say the woman is inferior to man, for both God and the woman are *'ezer*. God's choice of *'ezer* indicates that the woman is a man's first line of defense and an equal partner in the journey of life. The *'ezer* is God's gift to the husband. The woman's role is more than an assistant to man. She is the dynamic solution to man's loneliness as one who protects, reveals, and helps. Some see the ancient pictographic rendering of *'ezer* as *'E* (eye) - *Z* (man) - *R* (weapon), to mean "the revealer of the enemy." Both God and Adam wanted a partner. God wanted a man to till and work the garden, accomplishing God's purpose for man—to bring forth fruit. But Adam needed a bride, a partner for life who would be able to live and move and have her being in him. So, God gave Adam a job and a wife. All of this was to be a picture to Adam of God's yearning for a forever partner who will not just work alongside of him but also love and cherish him.

b 2:19 As he named each animal, Adam was expressing the authority God gave him to subdue and take dominion. With incredible intellectual abilities, Adam memorized the names of countless animals and all their subspecies. Adam was created with an organizational, administrative capacity which enabled him to identify and define the world around him.

c 2:21 Or "inner chamber." See also v. 22 and John 19:34. The word that is usually translated "side" or "rib" is an obscure one that can mean a structural element essential for something's existence (like a beam for a house or hull for a boat).

d 2:22 This verb is not used for anything else in the creation account, only for the woman. It takes one verse to describe the creation of man; six verses to describe the creation of woman.

e 2:22 Eve was not taken from Adam's feet to dominate her, but from his side, near his heart, to cherish her.

f 2:22 God instituted marriage by forming them and bringing them to each other. With the original genetics of man, the Lord fashioned a companion for Adam who powerfully expanded the graces and expression of himself. The great gift God gave to the woman was the ability to conceive and give birth. As the two came together, mankind would express a fuller, more complete picture of God. See Eccl. 4:9.

and her flesh from my flesh!
This one will be called: 'Woman,'
for she was taken from man."*a*

[24]For this reason, a man leaves his father and his mother to be *unselfishly* attached to*b* his wife. They become one flesh *as a new family!* [25]The man and his wife felt no shame, unaware that they were both naked.

The Fall

3 Now the snake*c* was the most cunning*d* of all living beings that Yahweh-God had made. He *deviously* asked the woman, "Did God really tell you, 'You must not eat fruit from any tree of the garden . . . ?'"

[2]But the woman *interrupted*, "—We may eat the fruit of any tree in the garden, [3]except the tree in the center of the garden. God told us, 'Don't eat its fruit, or even touch it,*e* or you'll die.'"

[4]But the snake said to her, "You certainly won't die. [5]God knows that the moment you eat it, your eyes will be opened, and you will be like God,*f* knowing both good and evil."

[6]When the woman saw that the tree produced delicious fruit, delightful to look upon, and desirable to give one insight, she took its fruit and ate it.*g* She gave some to her husband, who was with her, and he also ate it.*h* [7]*Immediately*, their eyes were opened, and they realized they were naked, *vulnerable,*

---

a 2:23 Or "from her man (husband)." Just as God reached into himself and took a portion of his being (image and likeness) to make man, he reached into man and took a portion of Adam to sculpt the woman. If Adam is dust refined, then the woman is double refined, for she was taken from man and shaped again by God's hand. There are many word plays found in this portion of Scripture. The word for man is *'ish* and the word for woman is *'ishsah*. The Son of Man also went into the deep sleep of death in order that his beloved bride would come forth. Eve was in Adam before she became the Bride; we were chosen in the Anointed One before we were born (Eph.1:4). Adam and Eve ruled together over this paradise; the Bride of Christ will rule and reign with him over a restored creation. The Spiritual Bridegroom and the Mystical Bride are the counterparts to this story.

b 2:24 Literally, "in his wife." This is the Hebrew word *dabaq* and means "to follow hard after" or "attaching oneself to another as an act of unselfishness," the opposite of looking out only for yourself. See Matt. 19:4–6. The Son of God likewise left his Father to join himself to (in) us, his Bride.

c 3:1 The Hebrew word for snake (serpent) is *nachash*, a very elastic term in Hebrew. It can function as a noun, a verb, or even as an adjective. When *nachash* functions as a noun, it means snake; when *nachash* serves as a verb, it means "to practice divination (deception)." When *nachash* has the definite article attached to it (as in this verse—the snake) it could be translated "the diviner (deceiver)." When *nachash* serves as an adjective, its meaning is "shining," or polished (as in—shiny). By adding the definite article to the word, *ha nachash* would then be rightly translated "the shining one." Angelic or divine beings are elsewhere described in the Bible as shining or luminous, at times with this very word, *nachash*. The shining one is the literal meaning of Lucifer. See Isa. 14:12.

d 3:1 There is a word play on the words *naked* in the previous verse and *cunning*. They both come from the same Hebrew triliteral root.

e 3:3 There is no mention of God forbidding touching the fruit tree; Eve was adding to God's command.

f 3:5 Or "like gods (divine beings)." See 2 Sam. 14:17; 2 Cor. 11:3.

g 3:6 See 1 Tim. 2:14.

h 3:6 Man's sin began with a tree and ended on a tree. See Rom. 5:12, 17–19.

and ashamed; so they sewed fig leaves*ᵃ* together for coverings.

God Manifests in the Garden

⁸Then Adam and his wife heard the sound*ᵇ* of Yahweh-God passing through*ᶜ* the garden in the breeze of the day.*ᵈ* So, they hid among the trees concealing themselves from the face of Yahweh-God.

⁹Then Yahweh-God called Adam's name and asked, "Where are you?"*ᵉ*

¹⁰Adam answered, "I heard your *powerful* presence moving in the garden, and I was afraid because I was naked; so I hid."

¹¹"Who told you that you were naked?" God said. "Did you eat the fruit of the tree that I commanded you not to eat?"

¹²Adam *pointed to the woman* and said,

"The woman you placed alongside me—
she gave me fruit from the tree,
and I ate it."*ᶠ*

¹³So Yahweh-God said to the woman, "What have you done?"
The woman *pointed to the snake* and said,
"The *shining* snake tricked me, and I ate."

¹⁴Yahweh-God then said to the snake:
"Because you have done this,
You are cursed above every wild animal,
Condemned above every creature of the field!

---

a 3:7 The fig tree was the only thing Jesus cursed while on earth (Matt. 21:19). Fig leaves are a picture of whatever we hide behind to cover our spiritual shame. This is the first attempt of man to cover his "nakedness." The works of man are never enough to cover our sinfulness, for it only partially covered them. The robe of righteousness that Jesus clothes us in is perfect. See 2 Cor. 5:21.

b 3:8 Or "voice."

c 3:8 Or "going (walking) back and forth repeatedly." That is, the sound or voice of God *was heard from all directions*. It is the voice that "walks" back and forth, back and forth, repeating the sound over and over. God has no feet, nor a body. His voice is coming into the Garden as if it were everywhere at once.

d 3:8 Or "walking in the spirit of the day," or "moving in the breeze (breezy time) of the day." The implication is that God had been doing this daily, wanting friendship and intimacy with his newly created couple.

e 3:9 When Adam first sinned, he should have gone immediately to God to beg for mercy and forgiveness. Instead he did just what millions are doing today: he ran and hid from God so that God had to come and look for him. God knew where he was hiding but wanted Adam to admit his shame. The first question God asks in the Bible: "Adam, where are you?" shows that we belong to God. He longs for each person to examine our own lives, be honest with him, and come out of hiding. The first question of the New Testament is, "Where is the child who was born King of the Jews?" And the first question Jesus asks is, "What do you seek?" Our answers to these three questions hold the keys to understanding the need of our heart, our life's passion, and God's plan for our lives. See Matt. 6:33; John 1:38–39.

f 3:12 Blame shifting was the beginning of marital disharmony. Only the love of Christ can heal the wounds between men and women.

You will slither on your belly
and eat dust[a] all the days of your
life!
[15]And I will place *great* hostility
between you and the woman,
and between her seed[b] and
yours.
He will crush your head
as you crush his heel."[c]
[16]Then God said to the woman,
"I will cause your labor pains
in childbirth to be
intensified;[d]
with pain,[e] you will give birth to
children.

You will desire[f] *to dominate* your
husband,
but he will *want to* dominate
you."[g]
[17]And to Adam he said,
"Because you obeyed your wife
instead of me,
and you ate from the *forbidden*
tree
when I had commanded you not
to;
the ground will be cursed because
of you.
You will eat of it through painful
toil[h] all the days of your life.

---

a 3:14 Adam was made from dust, now the snake is cursed to feed on dust (Isa. 65:25). Whatever we withhold from God becomes food for the enemy. We choose to make our dust-life the dwelling place for the demonic or the divine.

b 3:15 Or "offspring." The *seed* of the woman is Jesus Christ. The male carries *the seed*, but with Jesus Christ, he is the *seed* of the woman, for there was no human father to conceive him. See Rom. 16:20; Gal. 4:4; Heb. 2:14; Rev. 12:1–5. Christ has sown himself as the seed into our hearts. We have been born again, not by a corrupting seed, but by an Incorruptible Seed, the living and abiding Word of God (1 Peter 1:23).

c 3:15 Or "He will batter your head and you will batter his heel." However, the structure of the sentence (subject before the verb) implies a synchronic action, making the second clause concessive. This is the Protoevangelium, God's first announcement of a Savior, and presents a preview of Jesus Christ who would be wounded by the snake/sin on his heel but bring a death-blow to Satan by the power of his cross and resurrection. See Isa. 53:10; Col. 2:14.

d 3:16 Or "I will multiply your pain and your pregnancies," a likely hendiadys.

e 3:16 The Hebrew word for pain (*'etsev*) is a homophone that can also mean "creativity." God will use our painful situations to birth and express his beautiful creativity through us. How many works of art, compositions of music, and powerful acts of kindness have been birthed through the "labor pains" of our sometimes-troubled past. Pain can be the incubator of creativity and beauty.

f 3:16 Or "your craving" (noun). There is no verb in this clause; it is borrowed from the next.

g 3:16 Sin has brought a painful conflict and power struggle into the home. This is not a statement of God's ideal (that either husband or wife dominate) but a result of the fall of humanity (arguing over who will be first place in the home). Husband and wife are both meant to reign and take dominion, for they are one. The thematic context is that of pain/conflict; between the seed of the woman and the seed of the snake, conflict (pain) in childbirth and child rearing, and conflict in marriage. God's ideal for marriage is a mutual submission, deference, and sacrificial love that places the other above ourselves. See Eph. 4:32–5:2, 18–33. See also Susan T. Foh, "What is the Woman's Desire?" *Westminster Theological Journal* 37 (1975): 376–83; Irvin Busenitz, "Woman's Desire for Man: Genesis 3:16 Reconsidered." *Grace Theological Journal* 7.2 (1986) 203–12.

h 3:17 The irony of the narrative is hard to miss. Because they ate what was forbidden, pain enters the world. The man will produce food to eat through "painful toil," and the woman will experience "painful childbirth." Additionally, the ground (and all creation) now labors with painful contractions waiting for the unveiling of God's sons and daughters (Rom. 8:19–21).

¹⁸It will sprout weeds and
thorns,ᵃ
and you will eat the plants of the
field.
¹⁹You will painfully toilᵇ and
sweat
to produce food to eat,ᶜ
until your body—taken from
the ground—returns to the
ground.
For you are from dust,
and to dust you will return."ᵈ

Eve
²⁰The man named his wife Eve—"Life-
Giver,"ᵉ because she would become the
mother of every human being.
²¹Yahweh-God made garmentsᶠ from
animal skinsᵍ to clotheʰ Adam and Eve.
²²And Yahweh-God said, "The man has
become like one of us, knowing good
and evil. And now he might take in
his hands fruit from the Tree of Life,
and eat it, and live forever." ²³There-
fore, Yahweh-God expelled him from

---

a   3:18 Thorns are part of the curse brought about by the sin of man. Jesus wore a crown of
thorns (John 19:2) because he took our curse and set us free. For the topic of thorns, see also
Song. 2:2; Matt. 13:3–9, 18–23; 2 Cor. 12:7; Heb. 6:4–8.
b   3:19 This is the same word used for the woman having "pain" in childbirth. The cause of pain
in our human experience is the result of sin.
c   3:19 Or "eat your bread." Work is not a part of the curse, for Adam was given responsibility
for working and tending the garden before the Fall (Gen. 2:15). The punishment of the woman
touches her identity as a wife and mother; the punishment of man touches his identity in his
activity of work and being a provider.
d   3:19 See Job 10:9; 34:15; Ps. 103:14; Eccles. 12:7. Jesus experienced all the effects of the curse.
He sweat and labored in prayer and in carrying the cross; he was crowned with thorns and left in
the dust "for dead" (Ps. 22:15). It is true that our bodies will return to dust, but we have been lifted
out of the dust and have been seated in the heavenly realm (Eph. 2:1–6). Death no longer has the
victory over us because the resurrection of Christ is also our resurrection (Rom. 6:5).
e   3:20 Adam changes her name from "Woman" to Eve, the first of many name changes in the
Bible. The Hebrew contains a pun, or paronomasia, with the name Eve, for her name havvah
is very similar to the word for life (khayah, or "living one"). God gave the woman the ability not
only to have babies but to also release life in a variety of expressions. Eve brought life into the
structure of Adam's world. What does the Scripture tell us about a woman? She is God's chosen
'ezer (Gen. 2:18), a protector, provider, and a source of strength for a man. Secondly, she is taken
from man, equally a partner under the Lord and perfectly matched for re-union as one. Thirdly,
she is the carrier of life for all humanity. A woman enfolds all three roles in one person.
f   3:21 This could also be translated "coats," "robes," or "tunics."
g   3:21 Their first sight of death was an innocent sacrifice, killed for them.
h   3:21 Father God did what any good father will do when a child fails. He wrapped his love
around them and did not degrade them. This verb (to clothe) is mostly used for kings who
clothe others with robes (Gen. 41:42), or for priests who are clothed with sacred garments
(Ex. 28:41; 29:8; 40:14). When God clothed Adam and his wife, he did more than cover their
nakedness. Moved by love, he clothed them to cover their shame. The role of Adam and
Eve as rulers on the earth was not erased by their fall. They were still commissioned as a priest
and priestess by God himself. God's love shines through this episode, for he is the one who, as
an act of grace, caringly provides adequate covering for their bodies. For God to use blood-
stained animal skins as royal robes to clothe his beloved Adam and Eve meant that animals
had to be sacrificed to provide their covering. See also Ezek. 16:8.

Eden's paradise to till the ground from which he was taken.[a] [24]He drove them out of the garden, and placed[b] *fearsome* angelic sentries[c] east of the garden of Eden, with a turning fiery sword[d] to guard the way to the Tree of Life.[e]

The Story of Cain and Abel

4 Now Adam had slept[f] with his wife, and she conceived and bore a son named Cain.[g] She said, "By *the grace*[h] of Yahweh I have birthed a man!"[i] [2]Then later, she gave birth to Cain's brother, Abel.[j] Abel grew up to be a shepherd,

---

a 3:23 Taken from the earth, he now is given the earth to till. Turning over the soil is a picture of how man must guard his heart, his life. We must become those who have been loosened and opened to the rain of God. The Tree of Life must be planted in the soil of the human heart. When God charged man to till the ground, it meant that the soil of his heart must be broken up and prepared for this Beautiful Tree to come into him and branch out through him. See John 15.

b 3:24 This is the Hebrew word from which we get "Shekinah."

c 3:24 Or "cherubim," from the masculine word *kerub*, translated "one who intercedes" or "one with knowledge," borrowed from the Assyrian language from a root word meaning "to be near." See 1 Sam. 4:4; 2 Sam. 6:2; 2 Kings 19:15; 1 Chron. 13:6; Pss. 18:9–10; 80:1; 99:1; Isa. 37:16; Ezek. 10:1–22.

d 3:24 This is the first reference to the sword in the Bible. In Hebrews 4:12 and Ephesians 6:17–18 the sword is a metaphor of God's Word as it judges the intentions of the heart. We still must pass through the ministry of the flaming sword to return to the place where God desires us to dwell. This sword was "awakened" (Zech. 13:7) against the Lord Jesus Christ as he paid the full price to redeem us to God. The cherubim, embroidered into the fabric of the veil of the Holy of Holies, were like sentries, guarding the way to the Life within. When the veil was torn in two from the top to the bottom, it was as though the cherubim parted and granted access within the veil for every believer to come and feast upon the Tree of Life, Jesus Christ. See Ex. 26:31–35; Mark 15:37–38; Heb. 10:19–23.

e 3:24 The way to the Tree of Life is Jesus Christ. See John 14:6; Heb. 10:20.

f 4:1 Or "knew his wife." The Hebrew word for knew is *yada* and carries the implication of knowing intimately and experientially and implies a special relationship (i.e. sexually). It is possible that Eve's conception of Cain had taken place while they were still in the garden, which is also implied in Gen. 3:20.

g 4:1 Cain means "possessed" or "smith (fabricator)."

h 4:1 Or "Together with Yahweh," or "By the help of Yahweh." This utterance by Eve, was the first time anyone speaks the divine name in Scripture.

i 4:1 Or literally, "I gained a man-Yahweh," or "I brought him from Yahweh." Some have surmised that since God prophesied a coming "seed" of the woman, Eve believed that Cain was that promised deliverer. The triliteral root of the Hebrew verb *qanah* is the same root for the name Cain. Although the meaning of Cain is uncertain, some believe it could mean "acquired (one)" or "possession." Some Hebrew scholars believe a more accurate translation would read "I have brought forth a man-Yahweh (the God-man)," meaning Eve believed the promise of her "Seed" (Gen. 3:15) and presumed that Cain was the promised one. What a disappointment when Cain became a murderer!

j 4:2 Abel means "breath," "vapor," or "vanity." Adam and Eve had many sons and daughters (Gen.5:4), but Cain and Abel seem to have been the two eldest. Jewish tradition holds that they were twins. Abel means "vanity," "puff of air," or "fading away to nothingness." Perhaps this is because their hope for the Messiah had faded. Or maybe they saw from the thorns and thistles and hard ground that life was much more difficult outside the Garden than inside, their joy faded away. Paul tells us in Romans 8:20 that the world was made subject to vanity. Adam and Eve saw this vanity firsthand and named their son, Abel. The Syriac name for Abel is "herdsman."

and Cain became a farmer, working the ground.[a] ³After some time passed, Cain presented an offering to Yahweh from the produce of the land. ⁴Abel also brought his offering, from among the finest[b] of the firstborn of his flocks. Yahweh was *very* pleased[c] with Abel and *accepted* his offering, ⁵but with Cain and his offering, Yahweh was not pleased,[d] making Cain very furious and resentful.[e] ⁶So Yahweh said to Cain:

"Why are you so angry and bothered?
⁷If you offer what is right, won't you be accepted?[f]

But if you refuse to offer what is right,
sin, *the predator*, is crouching in wait[g] outside the door *of your heart.*
It desires to have you, yet you must be its master."

⁸*One day* Cain said to his brother, "Let's go out into the field."[h] When they arrived at the field, Cain rose and attacked and killed his brother Abel.
⁹Then Yahweh said to Cain, "Where is your brother Abel?"
He answered, "How do I know? Am I my brother's keeper?"[i]

---

a 4:2 Cain chose to work the ground, which was under the curse.

b 4:4 Or "fattest." Many Jewish scholars believe it was a lamb that Abel sacrificed to God. Sheep were not used for food prior to the flood (Gen.1:29), only for sacrifice. Abel had his heart set on the coming Sacrifice, confessed his sin, and brought the first and best of his flock as a sacrifice in faith. Abel acknowledged that he was worthy of death because of his sin and chose an acceptable sacrifice that was acceptable to God.

c 4:4 Or "to gaze upon (with favor and devotion)." It is possible that fire from heaven consumed Abel's offering as a sign that God was pleased and accepted Abel's blood sacrifice (Lev. 9:24; Judges 6:21). God also gazed upon Abel's heart and saw his longings and was pleased, for Abel offered a sacrifice to God with faith. See Heb. 11:4.

d 4:5 Cain's heart and character were not right with God (Prov. 15:8). Some believe Cain picked inferior portions of produce (no mention of firstfruits) to offer to God, much like trying to please God with good works without faith. The curse could not be broken by a product of the curse. See Rom. 4:4–5; Heb. 11:6.

e 4:5 Or "his face (countenance) fell," a Hebrew idiom.

f 4:7 Or literally, "If you do well, uplifting?" Scholars consider this verse to be one of the more difficult verses in Genesis to translate. The implication is that God would lift up Cain with favor (forgiveness) and accept Cain if he did well by bringing an acceptable offering. This is not condemnation, but an invitation for Cain to change his ways. The Hebrew word for "uplifting" is taken from the root word *nasa'*, which means "to carry away," "to take away," "to lift up," "to bear (iniquity)," or "to forgive." Abel's works were righteous, and Cain's works were evil. See 1 John 3:12.

g 4:7 Or "crouching" or "resting outside the portal." The Akkadian word for crouching (*rabisu*) is frequently associated with a demon. Sin is seen as a demon-beast crouching at the door of Cain's heart. However, the word for sin can also mean "sin-offering." God could be telling Cain that there is a sin-offering, as a resting lamb, lying outside his door to be the acceptable sacrifice. They were opening a portal to the presence of God. If the sacrifice was accepted the (Heb. *patach*) portal to God's presence would open. Both sin and Jesus are knocking on our heart's door waiting to come in. See Rev. 3:20.

h 4:8 The words of Cain are missing from most Hebrew manuscripts but are found in the Samaritan Pentateuch, LXX, Vulgate, and Syriac.

i 4:9 Or "guardian." In a sense, Cain is saying about his shepherd-brother, "Am I the shepherd's shepherd?"

¹⁰Yahweh said, "Listen—the voice of your brother's blood*ᵃ* is crying out to me from the ground! What have you done? ¹¹Now you are banished*ᵇ* from the land, from the very ground that drank your brother's blood from your hand!*ᶜ* ¹²When you try to cultivate the ground it will no longer produce crops*ᵈ* for you; and you will be a fugitive, a homeless wanderer!"*ᵉ*

¹³Cain said to Yahweh, "My punishment is more than I can bear!*ᶠ* ¹⁴Look—you've thrown me off the land today, and now I must hide from your presence. As a fugitive and wanderer on the earth, anyone who meets me may choose to kill me!"

¹⁵Yahweh responded, "Not so! If anyone kills you, I promise the seven-fold*ᵍ* vengeance of Cain will be released upon him!" So, Yahweh put an *identifying* sign*ʰ* on Cain as a warning so that no one would dare kill him. ¹⁶Then Cain left the presence of Yahweh and journeyed to the Land of Wandering,*ⁱ* east of Eden.

The Family Line of Cain

¹⁷Cain slept with his wife and she conceived and bore Enoch.*ʲ* Cain

---

a 4:10 Or "bloods" or "drops of blood." Blood crying is a symbol of the soul crying out for the right to live, demanding for the punishment of the murderer. Bloodguilt calls for justice, even from the ground. It is as if the face of the earth blushes as it becomes stained by blood. Blood (spilled) outside the body is always plural in Hebrew, "Your brother's bloods." This speaks of his descendants that could have lived—their blood, too, cries out against Cain. The blood of Abel cries out for vengeance, but the blood of Christ cries out for mercy and pardon. Therefore the blood of Christ speaks a better word than the blood of Abel (Heb.12:24).

b 4:11 Or "cursed (punished)."

c 4:11 Blood-guilt not only stains the conscience, but it also defiles the ground. See Num. 35:33. We are told to avoid the way of Cain (Jude 11), which would include (1) offering God what is cursed, (2) jealous anger toward another, (3) refusing to repent, (4) murder, (5) wandering away from God's presence.

d 4:12 Or "yield its strength."

e 4:12 Or "you will be a totterer and a wanderer." Alienation from God is the ultimate consequence of sin.

f 4:13 Or "Is my sin too great to be forgiven?" (LXX). The Hebrew word *'avon* means sin and its punishment. The Hebrew can be translated, "My sin (or "my punishment") is too great to bear."

g 4:15 That is, seven times over—seven lives will be taken to avenge Cain's death. Or it could mean, seven generations will be avenged. The next murderer we find in Scripture is Lamech, seventh generation from Cain. Jewish sages believe it was Lamech who killed his ancestor Cain.

h 4:15 Or "mark." It could have been a visible mark upon Cain as a warning that he was under divine protection. See Ezek. 9:4, 6. However, it is also possible that God showed a supernatural, authenticating sign to confirm to Cain that he would not be harmed. Ancient rabbis taught that the mark of Cain was a horn that grew on his head.

i 4:16 Or "Nod," the Hebrew word for *wandering*, likely a symbolic place. There was a span of 130 years from the creation of Adam to the murder of Abel, which would have allowed for other sons and daughters of Adam to have spread over the earth. Some have calculated there could have been over half a million people alive at that time. See Gen. 4:25; 5:3. Scripture does not mention the line of Cain after this chapter nor mention Cain's death. Within Jewish tradition there is a reference to Cain marrying his sister. See *Jubilees* 4:9; Sanhedrin 58b.

j 4:17 Enoch means "dedicated," "teacher," or "initiated."

was building a city at the time,[a] so he named it the Village of Enoch, after his son. [18]Enoch's son was Irad,[b] and Irad's son was Mehujael,[c] and Mehujael's son was Methushael,[d] and Methushael's son was Lamech.[e]

[19]Lamech married two women, Dawn[f] and Dusk.[g] [20]Dawn gave birth to Jabal,[h] the first[i] of those who lived in tents and raised livestock. [21]Jabal's brother was Jubal,[j] the first of *musicians* who played instruments.[k] [22]Dusk gave birth to Tubalcain,[l] the first of blacksmiths who forged all kinds of bronze and iron tools. His sister was Naamah.[m]

[23]Lamech boasted to his wives:[n]

"Listen to me, Dawn and Dusk!
Mark my words, O wives of
  Lamech!
I have killed a man for wounding
  me,
and a young man for bruising
  me.[o]
[24]If killing Cain costs seven lives,
for Lamech, it will cost
  seventy-seven!"[p]

[25]Adam slept with his wife again and she bore a son whom she named Seth, meaning "appointed," for she

---

a 4:17 Or "walled village." God banished Cain to wander as a fugitive, but instead he builds a city in rebellion to God.

b 4:18 *Irad* means "city of witness," "wild donkey," or "fugitive."

c 4:18 Mehujael means "God is combatting" or "smitten by God." The Akkadian word *mahlu* means "ecstatic (seer)."

d 4:18 Methushael means "My god is husband" or "man of god." Some suggest it is taken from a word in Ugaritic, *mutba'al*, which means "man of Baal." Others view it as "man of Shael" or "man of Sheol," the underworld.

e 4:18 *Lamech* means "overthrower" or "one who brings low." The Arabic meaning of Lamech is "strongman." Lamech, the first polygamist, was the seventh from Adam in the line of Cain. He denotes the antichrist spirit with his prideful boasting.

f 4:19 Or "Adah," which means "dawn," possibly related to the Hebrew word *'adi*, meaning "jewel."

g 4:19 Or "Zillah," which means "dusk" or "shadow."

h 4:20 Jabal means "nomad" or "flowing."

i 4:20 Or "the father," used also in v. 21.

j 4:21 Jubal means "joyful sound."

k 4:21 Or "the harp (stringed instrument) and flute (wind instrument)." The Hebrew word for *play* means "to hold" or "to handle" and later became associated with "to play skillfully." Jubal invented musical instruments and taught others to play them. See Job 21:12; 30:31. Musicians today should dedicate their gifts and talents to God for heaven to be glorified.

l 4:22 Tubalcain means "flowing from Cain." He invented and taught others metallurgy.

m 4:22 *Naamah* means "pleasant" or "gracious." The triliteral root, *n-'-m* can also mean "to sing." At least one Targum reference describes her as a professional singer. Ancient Jewish writings suggest that Naamah became Noah's wife.

n 4:23 The form of v. 23–24 is the first example of poetry in the Bible, known as parallelism. Many Jewish scholars view this "Song of Lamech" as a summary of a larger poetic composition describing the exploits of Lamech.

o 4:23 Or "I would kill a man for my wounding, in fact a boy for a bruise." There is a Jewish legend that states that Lamech killed Cain. If Lamech was boasting that killing others will be his practice, he became the world's first terrorist.

p 4:24 See Matt. 18:21.

declared, "God has appointed for me another son[a] to replace Abel, because Cain killed him." [26]*After many years* Seth had a son named Enosh.[b] During his lifetime, people[c] began to *worship* Yahweh and pray to him.[d]

Family History of Adam and Eve

[1-2]When God created human beings he made them in the likeness of God and created them as male and female. After he had created them, he *lovingly*[e] blessed them and named them "humanity."[f]

So here is the family history[g] of Adam *and Eve:*[h]

[3] When Adam was one hundred and thirty,[i] he fathered a child in his own likeness and in his own image, and he named him Seth. [4]Adam lived an additional eight hundred years after Seth was born and had *many* other sons and daughters. [5]The life span of Adam was nine hundred and thirty years, and then he died.[j]

[6]When Seth was one hundred and five, he fathered Enosh. [7]Seth lived an additional eight hundred and seven years after Enosh was born and had *many* other sons and daughters. [8]The life span of Seth was nine hundred and twelve years, and then he died.

[9]When Enosh was ninety, he fathered Kenan.[k] [10]Enosh lived an additional eight hundred and fifteen years after Kenan was born and had *many* other sons and daughters. [11]The life span of Enosh was nine

---

a 4:25 Or "seed."

b 4:26 *Enosh* means "mortal" or "frail (man)." Seth humbly names his son Enosh, emphasizing the frailty of man.

c 4:26 Or "he (Enosh)." With Enosh and his family line, we see the restoration of a longing to commune with God.

d 4:26 Or "call upon his name," a Biblical description of prayer that includes praise and worship. The name *Yahweh* expresses his personality, "He who Is and Causes to Be," and reveals his desire to commune with human beings.

e 5:1–2 Love is implied in God's blessing upon the human family. God's blessing is upon man and woman, empowering them to live on this planet. Inherent in this "blessing" is being infused with power and favor to succeed in life and to multiply. Father God loves to bless his people.

f 5:1–2 Or "Adam." No stronger statement could be made that male and female are co-equal before their creator. There is really only one man in the Old Testament, and that is Adam. There is really only one Man in the New Testament, and that is Jesus. There are really only two men who have represented the human race: the first Adam and the Last Adam, Jesus Christ. The books of Genesis and Matthew both are introduced with the record of the generations of Adam and Christ.

g 5:1–2 Or "book" or "written record." What follows is a genealogy. The reason God includes so many genealogies is because he loves families and they are important to God. Each name represents a family.

h 5:1–2 See 1 Chron. 1:1–4; Luke 3:36–38.

i 5:3 Or "230" (LXX, Samaritan Pentateuch). The ages given of individuals in this chapter are taken from the Hebrew. Both the Septuagint and Samaritan Pentateuch give different ages, usually adding 100 years to each.

j 5:5 People experienced lengthy life spans in the antediluvian age. It is plausible that Adam and Noah knew each other, since their lives overlapped 243 years. Perhaps Adam orally passed down the creation story to his entire lineage, including Noah. One Jewish tradition states that Adam had 300 sons and daughters. The history of man begins with death and pain, but will one day end with delight and pleasure, as the redeemed become the dwelling place of God.

k 5:9 The probable meaning of Kenan is "one who laments (over death or dying)."

hundred and five years, and then he died.

¹²When Kenan was seventy, he fathered Mahalalel.ª ¹³Kenan lived an additional eight hundred and forty years after Mahalalel was born and had *many* other sons and daughters. ¹⁴The life span of Kenan was nine hundred and ten years, and then he died.

¹⁵When Mahalalel was sixty-five, he fathered Jared.ᵇ ¹⁶Mahalalel lived an additional eight hundred and thirty years after Jared was born and had *many* other sons and daughters. ¹⁷The life span of Mahalalel was eight hundred and ninety-five years, and then he died.

¹⁸When Jared was one hundred and sixty-two, he fathered Enoch.ᶜ ¹⁹Jared lived an additional eight hundred years after Enoch was born and had *many* other sons and daughters.

²⁰The life span of Jared was nine hundred and sixty-two years, and then he died.

²¹When Enoch was sixty-five, he fathered Methuselah.ᵈ ²²Enoch walked with God for three hundred years after Methuselah was born and had *many* other sons and daughters. ²³⁻²⁴Enoch and God walked together as intimate friends; then God took him to himself,ᵉ and he was seen no more. The life span of Enoch was three hundred and sixty-five years.

²⁵When Methuselah was one hundred and eighty-seven, he fathered Lamech. ²⁶Methuselah lived an additional seven hundred and eighty-two years after Lamech was born and had *many* other sons and daughters. ²⁷The life span of Methuselah was nine hundred and sixty-nine years, and then he died.

---

a 5:12 Mahalalel means "the splendor of God" or "praising God."

b 5:15 Or "Yered." Jared means "to descend" or possibly "servant."

c 5:18 *Enoch* means "he teaches," "he initiates," or "dedicated one." As the seventh from Adam, the life of Enoch teaches us what a life of dedication to God looks like. Enoch shows us what mature sonship could be. He was a prophet who foretold of the "second coming" (Jude 14–15). God told Adam and Eve about the first coming (Gen. 3:15, 21), yet Enoch received even more revelation as he prophesied of the return of Christ.

d 5:21 *Methuselah* is a complex name with at least two words embedded within it: "death" and "send/let go." Some scholars believe his name means "when he dies, it will be sent," or "his death will bring." This is a prophecy hidden in his name, for the year he died was the year God sent the flood. Jewish writers say that Methuselah, Noah's grandfather, died seven days before the flood and that Noah and his family entered the ark the day Methuselah died (Gen. 7:10). For 969 years, the world had a walking warning of the coming judgment. An alternate meaning of Methuselah is "man of the spear (weapon)."

e 5:23–24 God *took him* is a Hebrew word *laqach* that can also mean "God took him in marriage," as a man takes a bride in marriage. Luke included Enoch in the genealogy of the Son of God (Luke 3:23–38). He was a man who walked in faith and was translated from earth to heaven without dying (apotheosis). His life was pleasing to God (Heb. 11:5). He also was a prophet who prophesied about the coming of Christ with myriads of holy ones (Jude 14–15). Ancient Jewish and Arabic writings often refer to him as one who possessed the secrets of heaven and invented mathematics, astronomy, and a lunar-based calendar. The Book of Jubilees states that he was carried into paradise, where he writes down the judgment of all men.

²⁸When Lamech was one hundred and eighty-two, he fathered a son ²⁹and named him Noah,ᵃ saying, "He will relieve us from our *hard* work and painful toil, and from the ground that Yahweh cursed." ³⁰Lamech lived an additional five hundred and ninety-five years after Noah was born and had *many other* sons and daughters. ³¹The life span of Lamech was seven hundred and seventy-seven years, and then he died.

³²After Noah had lived five hundred years, he fathered Shem, Ham, and Japheth.

God Grieves over Human Wickedness

6 When people began to populate the earth, they had *many lovely* daughters. ²Divine beingsᵇ found them very appealing, so they took the women they wanted as their wives.

³Yahweh said, "My Spiritᶜ will not striveᵈ with humanity indefinitely,ᵉ for

---

ᵃ 5:29 This is a pun, for *Noah* and the Hebrew words for "relief," "comfort," or "rest" are very similar. Noah was the tenth generation from Adam. Ten is the Biblical number of trial and human responsibility (i.e. 10 Words/Commandments, Ex. 20:1–17). See also Dan. 1:12; Rev. 2:10. There are ten more generations between Noah and Abraham. Notice the meaning of the ten names of the men of the line of Seth: man, appointed, mortality, lament of death, splendor of God, descends, teaching, his death will bring, powerful-overcoming, rest and comfort. When the meanings of the ten names are joined together it is an obvious theme hidden in the genealogy of Adam: *Man* is *appointed* to *mortality* and the *lament of death*, but the *splendor of God* (Jesus Christ) will *descend*, and *his death will bring* the *powerful overthrow* of (death and sin) to bring to us *rest and comfort*.

ᵇ 6:2 Or "the sons of the gods" or "angels of God" (LXX). This is one of the most difficult verses in Genesis to interpret. There is much debate over the identity of these *divine beings*, yet we see that they are linked to the "Nephilim (giants)," the corrupting of the divine "seed of the woman" (Gen. 3:16) who was to come, and the judgment of God through the flood. Many scholars view "the sons of the gods" as sons of Seth (the godly lineage), but the line of Seth is nowhere stated to be a godly line; in fact, only Noah was considered righteous in God's eyes. Other scholars see them as a reference to a group of fallen angels who *in rebellion went outside their rightful domain of authority and abandoned their appointed realms* to have sexual relations with women. Consequently, they were *bound in everlasting chains in the dark abyss of the underworld* (Jude 6; 2 Peter 2:4–5). The argument that they could not be fallen angels because angels cannot marry (Matt. 22:30) is in reference to angels who are in heaven, not the angels who came to earth as part of Satan's plan to cohabitate with women and corrupt the human race. Virtually all of the earliest writings of Jewish and Christian literature interpret the phrase "the sons of the gods" as heavenly beings known as fallen angels or "watchers." See also Job 1:6; 2:1; 4:18–19; 38:7; Dead Sea scrolls 1QapGen, 4QDtj and 4QDtq; the Damascus Document 4Q180; the *Book of Jubilees*; *2 Baruch*; *the Book of Enoch*; the Jewish historian Josephus; and church fathers Justin Martyr, Eusebius, Clement of Alexandria, Origen. The coming (Gr. "parousia") of the Lord is also going to take place in a time just like the days of Noah (Gen. 6).

ᶜ 6:3 Or "breath."

ᵈ 6:3 Or "shield man (from judgment) indefinitely." Although many scholars translate this hapax legomenon as "abide," the cognate Akkadian word means to "shield" or "protect."

ᵉ 6:3 Or "forever."

they are mortal. Their life span will be *shortened* to only one hundred and twenty years."[a]

[4]Back then, and later, there were giants[b] on the earth, who were born as a result of the *unholy* union of heavenly beings with the human daughters. They were the mighty ones of old, warriors of renown.

[5]But Yahweh saw how extremely wicked humanity had become, for they imagined only evil, for all they thought about was doing evil all the time. [6]And Yahweh was saddened[c] that he had made humanity, and his heart was filled with pain. [7]So Yahweh decided, "I will do away with *my ruined creation*—human beings that I created—people and animals, creeping things and flying birds, for it breaks my heart that I made them!"

[8]But *one man* found grace[d] in the sight of Yahweh: Noah.[e]

Noah Pleases God

[9]This is the story of Noah.

Noah was a godly man of integrity, without fault in his generation,[f] and he lived close to God. [10]Noah

---

a 6:3 Or "they will only live another 120 years," possibly a prophecy of when the flood was coming.

b 6:4 This is the Hebrew word *Nephilim*, or "giants." The triliteral root is also used for "fallen ones." They appear to be the offspring of the *divine beings* and women. They were monsters of iniquity, meant to corrupt the earth and destroy the godly *seed*. See Num. 13:33. There are only two ways to kills giants in the Bible: (1) Like David, prophesy their downfall, run straight toward them, knock them down and cut off their head (1 Sam. 17:48–51), or (2) Like Caleb and Joshua, conquer them, see them as "bread" to strengthen us. Intimidation never works when you are facing a giant. Num. 13–14. David also raised up giant killers among his mighty men (2 Sam. 21:18–22; 1 Chron. 20:4–8).

c 6:6 Or "God sighed within himself" or "God regretted." This is the Hebrew word *nacham*, which is nearly impossible to translate adequately into English. It is a word that expresses grief, comfort, compassion, and hope all at the same time. God felt all of these emotions over the creation of man. God's heart was filled with sorrow, compassion, and hope, not simply anger.

d 6:8 Or "Noah found favor." The Hebrew word for favor is the name Noah written backwards, an obvious Hebrew play on words.

e 6:8 Noah found another age—the age of grace. He laid hold of grace and knew that God was merciful, even in an age of judgment and wickedness. It is possible to translate this sentence, "Noah laid hold of grace in the eyes of Yahweh." It was not the virtue of Noah that saved him, but the grace of God. This is the first mention of grace in the Bible.

f 6:9 Ezekiel described Noah as one of the godliest of men (Ezek. 14:14, 20). No matter how evil the world may be around us, God has enough grace to purify our hearts and enable us to live godly lives for his glory.

had three sons, Shem,[a] Ham,[b] and Japheth.[c] [11]Injustice and violence filled the world; the earth was ruined[d] in the sight of God, [12]for he saw how debased the world had become, for everyone was corrupt to the core. [13]So God said to Noah,[e] "I have decided[f] that all living creatures must die, for their violence has filled the earth, and I will wipe them off the face of the earth!

[14-15]Build a boat for yourself—an ark[g] of sturdy timber.[h] And this is how you are to design it: make separate compartments[i] within it, and seal it inside and out with thick tar.[j] The length is to be 450 feet, its width 75 feet, and its height 45 feet.[k] [16]Cover it with a roof,[l] but leave a gap of eighteen inches[m] at the top *for ventilation*. Construct a door on the side of the ark, and design it with lower, middle, and upper decks. [17]I

---

a 6:10 Shem, from whom descended the "Semitic" races, means "name," "upright," "brilliant," "prosperity," or "dignity." According to some Jewish traditions and rabbinical teachings, Shem is sometimes identified as Melchizedek (B. Talmud Nedarim 32b; Genesis Rabbah 46:7; Genesis Rabbah 56:10; Leviticus Rabbah 25:6; Numbers Rabbah 4:8). Jesus was a descendant of Shem (Luke 3:36). The *Book of Jubilees* mentions Shem's wife, who survived the flood, as Sedeqetelebab. It also states that each of Noah's three sons built cities named after their wives.

b 6:10 *Ham* means "hot," "he raged," or "tumult." The Egyptian word for Ham is "servant." The historian Josephus states that the Hamites populated northern Africa and adjoining regions of Asia. Egypt is called the land of Ham (Ps.105:23, 27). The *Book of Jubilees* mentions Ham's wife, who survived the flood, as Na'eltama'uk. Pakistan claims to have Ham's burial site and its people considered him to be a prophet.

c 6:10 *Japheth* means "let him spread out," "enlargement," "increase," or "expansion." Japheth is taken from a root word for "beautiful." He is considered the father of the European, Anatolian, and east Asian peoples. In Greek tradition, he is considered the ancestor of the Greeks. The *Book of Jubilees* mentions Japheth's wife as 'Adataneses. In Acts, we have God bringing the sons of Noah into his kingdom: Ham (the Ethiopian, Acts 8), Shem (the Jewish man, Saul, Acts 9), and Japheth (Cornelius, Acts 10).

d 6:11 That is, everyone had corrupted their lives with wickedness.

e 6:13 God speaks directly with Noah seven times in this narrative.

f 6:13 Or "it is in front of me" or "The time of every man is come before me" (LXX).

g 6:14–15 The Hebrew word for ark (*tevah*) is found seven times in this chapter and seven times in Chapter 8.

h 6:14–15 Or "gopher wood," possibly cypress or cedar.

i 6:14–15 Or "nests."

j 6:14–15 This is the Hebrew word *kopher*, which is a homonym that also means "atonement." Noah was told to seal (literally, "atone") the ark, as it were, in the atonement. Christ's blood now preserves us from judgment. He endured judgment in our place, and we are now sealed until the day of redemption. See Eph. 4:30. This homonym also has the meaning of "henna." Jesus is like a cluster of henna (atonement). See Song. 1:14.

k 6:14–15 Or "300 cubits long (130 meters), 50 cubits wide (22 meters), and 30 cubits high (13 meters)." The Hebrew word for "cubit" literally means "forearm." The measurement of a cubit is thought to be about 18–20 inches (45–50 cm). This suggests a vessel of over 43,000 tons. See A. Heidel, *The Gilgamesh Epic and Old Testament Parallels*, 1946, p. 236. Even with the smallest estimate for a cubit, the ark would have three floors of 33,750 square feet each, making a total space of over 101,000 square feet.

l 6:16 Or "Make a window." The meaning of the Hebrew word is uncertain.

m 6:16 Or "one cubit."

am going to release a great flood that will destroy all life upon the earth, and every breathing thing under heaven will perish—everything on earth will die. [18]But as for you, I will establish my covenant *of friendship*, and you will escape destruction by coming into the ark,[a] you and your wife, your sons and their wives. [19]Bring with you into the ark a pair of every animal, male and female; and they will also be spared. [20]Different kinds of birds, animals large and small[b]—two of every kind I will send to you to be kept alive. [21]Also take with you every kind of food, both for you and them."

[22]So Noah completed all these preparations and did everything exactly as God had commanded him.[c]

The Great Flood

7 *The day came when* Yahweh said to Noah,[d] "Come[e] into the ark, you and your entire household, for I have found you to be the only one righteous in my eyes in this generation.[f] [2]Take with you seven pairs of all the clean animals,[g] both male and female, and

---

a 6:18 Noah's ark is a beautiful picture of Jesus Christ. It was made from sturdy wood (the humanity of Christ, Isa. 53:2; Dan. 9:26) and is sealed with tar (blood atonement). It was a place of salvation and preservation (Jesus our Savior). Into this ark, man is invited to come to find a place of security from judgment, and so we are hidden in Christ (Col. 3:3). All who entered the ark were kept safe and none perished. The dimensions of the ark are significant. It was 300 cubits long (300 is the number of complete victory in Christ [Judges 7:7–22; 1 Kings 10:17; Mark 14:3–6]), 50 cubits wide (50 is the number of Jubilee, Pentecost [Acts 2:1–47]), and 30 cubits high (30 is the number of maturity, authority, and full stature [Gen. 41:46; 2 Sam. 5:4; 1 Kings 6:2; Luke 3:23], and priests began their ministry at 30). The ark only had one door, and there is only one door of salvation (John 10:9; 14:6). The door was on the side of the ark (John 19:34). There were three stories or levels to Noah's ark, which points to a full salvation for man's body, soul, and spirit (1 Thess. 5:23, Noah's family lived on the third level). There were many rooms ("nests") in the ark (John 14:1–3). The ark rested in the seventh month on the seventeenth day. The Passover was the fourteenth day of the seventh month, and three days later (seventeenth) was the Resurrection (Christ "resting" on high). The ark rested on Mt. Ararat, which means "the curse is reversed" or "high and holy land." To be "in the ark" is to be "in Christ" (Eph. 1–3). The Bible mentions three arks, and each point to Christ: Noah's ark, the ark for baby Moses (Ex. 2:2), and the ark of the covenant (Ex. 25:10–22).

b 6:20 Or "animals, and creeping things (everything that walks or moves on the ground)."

c 6:22 Noah's response to the grace of God was obedience to his commands. This sentence is repeated four times concerning Noah (Gen. 6:22; 7:5, 9, 16). It is God's grace that leads us to obedience, not independence. See Phil. 2:12–13.

d 7:1 How did God speak to Noah? Did he come in human form? Perhaps he appeared in a burning bush, or as an angel, or in a dream. God is able to speak in whatever way he chooses. We have a God who speaks to those whose ways are blameless. Noah moved with faith and acted on the revelation given to him. Do you respond when God speaks?

e 7:1 The implication is that God is in the ark waiting for Noah to enter and come to him. He has always gone before us and knows what we will face. This Hebrew word for come is used in contemporary Jewish weddings and songs—"Come to me."

f 7:1 This statement shows that the sons of Seth could not rightly be called the sons of God (Gen. 6:2), for only Noah was righteous. God needed Noah. There must be a righteous man who would save mankind. When God comes down, he comes looking for human vessels he can use to bring deliverance and salvation (1 Sam. 16:7; 2 Chron. 16:9).

g 7:2 Seven pairs of clean animals (ritually acceptable) were spared so that Noah could use them for sacrifices. See Lev. 11:1–12.

one pair of all the unclean animals, both male and female. ³Take seven pairs of flying birds of all kinds, male and female, to make sure they survive on the earth. ⁴For in seven days I will send rain and flood the earth for forty days and forty nights.ᵃ Every living thing that I made I will wipe off the face of the earth."ᵇ

⁵Noah obeyed all that Yahweh had commanded him.

⁶Noah was six hundred years old when the great flood came on the earth. ⁷Noah and his wife and his sons and their wives boarded the ark to escape the flood. ⁸⁻⁹Two of each animal: the male and female, clean and unclean, large and small, along with birds and crawling things, entered the ark with Noah as God had commanded. ¹⁰Then seven days later, *massive* floodwaters covered the earth.

¹¹It started in the six hundredth year of Noah's life, in the second month on the seventeenth day.ᶜ *On that day,* all the fountainsᵈ of the subterranean deep cracked open and burst up through the ground. Heaven's floodgates were opened,ᵉ ¹²and heavy rains fell on the earth for forty days and forty nights.ᶠ

¹³On that very day, Noah and his wife, their sons, Ham, Shem, and Japheth, and their wives, entered safely into the ark. ¹⁴⁻¹⁵Pairs of every species of animal entered with them—wild animals, domesticated animals, large and small, and every species of bird and winged creatures—every animal that has the breath of life came into the ark with Noah. ¹⁶Both male and female went inside as God had commanded Noah; and Yahweh himself shut them in.ᵍ

¹⁷For forty days, the flood engulfed the earth. The swelling floodwaters lifted up the ark until it rose high above the ground. ¹⁸The *raging* flood completely inundated the earth, but the ark floated *safely,* drifting upon the surface of the water, ¹⁹until the highest mountains were completely submerged beneath

---

a 7:4 The number forty is a symbolic number in the Bible that represents testing and purification. See Ex. 16:35; Num. 14:34; Deut. 25:2–3; Jonah 3:4; Mark 1:13.

b 7:4 In the days of Noah, the flood took away the wicked and left behind the righteous. See Matt. 24:37–41; Luke 17:27.

c 7:11 The exact date is given of the deluge, a miracle pointing to the divine inspiration of Scripture. God noted and had recorded the exact day the flood began. He gave us amazing details of these events as they happened. The flood began, according to the Jewish scribes, the year 1656 from creation.

d 7:11 The Hebrew word *mayanot,* or "fountains," here has the same root as *mayan* in Song. 4:15. As my inward life sprouts and brings forth fruit, it has the loving power of a subterranean fountain.

e 7:11 It is as though God returned the earth back to the chaos of chapter one. He once separated the waters and raised up the dry ground; now he is covering the earth again with water and removes the separation that he spoke into existence (Gen. 1:6–10).

f 7:12 God, at creation, had fixed a "boundary," setting "doors and bars in place" that the waters could not pass (Job 38:8–11; Ps. 104:9). Now he simply removes those restraints, and the waters gushed forth and flooded the earth as they had done at first (Gen.1:9). The floodgates of the heavens were similarly opened up.

g 7:16 Closing the door of the ark was a supernatural act of God. It was Elohim ("the Mighty One") who commanded Noah to enter the ark, and Yahweh (the covenant-keeping God, the Friend of Sinners) who shut him in. The God of Israel is known by both names.

the rising waters. ²⁰The waters rose over twenty-two feet*a* above the highest mountains.*b* ²¹Every living thing on the earth perished—domesticated animals, wild animals, birds, everything that moved on the earth, and all mankind perished. ²²Everything perished—every animal on earth with the breath of life in its nostrils died. ²³All life on earth was blotted out—all that he had made, animals large and small, wild and domesticated, birds and reptiles, including humanity—was wiped off the face of the earth. Only Noah was left behind,*c* and those who were in the ark with him. ²⁴And the waters covered the earth for 150 days.

Noah Leaves the Ark

8 God's heart *was moved with compassion as he* remembered*d* Noah and all the animals, large and small,*e* that were with him in the ark.*f* And God caused a wind*g* to sweep across the earth *again*ʰ and the waters subsided. ²He closed the subterranean fountains and the floodgates of heaven and held back the rain. ³After 150 days, the floodwaters gradually receded from the earth and the waters began to subside. ⁴And on the 17th day of the 7th month,*i* the ark came to rest*j* on the highest peak in Ararat.*k* ⁵The waters continued to recede until the 10th month. And on the 1st day of

---

a 7:20 Or "fifteen cubits (22.5 feet)." Waters covered the earth for a depth of three miles above normal sea level. All the mountains of the pride of man were covered up,

b 7:20 This indicates a universal flood, not just regional. See Ps. 104:6; 2 Peter 3:5–7.

c 7:23 In the days of Noah, the wicked were taken away, swept off the earth by the flood. It was the righteous who were left behind to inherit the earth. See Matt. 24:37–41; Luke 17:27.

d 8:1 God had not forgotten and then suddenly remembered them; his heart of compassion focused on Noah and all that survived in the ark. Mercy triumphs over judgment (James 2:13).

e 8:1 Or "wild and domesticated animals."

f 8:1 Being in the ark assured their salvation. Being "in Christ" likewise assures our salvation.

g 8:1 Or "(his) Spirit" or "breath." See Ps. 148:8.

h 8:1 God repeated what he did at creation; his Spirit hovered over the face of the waters. And it happened again thousands of years later, as God's Spirit hovered over and filled 120 believers at Pentecost, giving them new creation life.

i 8:4 At the institution of the Feast of Passover the Lord made the seventh month into the first month, the month of great importance for Israel (Ex. 12:2). Passover was the fourteenth day of the month. Three days later would be the seventeenth day of the month; the very day Jesus rose from the dead. The final resting place of our ark of salvation was the top of the mountain. Jesus was raised on high, seated at the right hand of the Most High. What inspiration lies within the Bible!

j 8:4 This is a play on words, for Noah's name means "rest." God's covenant of peace with Noah would remain (Ps. 32:6; Isa. 54:10). Who measured all these things? Who knew the mountains were covered by fifteen cubits? It could not have been Noah or Moses, unless God had showed them. The amazing details of the account of the flood all point to divine inspiration of Scripture.

k 8:4 Mt. Ararat is believed to be on the border of Turkey, Armenia, and Iran, known as Urartu in Assyrian inscriptions. See 2 Kings 19:37; Isa. 37:38; Jer. 51:27. *Ararat* means "the curse is reversed" or "high and holy land." The resting place of God's sons and daughters is where *the curse is reversed* (the cross and empty tomb), in the *high and holy land* of being seated with Christ in the heavenly realm (Eph. 2:6).

the 10th month, all the mountaintops appeared.[a]

[6]After 40 more days Noah opened the window he had made in the ark [7]and released a raven. It flew back and forth *from the ark* until the earth was dry.[b]

[8]Then he sent out a dove[c] to see if the waters had receded from the surface of the ground. [9]But the dove found no place to rest, so it returned to Noah in the ark because the waters still covered the face of the earth. Noah put out his hand and grasped the dove and put it back into the ark. [10]He waited another seven days and released the dove from the ark again. [11]Before evening, the dove came back to him—and there in its beak was a freshly plucked olive leaf![d] So Noah realized that the waters had finally subsided from the earth.

[12]Then he waited another seven days and sent the dove out again, but this time it did not return to him in the ark.[e]

[13]In Noah's six hundred and first year, on the first day of the first month, the waters were dried up from the earth. Noah lifted the hatch, looked out, and saw the dry ground. [14]On the twenty-seventh day of the second month,[f] the earth was dry. [15]Then God said to Noah, [16]"Come out of the ark, you and your wife, your sons, and their wives.[g] [17]Release all the animals with you and set them free—birds, animals large and small—every living thing. And they will multiply and abound and flourish on the earth *and in the sky*." [18]So Noah and his family left the ark; [19]and every animal large and small, every bird and crawling thing came out of the ark by families.[h]

---

a 8:5 The mountaintops became visible seventy-three days after the ark rested. This new age now begins with eight people. Eight is the Biblical number of a new beginning.

b 8:7 In other words, the unclean raven apparently did not return to the ark.

c 8:8 Or "sent out a dove from him," an awkward construction in English. The next verse shows that Noah took the dove back into the ark with his hand to see if there was any clay or mud on its feet.

d 8:11 The contrast of the raven and the dove is an allegory. The raven symbolizes the Law, which was sent out first, but gave no assurance that waters of judgment had lifted. The dove, returning with an olive branch, the symbol of peace, symbolizes the gospel of grace given to us by the Holy Spirit. The gospel of our Lord Jesus Christ brought a better hope to the believer—judgment has retreated. Every time the Dove of God comes, he brings a fresh olive branch—fresh oil for the sons and daughters of the highest.

e 8:12 The Dove (Holy Spirit) cannot rest where there is corruption and death. For generations, the Dove, seeking a place to rest, flew over Abraham, Moses, the Prophets and kings unable to find a resting place. Until at last, at the river Jordan, the Dove came from the open heaven and rested on the perfect man, Jesus, the Son of God (Matt. 3:16). Has the gentle Dove found a nest in your heart? In order to have the gifts (Gal. 5:22–23) and power of the Dove, you must seek first the nature of the Lamb.

f 8:14 Noah was obedient to God, refusing to move until he heard the Word of the Lord. Just as he waited for the command to enter, he waited for the command to disembark.

g 8:16 Noah waited over six weeks in the ark on top of Ararat while the waters completely receded, and the ground was dry. This took great discipline, for no one likes to wait. But God's timing is always perfect. Noah was in the ark for a total of one year and seventeen days.

h 8:19 That is, by species. Noah and his family would never forget the moment they pushed open the door of the ark and walked out into a new world. Eight human beings found a new beginning with God. Like a new Adam and a new Eve, they began all over again. What a spine-tingling moment it was! The bright sunlight, the fresh air, the gentle breeze—God had seen them through!

God's Promise to Noah

20Noah erected an altar dedicated to Yahweh.*a* Then he selected ritually clean animals and birds of every species and offered them as burnt sacrifices on the altar. 21And when Yahweh smelled the sweet fragrance of Noah's offerings, *his heart was stirred,*b* and he said: "Never again will I curse the earth because of people, even though the imagination of their hearts are evil from their childhood; nor will I ever again destroy every living creature as I have done. *I promise this:*

22"As long as earth exists
there will always be *seasons
of* planting and harvest,
cold and heat,
summer and winter,
day and night."

God's Covenant with Noah

9 God *lovingly* blessed Noah and all his family and said to them, "Reproduce, be fruitful, and populate the earth. 2I will cause every living creature of earth, sky, and sea*c* to fear and dread you from this time forward. They are now under your authority.*d* 3You may now eat the meat of animals*e* as well as green plants; I now give you everything *for food for you.* 4However, you must not eat meat with its lifeblood still in it, *for its life is in the blood.* 5If anyone takes another person's life, I will demand an account—whether from man or beast, I will demand an account for taking a human life.

6"Whoever sheds human blood,
by other humans, he must have
his own blood shed;
for *to kill a person is to kill* one
made
in God's own *beautiful* image.

7Now all of you, *with my blessing,*
reproduce,
be fruitful and repopulate the
earth."*f*

8Then God said to Noah and his family, 9"I establish my *loving* covenant*g* with you, your descendants, 10and every living creature that is with you; animals large and small, birds, and every living thing that came out of the ark. 11I will maintain my *loving* covenant with you. I will never again completely destroy life on earth by means of a flood. *Yes,* never again will a flood destroy the whole earth!"

The Rainbow

12"Here is the sign for you and future generations that my *loving* covenant will endure between me and you and

---

a 8:20 The first thing Noah did when he gets out of the ark is to worship Yahweh. Noah realized the great love of God that was upon his life and offered himself to God. The kindness of God is also seen in Jesus. God is always ready to renew a relationship with people when they turn to him.

b 8:21 Or "he said to his heart."

c 9:2 Or "every animal of the earth, every bird of the air, everything that creeps on the ground, and all the fish of the sea."

d 9:2 Or "are delivered into your hands."

e 9:3 Or "every moving thing that lives." See Col. 2:16; 1 Tim. 4:3–5.

f 9:7 Or "swarm throughout the earth."

g 9:9 The Hebrew word for covenant is *berit* and is found in the Hebrew in this chapter. God's covenant turns judgment into grace. See vv. 9, 11, 12 (twice), 13, 15, 16, 17.

every animal that came with you out of the ark: [13]I have placed[a] my rainbow[b] among the clouds, and it will be a sign of my *loving* covenant between me and the earth. [14]Whenever I bring clouds over the earth, and the rainbow appears in the clouds, [15]I will remember my covenant with you and with every living thing upon the earth. Never again will the waters become a flood to destroy life from the earth. [16]When the rainbow is in the clouds, I will see it and remember the everlasting covenant I made with you and every living thing of every kind upon the earth."

[17]So God said to Noah, "The rainbow is my *signature* in the sky, my seal of love[c] to confirm that I have kept my covenant between me and every living thing on earth."

Noah's Sons

[18]Noah's sons came out of the ark with him: Shem, Ham (the father of Canaan), and Japheth. [19]From these three sons of Noah the entire world was repopulated.

[20]Noah, a farmer, was the first to plant a vineyard. [21]He drank so much of the wine he made that he got drunk and passed out naked inside his tent.[d] [22]And Ham, the father of Canaan, *went into the tent and* gazed on his *shamefully* exposed father.[e] Then he went out and informed his brothers. [23]So, Shem and Japheth took their father's[f] cloak and walked backwards with the cloak on their shoulders into the tent to cover up their naked father. *Respectfully*, they turned their faces away so as not to see their father lying there exposed. [24]When Noah sobered up and realized what his youngest son had done to him, [25]he uttered these words:

"Cursed be *your son*, Canaan,[g]
and let him be the lowest of servants[h] to his brothers."

---

a 9:13 This is the Hebrew word *nathan*, which means "give" or "grant." This same word is used in Gen. 1:19.

b 9:13 Or "bending," most often translated "warrior's bow," for just as a warrior hangs up his bow after the battle, so God's bow, without arrows, is now surrendered to the sky, and not aimed on earth because of his love for humanity. The rainbow around God's throne is a full circle, for the earth does not cut off God's rainbow promises. And it is an emerald color rainbow around the throne, for it is the promise of life. See Rev. 4:3; 10:1.

c 9:17 Or "sign of confirmation."

d 9:21 Chronologically, this would likely have been years after they exited the ark.

e 9:22 Various Hebrew scholars surmise that this was a euphemistic account of Ham doing some act of gross indecency, not mere voyeurism. See also Prov. 30:17; cf. 1 Peter 4:8.

f 9:23 Or "the garment," it is possible that Ham brought his father's garment outside the tent to show it to his brothers.

g 9:25 Although it was Ham, Noah's son, who violated his father, Ham's son Canaan was the one who was cursed. Some see the possibility that Canaan was complicit with what Ham did.

h 9:25 Or "slave of slaves." Canaan was the ancestor of the Canaanites. *Canaan* means "bow down." See Josh. 9:23; Judg. 1.

²⁶He also said,

"Worthy of praise is Yahweh,
the God of Shem!ᵃ
Let Canaan be Shem's slave.
²⁷May God enlarge Japheth's family
and increase his *territory*.ᵇ
May he *share in the blessing of
Shem*,
and his descendants make their
homes

among the tents of Shem,ᶜ
and may Canaan be his slave also!"ᵈ

²⁸After the flood, Noah lived another
three hundred and fifty years. ²⁹Noah's
entire lifetime was nine hundred and
fifty years, and then he died.ᵉ

10 This is the story of the descendants of Noah's three sons,
Shem, Ham, and Japheth. After the great
flood, they fathered many children.ᶠ

---

a 9:26 Jesus Christ came through the lineage of Shem (Luke 3:23–38), the father of the Semitic peoples. This is a prophecy that Shem would have a special relationship with Yahweh.

b 9:27 Or "May God make room for Japheth." This a play on words, for the Hebrew triliteral root for *Japheth* (y-p-t) is identical for "make room," "increase," or "enlarge (enrich, prosper)." Japheth was to become the father of enlarged nations, spreading out over the globe.

c 9:27 Many scholars view this as an alliance between Shem and Japheth that would include sharing the blessing of prosperity among them.

d 9:27 This account of Noah's curse and blessing of his three sons illustrates the power of a father's words over his children (and grandchildren) and how those words create the reality of their future. Descendants of each of Noah's sons were present at the crucifixion of the Lord Jesus. The descendants of Shem were present in the Jewish religious leaders who conspired to crucify the Messiah. Japheth was present in the Romans who participated jointly with the Jews to crucify the Lord Jesus. And a descendant of Ham was present in the person of Simon of Cyrene, who bore the cross of Christ in servitude (Luke 23:26). The sons of Noah are brought before us again in Acts 8–10. The Ethiopian eunuch was a descendant of Ham whom Philip blessed with the gospel (Acts 8). Saul of Tarsus (Paul) was from Shem and also converted by the revelation of Jesus (Acts 9). Cornelius the centurion was a son of Japheth who believed the good news of Christ (Acts 10).

e 9:29 There are numerous parallels of Noah and Adam. Both came onto an earth that had been submerged by water. Both were given lordship over creation. Both were blessed and told to multiply. Both were men of the soil, working the ground. Both sinned in a garden (vineyard). Both experienced the exposure of nakedness. Both men's sins affected their posterity. Both had three sons. And both experienced a prophecy following their fall.

f 10:1 This begins the second ten-generation account in Genesis and is incredibly important in understanding human history. This chapter contains what many have described as the "Table of Nations," the earliest ethnological table found in literature of the ancient world. Virtually all the names included here have been verified and found in archeological sites over the past one hundred years. There are precisely seventy names mentioned here, and seventy followers of Jesus were sent out as a testimony that the gospel of his kingdom is meant for all people (Luke 10:1–24). This chapter includes more than the names of people; it lists the names of cities, tribes, and nations. The underlying theme in this chapter is that God determines the boundaries of nations and seasons of history. See Pss. 82:8; 96:7–10; Jer. 10:7.

Descendants of Japheth

²The sons of Japheth were: Gomer,ᵃ Magog,ᵇ Madai,ᶜ Javan,ᵈ Tubal,ᵉ Meshech,ᶠ and Tiras.ᵍ ³The sons of Gomer were: Ashkenaz,ʰ Riphath,ⁱ and Togarmah.ʲ

⁴The sons of Javan were: Elishah,ᵏ Tarshish,ˡ Cyprus,ᵐ and Rhodes.ⁿ ⁵All of Japheth's descendants lived in their respective tribes and regions, each group speaking its own language. From there, the people spread to distant shores and faraway lands.

---

a 10:2 Gomer means "complete" and was the ancestor of the ancient Cimmerians who are believed to have originated in southern Russia and northern Iran. Gomer is mentioned in Ezek. 38:6 as an ally of Gog and enemy of Israel. Romans, Gauls, Germans, Celts, and Britons could all be considered as descendants of Japheth and Gomer.

b 10:2 Magog means "region of Gog" and was a Scythian (Iranian) or Tartar (Russian) tribe. One church father, Jerome, states they were "Scythian nations, fierce and innumerable, who live beyond the Caucasus and the Lake Maeotis, and near the Caspian Sea, and spread out even onward to India." It is possible that the Chinese, Japanese, Alaskans, Russians, and Native Americans could be traced back as descendants of Japheth and Magog.

c 10:2 Madai means "middle land" and was the ancestor or the Medes who lives east of Assyria, south of the Caspian Sea. It is possible that Madai (Medes) can also include Persians. Isa. 13:17; 21:2; Jer. 51:11, 28.

d 10:2 Javan means "Ionia," or "Greece" and is the ancestor of a branch of Greek people.

e 10:2 Tubal means "brought forth" and in contemporary scholarship is Tabal, an Anatolian state and region north of the Black Sea, identified in Assyrian sources. There is a city in Russia named "Tubolsk."

f 10:2 Meshech means "drawing out" and was the ancestor of people identified by Assyrian records as Muscu and by Flavius Josephus with the Cappadocian "Mosocheni" (Mushki, possibly Moscow).

g 10:2 Tiras, or Tirana, meaning "desire," was the ancestor of the Thracians who were also called "Sea People." According to the Book of Jubilees, they inhabited four islands in the Mediterranean. This possibly includes the people who settled in the Balkans, Romania, Bulgaria, Moravia, and Italy.

h 10:3 Ashkenaz means "scattered" and was the ancestor of the northern Indo-Germanic tribes and the father of the Saxons and Scandinavians.

i 10:3 Riphath means "spoken" and was the ancestor of those that settled in Carpathia and Paphlagonia.

j 10:3 *Togarmah* means "you will break her" and is the ancestor of those who settled in modern-day Turkey and possibly Azerbaijan, Uzbekistan, and Kazakhstan.

k 10:4 Elishah means "God of the coming," or "God of the coming one" and was the ancestor of those who populated modern day Cyprus. He is mentioned in Ezek. 27:7 as the source of the purple dye shipped to Tyre.

l 10:4 Tarshish means "yellow stone" and is mentioned twenty-eight times in the Bible but is difficult to identify. Some believe he was the ancestor of those who settled in southern Turkey, although there is evidence that Tarshish was the ancestor of Sardinia, or Tartessos (Spain). See 1 Kings 10:22; Jer. 10:9; Jonah 1:3.

m 10:4 Or "Kittim" which means "bruisers" and is an ancient name for Cyprus. There is a Cyprian city named Kition.

n 10:4 *Dodanim* means "leaders" or *Rodanim* (1 Chron. 1:7) and is most often associated with Greece (Rhodes, Dardanelles).

Descendants of Ham

[6]The sons of Ham[a] were Ethiopia,[b] Egypt,[c] Libya,[d] and Canaan.[e] [7]The sons of Cush were Seba,[f] Havilah, Sabtah,[g] Raamah,[h] and Sabteca.[i] The sons of Raamah were Sheba[j] and Dedan.[k]

[8]Cush also had a son named Nimrod, who became known as the first mighty conqueror.[l] [9]He was a mighty despot[m] before Yahweh. There was a saying, "Like Nimrod, a mighty despot before Yahweh." [10]The centers[n] of his kingdom, Babel,[o] Erech,[p] and Akkad,[q] were in the land of Shinar.[r] [11]From there, he went into Assyria and built *the cities of* Nineveh,[s] Rehoboth-Ir,[t] Calah,[u] [12]and Resen[v] (which is

---

a 10:6 The Hamites are listed in four primary subgroups from south to north. The first three are in Africa and last in the land bridge between Africa and Asia.

b 10:6 Or "Cush" or "Kesh" (Egyptian), whose descendants settled in Ethiopia and southern Sudan.

c 10:6 Or "Mizraim," which means "land of the Copts," whose descendants settled in Egypt. See Ps.105:23.

d 10:6 Or "Put," which means "a bow," whose descendants settled in Libya and possibly Somalia. See Jer. 46:9.

e 10:6 The descendants of Canaan settled in Palestine (Phoenicia).

f 10:7 *Seba* means "drink" and is the ancient name for Meroe in northeast Africa. See Ps. 72:10; Isa. 43:3.

g 10:7 This is the only place Sabtah (striking) is mentioned in the Bible. It is likely a region in southern Arabia.

h 10:7 *Raamah* means "horse's mane" and is perhaps a south Arabian city mentioned in ancient inscriptions. See also Ezek. 27:22.

i 10:7 The descendants of Sabteca settled eastward in Samudake, along the Persian Gulf.

j 10:7 The descendants of Sheba, which means "an oath," were the Sabaeans who lived in southwest Arabia and were trading merchants. See Isa. 60:6.

k 10:7 The descendants of Dedan, which means "lowlands," are mentioned as traders with caravans of camels. See Isa. 21:13; Jer. 25:23; 49:8. Dedan may be identified as the present day oasis of Al-'Ula in northern Arabia or possibly Kuwait.

l 10:8 Or "strong man," or "giant" (LXX).

m 10:9 Or "a mighty hunter before Yahweh." Nimrod was a hunter of men (not simply animals), a potentate, a terrorist. See Jer. 16:16; Mark 3:22. Some etymological studies link Nimrod to the word for "rebel" or "we will rebel." Nimrod was the first despot and anarchist. Many believe that Nimrod was also named "Marduk," whom scholars identify as the god of the Babylonian religions. His wife was Semiramis. They bore a child that is identified by some as the Egyptian Osiris and the Hindu Vishnu. See 1 Chron. 1:10.

n 10:10 Or "The beginning of his kingdom."

o 10:10 Or "Babylon," which means "confusion," "mixed," or "chaos." Babel was a famous city on the Euphrates in modern Iraq.

p 10:10 A region southeast of Babylon known as Uruk (modern Warka). Erech means "long."

q 10:10 A region north of Babylon known as Agade. Akkad means "subtle."

r 10:10 Or "Babylonia."

s 10:11 Nineveh, which means "abode of the god Ninus," was the capital of Assyria 250 miles northwest of Baghdad. It is presently identified with the mounds of Kuyunjik and Nebi Yunus which means "the prophet Jonah."

t 10:11 Rehoboth-Ir means "(city of) broad streets."

u 10:11 Calah, which means "enthusiasm," was one of the four great cities of Assyria.

v 10:12 Resen, which means "fountainhead," was one of the four great cities of Assyria.

between the great city of Calah[a] and Nineveh).

[13]Egypt[b] was the father of the Ludites,[c] Anamites,[d] Lehabites,[e] Naphtuhites,[f] [14]Pathrusites,[g] Casluhites, and Caphtorites (the ancestors of the Philistines).[h]

[15]Canaan was the father of Sidon[i] (his firstborn), the Hittites,[j] [16]the Jebusites,[k] the Amorites,[l] the Girgashites,[m] [17]the Hivites,[n] the Arkites,[o] the Sinites,[p] [18]the Arvadites,[q] the Zemarites,[r] and the Hamathites.[s] The families of the Canaanites eventually scattered across [19]the Canaanite territory extending from Sidon toward Gerar[t] to Gaza[u] including Sodom,[v]

---

a 10:12 This is modern Nimrud in Iraq, south of Mosul. It is likely called the great city because it was at one time the royal capital of the Assyrians.

b 10:13 Or "Mizraim."

c 10:13 The Ludites, which means "firebrands," are difficult to identify. They are known as warriors and descendants of the Egyptian people. Some scholars see them as Lybians and others as Lydians.

d 10:13 The Anamites, which means "affliction of the waters," were an unidentified people who were descendants of Egypt.

e 10:13 The Lehabites were considered descendants of Libya. See 2 Chron. 12:3; 16:8; Dan. 11:43.

f 10:13 Naphtuhites may mean "people of the (Nile) delta."

g 10:14 The Pathrusites (related to Pathros, "southland") were inhabitants of Upper Egypt. See Jer. 44:15.

h 10:14 Some scholars link this parenthetical information with the previously noted Casluhites. The Philistines were from the area of the Aegean Sea and invaded the land of Canaan and Egypt in the 13th Century BC See Amos 9:7.

i 10:15 Sidon, which means "hunting," likely represents all of Phoenicia. See Judges 18:7; 1 Kings 5:6; 16:31.

j 10:15 Or "Heth," which means "terror," the father of the Hittites, a dominant tribe in Canaan.

k 10:16 The Jebusites, which means "people of the threshing floor," were the ancient inhabitants of the Jebus, a stronghold that was conquered by David when he established Jerusalem. David purchased from Araunah, the Jebusite, the plot of land upon which the Temple would later be built. See Josh. 15:8; 2 Sam. 5:6–9.

l 10:16 The Amorites, which means "talkers," inhabited the promised land west of the Jordan before the arrival of the Israelites. See Amos 2:9–10.

m 10:16 The Girgashites, which means "clay-dwellers," lived on the east of Lake Galilee.

n 10:17 Hivites, which means "villagers," were located in the vicinity of Gibeon (Josh. 9:7; 11:19) near Shechem (Gen 34:2) and near Mount Hermon (Josh. 11:3).

o 10:17 Beginning with the Arkites, which means "gnawing," verses 17–18 list inhabitants of cities. The Arkites are identified with modern Arqa in Lebanon.

p 10:17 The Sinites, which means "those of clay," are connected to an unidentified city, likely near Arqa in Lebanon. See 1 Chron. 1:15.

q 10:18 The Arvadites, which means "those who break loose," are connected to a coastal city in Lebanon, modern Ruad. See Ezek. 27:8, 11.

r 10:18 The Zemarites, which means "double woolen," are a people of a city south of Arvad.

s 10:18 The Hamathites, which means "fortress dwellers," are the people of the city of Hamath, modern Hama in Syria. See Num. 13:21; Josh. 13:5; Judges 3:3.

t 10:19 Gerar, which means "lodging place," was a Philistine town in Gaza, modern Umm.

u 10:19 Gaza, which means "the strong one," was a Philistine city in the southwest coastal region of Israel, modern Gaza City.

v 10:19 Sodom, which means "burning," was a Canaanite city located in the region of the Dead Sea, possibly identified with Tell el-Hammam in Jordan near the Israel border, and was destroyed by God's judgment of fire and brimstone. See Gen. 19:1–29.

Gomorrah,[a] Admah,[b] and Zeboiim,[c] as far as Lasha.[d] [20]These were the descendants of Ham by families, lands, languages, and nations.

Descendants of Shem

[21]Shem, the older brother of Japheth, also had sons and was the ancestor of all the sons of Eber, *who were also known as "Hebrews."*[e]

[22]The sons of Shem were Elam,[f] Assyria,[g] Arphaxad,[h] Lud,[i] and Aram.[j] [23]The sons of Aram were Uz,[k] Hul,[l] Gether,[m] and Mash.[n] [24]Arphaxad was the father of Shelah,[o] the father of Eber.

[25-26]Eber was the father of two sons: Peleg, (or *"Division,"*[p] for during his lifetime the earth was divided),[q] and his brother Joktan,[r] the father of Almodad,[s] Sheleph,[t] Hazarmaveth,[u] Jerah,[v]

---

a 10:19 Gomorrah, which means "submersion," was a Canaanite city, perhaps a twin city of Sodom located in the region of the Dead Sea.

b 10:19 Admah, which means "red earth," was a Canaanite city in the Siddim Valley.

c 10:19 *Zeboiim*, which means "gazelles," was a neighboring city of Sodom.

d 10:19 *Lasha*, which means "fissure," was a city of the Dead Sea Valley.

e 10:21 *Eber*, which means "the region beyond" or "the opposite side," was the eponymous ancestor of the Hebrews.

f 10:22 *Elam*, which means "eternal one" or "eternity," settled in Babylonia. Their capital city was Susa. See Gen. 14:1; Isa. 11:11.

g 10:22 Or "Asshur," the Hebrew word for Assyria.

h 10:22 Arphaxad, which means "he cursed the breast," is associated with Babylon, and some Jewish scholars identify him as the founder of the Chaldean city of Ur, the future home of Abram.

i 10:22 Lud, which means "strife," settled in northern Africa and may be the ancestor of the Lydians of Anatolia.

j 10:22 Aram, which means "exalted," refers to the Arameans who eventually settled in Syria and through their influence the Aramaic language shaped commerce and diplomacy.

k 10:23 Uz, which means "woodland," was the land of Job, possibly in Arabia.

l 10:23 Hul, which means "circle," was the ancestor of a Syrian people group, possibly the Armenians.

m 10:23 Gether, which means "fear," according to Josephus, was the ancestor of the Bactrians of Central Asia.

n 10:24 Or "Meshech" (LXX, 1 Chron. 1:17). Mash means "drawn out."

o 10:24 Shelah means "sent/shot forth (like a prayer)."

p 10:25 Or "earthquake."

q 10:25 Division is a play on words for *Peleg*, which means "disperse," "divide," or "cut into channels." The Hebrew word *'eretz*, which means "earth," is more commonly translated "land." In that case, "the earth was divided" could point to a tectonic dividing of the continents during the lifetime of Peleg. The Greeks call the Aegean Sea "the Archi*pelago*," the "first sea." There is some evidence to link this with the scientific theory of continental drift; the parting of the continents during the days of Peleg. Most scholars, however, view this "division" as the dividing of languages and dispersing of nations at the Tower of Babel.

r 10:25–26 Joktan, which means "he will be made little," was the ancestor of various Arabian tribes. His Arabic name means "wakeful."

s 10:25–26 Almodad means "not measured," or "God is friend" (LXX).

t 10:25–26 Sheleph, which means "drawn out," was the possible ancestor of various Yemenite tribes.

u 10:25–26 *Hazarmaveth*, which means "oasis of Mot" or "the god of death," was the possible ancestor of people who settled east of Yemen. He is equated with modern Hadramaut in Yemen.

v 10:25–26 Jerah, which means "moon" or "month," likely settled in south Arabia.

²⁷Hadoram,ᵃ Uzal,ᵇ Diklah,ᶜ ²⁸Obal,ᵈ Abimael,ᵉ Sheba,ᶠ ²⁹Ophir,ᵍ Havilah,ʰ and Jobab.ⁱ All the descendants of Joktan ³⁰lived in the territory that extends all the way from Meshaʲ toward the eastern hills of Sephar.ᵏ ³¹These were the families of Shem according to their genealogies, by their families, lands, languages, and nations. ³²After the flood, Noah's descendants formed nations as the people spread throughout the earth.

The Tower of Babel

11 Now everyone at that time spoke a single languageˡ with one vocabulary. ²As people migrated eastward,ᵐ they found a large plain in the land of Shinar and settled there.

³They said to one another, "Come, let's unite together and make bricks *of clay*ⁿ and burn them until they become hard." So, they piled up the bricks they made to serve as stones and collected tar for mortar. ⁴Then they said, "Come, let's begin work to build ourselves a city with a lofty tower that rises into the heavens. We'll make a name for ourselves, *a monument to us*,ᵒ instead of being scattered all over the earth."

⁵But when Yahweh came down to see the city and the tower which mortals had started building, ⁶he said, "If they have begun this as one people sharing a common language, then nothing they plan to do will be impossible for them. ⁷Come, let usᵖ go down and confuse

---

a 10:27 Hadoram, which means "the god Hadad is exalted," was the possible ancestor of Yemenite people (Sabeans).

b 10:27 Uzal (or Azal) was the ancient name of Sanaa, capital of Yemen.

c 10:27 Diklah means "date palm."

d 10:28 Obal means "stripped bare." There are a number of possible locations in Yemen of a city of Obal.

e 10:28 Abimael means "a father sent by God" or "truly, God is my father." Abimael was an ancestor of Arabian tribes.

f 10:28 Descendants of Sheba settled in southern Arabia. Sheba is sometimes identified with the entire Arabian Peninsula. See also 1 Kings 10.

g 10:29 Ophir is known as the east coast of Arabia and is frequently connected to gold, i.e. "the gold of Ophir."

h 10:29 Havilah is not believed to be the same Havilah mentioned in 2:11. This region of Havilah was in Arabia toward the Red Sea.

i 10:29 Jobab, which means "desert," is an unknown region likely in Arabia.

j 10:30 Mesha, which means "freedom," is the region on the east coast of the Red Sea.

k 10:30 Sephar, which means "a numbering," is the hilly region near the Red Sea.

l 11:1 Or "one lip."

m 11:2 Or "from the east." The Hebrew is ambiguous.

n 11:3 God's building never includes bricks, only stones. Man makes bricks; God is the Maker of stones. The New Jerusalem will not be made from bricks but from precious stones (Rev. 21:18–20). Pharaoh made his treasure cities out of bricks; God raises up his temple using living stones (1 Pet. 2:5).

o 11:4 An ancient historian, Philo Judaeus, says that each worker engraved their names on the bricks to memorialize themselves. Today their names are forgotten, and the Name of God stands as a High Tower. Seeking to make a name for ourselves is self-worship. We are to lay aside our reputation to make the Name of Jesus famous (Phil. 2:3–11). Jesus emptied himself of his outward glory.

p 11:7 In the plural pronoun, many theologians see the three members of the Godhead.

their language and prevent them from understanding each other."[a]

[8]So Yahweh scattered them over the entire earth, and they stopped building their city.[b] [9]That is why the city was called Babel—because it was there that Yahweh confused[c] the language of the whole world and from there the people were scattered over the face of the earth.

Genealogy of Shem

[10]These are the descendants of Shem:[d]

Two years after the flood, at the age of one hundred, Shem had a son named Arphaxad.[e] [11]And after Arphaxad was born, Shem lived another five hundred years and had other sons and daughters.

[12]When Arphaxad was thirty-five, he had a son named Shelah.[f] [13]And after Shelah was born Arphaxad lived another four hundred and three years and had other sons and daughters.

[14]When Shelah was thirty, he had a son named Eber.[g] [15]And after Eber was born, Shelah lived another four hundred and three years and had other sons and daughters.

[16]When Eber was thirty-four, he had a son named Peleg.[h] [17]And after Peleg was born, Eber lived another four hundred and thirty years and had other sons and daughters.

[18]When Peleg was thirty, he had a son named Reu. [19]And after Reu was born, Peleg lived another two hundred and nine years and had other sons and daughters.

[20]When Reu was thirty-two,[i] he had a son named Serug. [21]And after Serug was born, Reu lived another two hundred and seven years and had other sons and daughters.

[22]When Serug was thirty,[j] he had a son named Nahor. [23]And after Nahor was born, Serug lived another two hundred years and had other sons and daughters.

[24]When Nahor was twenty-nine, he had a son named Terah.[k] [25]And after Terah was born, Nahor[l] lived another

---

a   11:7 Some linguists believe there are nearly seven thousand languages in the world. Although God confused the language of earth, he will one day purify (clarify) the language so that people will serve him in unity. See Zeph. 3:9. Acts 2 is the reversal of Babel, for God gave men unlearned languages as they spoke in tongues.

b   11:8 The Bible ends with two figurative cities, Babylon and the New Jerusalem. Babylon-builders will always seek to make a name for themselves. Those who are a part of the New Jerusalem only long to see the name of Jesus exalted. The overcomer's name will be engraved on a pillar forever in the "City" of our God where he makes his dwelling with man.

c   11:9 Babel comes from the word "to confuse." However, in the Babylonian language, the city was called Bab-ilu, "the gate of God."

d   11:10 See 1 Chron. 1:17–27; Luke 3:34–36.

e   11:10 See Gen. 10:22.

f   11:12 See Gen. 10:24.

g   11:14 See Gen. 10:24.

h   11:16 See Gen. 10:25.

i   11:20 Or "132" (LXX, Sam. Pent.). It is Jewish tradition that Reu was born when the Tower of Babel had begun to be built. Reu means "friend" or "shepherd."

j   11:22 Or "130" (LXX, Sam. Pent.). Serug means "interwoven" or "strength." According to the book of Jubilees, Serug was the first one of Shem's descendants to turn from Yahweh to worship idols. It is said he taught sorcery to his son Nahor.

k   11:24 Terah means "wild goat" or "wanderer."

l   11:25 Jewish tradition states that Nahor lived in Ur, on the Euphrates in lower Mesopotamia, the place where God appeared to Abraham. Nahor means "angry," "passionate."

one hundred and nineteen years and had other sons and daughters.

²⁶When Terah was seventy, he had sons named Abram,ᵃ Nahor, and Haran.ᵇ

The Story of Terah

²⁷Here are the descendants of Terah: Terah was the father of Abram, Nahor, and Haran, and Haran was the father of Lot. ²⁸Haran preceded his father, Terah, in death in the land of his birth, in the Chaldean city of Ur.ᶜ ²⁹*The brothers*, Abram and Nahor, were both married. Abram's wife was Sarai.ᵈ Nahor married the daughter of *his deceased brother* Haran; her name was Milcah,ᵉ and her sister was Iscah.ᶠ ³⁰Now Sarai was barren and childless.

³¹Terah took his son Abram, his grandson Lot,ᵍ the son of Haran, and his daughter-in-law Sarai, his son Abram's wife, and they all departed together from the Chaldean city of Ur to go into the land of Canaan.ʰ But when they journeyed as far as Haran,ⁱ they settled there. ³²Terah lived two hundred and five years and died in Haran.

God Appears to Abram

12 Now Yahweh said to Abram:ʲ

"Leave *it all behind*ᵏ—

---

a 11:26 This was the Patriarch who would later have his name changed to Abraham. Abram means "exalted father." *Abraham* means "father of a multitude." There were ten generations from Adam to Noah and ten generations from Shem to Abram.

b 11:26 *Haran* means "living in the high place" or "mountaineer."

c 11:28 The word *Chaldea* means "demonic;" *Ur* means "flame." Ur was an ancient city-state in Mesopotamia (modern Iraq), which was approximately fifty miles south of Babylon. The ruin of Ur can still be seen at modern Tell el-Muqayyar. In 2000 BC, Ur was perhaps one of the largest cities of the world. It is clear that Abram and his father served foreign gods. Ur was named after the moon goddess and was her center of worship. The Chaldeans were astrologers, occultists, and idol worshippers. Ancient traditions state that Terah was an idol-maker until his death. The Jewish writers have a tradition that Abram and his father were cast into a fiery furnace for refusing to worship idols and were miraculously delivered. See Josh. 24:2.

d 11:29 Sarai means "ruler" or "my princess." God will later change her name to "Sarah."

e 11:29 Nahor married his orphaned niece. Milcah means "queen."

f 11:29 Iscah means "discerner" or "one who scans abroad." Iscah is Jessica in English.

g 11:31 Lot means "to wrap a covering" or "to envelop."

h 11:31 The land of Canaan takes its name from the son of Ham, Canaan. The land of Canaan is found sixty-six times in the Old Testament but not found in the New Testament.

i 11:31 Most scholars identify Haran with a city, now in ruins, called Harran in Turkey, approximately six hundred miles from Ur. It is the city that Jacob fled to (Gen. 27:43; 28:10) and, later, the Assyrians destroyed in the days of Hezekiah (2 Kings 19:12; Isa. 37:12).

j 12:1 The God of Glory appeared to Abram and spoke with him (Acts 7:2–5). God's appearance to Abram was sudden and without warning. The same voice of creation now proclaims a message of hope and blessing to all the world. Abram had no burning bush to inspire him, no tablets of stone to guide him, and no ark of the covenant as a centerpiece of worship. Neither did Abram have a Temple to worship in, a Bible to read, nor a priest to counsel him. Nor did Abram have a pastor to pray for him, nor a prophet to prophesy to him. But Abram had a divine encounter.

k 12:1 Or "Go yourself," from *lech-lecha*, which is a Hebrew play on words. The implication is that although Abram must undergo a traumatic departure from his native land, he is actually traveling to find his more authentic self. Perhaps, "Go and find yourself" conveys the meaning.

your native land,[a]
your people,
your father's household,[b]
and go to the land that I will show
  you.[c]
[2]*Follow me,*
and I will make you into a great
  nation.[d]
I will exceedingly bless and prosper you,
and I will make you famous,[e]
so that you will be a *tremendous*
  source of blessing for others.
[3]I will bless all who bless you
and curse all who curse you.[f]
And through you all the families
  of the earth will be blessed."[g]
[4]So Abram obeyed Yahweh and left;
and Lot went with him.

Now Abram was seventy-five years
old when he departed from Haran
after his father died.[h] [5]He took his wife
Sarai, his nephew Lot, and all the possessions and people[i] he had acquired
in Haran; and they departed for the
land of Canaan. When they arrived
in the land of Canaan, [6]Abram passed
through the land and stopped at the
sacred site of Shechem,[j] famous for
the great oak tree of Moreh.[k] At that

---

a 12:1 The Hebrew word *eretz* is etymologically linked to the Canaanite word *ratzon*, which means
   "firmness of will" or "stubbornness." God is saying to Abram with double meaning, leave your
   country but also leave your own will behind in order to enter God's plan. We need to leave it all
   behind, including our ideas of how God will work.

b 12:1 God was calling Abram out from more than just his relatives. He was calling Abram out
   from specific deity worship connected to nations, clans, and ancestors.

c 12:1 Leaving all that is familiar would display an incredible act of faith on Abram's part (Heb.
   11:8–10). He is told to go into an unknown land, but it would result in the seven-fold blessing
   of verses 2–3.

d 12:2 This would take a miracle, for Sarai was barren. This would have greatly stretched his
   faith, yet he believed. Because he had left his nation, God would make Abram into a great
   nation. God gave creative ability to Abram, not only to produce offspring, but applied creative
   ability to form lasting enterprises that would shape a nation. God gave the ability to create
   community to Abram and his seed.

e 12:2 Or "I will make your name great," which in ancient Near East also implies being highly
   esteemed for his character. Also, the building of the Tower of Babel was so that men could
   "make a name" for themselves. This was intended to be the gift of God and not something to
   be seized for oneself.

f 12:3 Or "All who cause you harm I will punish."

g 12:3 Or "And by you all the families of the earth will bless themselves" or "Every nation will
   long for me to bless them as I have blessed you." See Num. 24:9; Isa. 49:6; Gal. 3:8.

h 12:4 See Acts 7:4.

i 12:5 Or "souls." Jewish tradition states that Abram preached the revelation of Yahweh, the
   true God. Also, Abram was wealthy before Pharaoh gave him gifts (Gen. 12:16).

j 12:6 Or "the sacred site of Shechem." The Hebrew word *maqom* (a generic place) is never used to
   describe a city. In this context it is likely linked to the Arabic word *maqam*, which means "sacred
   site." The word *Shechem* means "between the shoulders." See Isa. 9:6; 22:22; Luke 15:4–5. The
   shoulder represents all power and authority (Isa. 9:6). The site of Shechem was the actual physical
   center of modern Israel and mentioned as a sacred place (Gen. 35:4; Josh. 24:25; Judg. 9:6, 37).

k 12:6 Or "the oak (cluster of oaks) of Moreh (oracle giver, instruction)." Undoubtedly, this was a
   place of mystery, and it was so famous that people used the tree as a landmark. See Deut. 11:30.
   At the great tree of Moreh, Yahweh taught Abram to walk by faith not by sight. God will lead us
   to a place of true strength (Shechem) and instruct our heart (Moreh) to trust in him alone.

time, the Canaanites were also in the land.

[7]Then Yahweh appeared[a] before Abram and said, "This is the land I will personally deliver to your seed."[b] So Abram erected an altar there to Yahweh, who had appeared before him. [8]From there, he journeyed on toward the hill country east of Bethel[c] and pitched his tent[d] with Bethel on the west and Ai[e] on the east. And there he built *another* altar to Yahweh where he prayed and worshiped Yahweh.[f] [9]Then Abram journeyed from there by stages through the southern desert region.[g]

Abram Detours to Egypt

[10]At that time, a severe famine struck the land of Canaan,[h] forcing Abram to travel down to Egypt and live there *as a foreigner.* [11]When he drew near to Egypt, he said to his wife Sarai, "Look, *I'm worried* because I know that you are a beautiful, gorgeous woman. [12]When the Egyptian men take one look at you, they will say, 'She is his wife.' Then they will kill me in order to have you. [13]Just tell them you are my sister[i] so that they will treat me well for your sake and spare my life."

[14]When Abram entered Egypt, everyone noticed Sarai's stunning beauty.[j] [15]When Pharaoh's dignitaries spotted her, they went to Pharaoh and raved about her beauty. Then they took Sarai into the palace *and made her part of Pharaoh's harem.* [16]Because she pleased Pharaoh, Abram got along

---

a 12:7 Or "made himself visible." Scripture records at least nine appearances of God (theophanies) to Abraham (Acts 7:2). The first was when he was still in Ur. See also Gen. 13:14; 15:1–21; 17:1–27; 18:1–33; 21:12; 22:1, 15.

b 12:7 Or "to your future descendants." Rom. 4:13; Heb. 11:12. God's divine declaration assigned the land of Israel to Abram and his descendants.

c 12:8 Bethel means "House of God." This is modern Beitin, a city about eleven miles north of Jerusalem. It is clear Abram adored Yahweh and was faithful to his voice.

d 12:8 While Abram lived in a tent without foundations, he was looking and waiting for a city with foundations (Heb.11:10). Likewise, we are living in the "tent" of church life today, waiting for its ultimate consummation—the New Jerusalem, the City of God with foundations. Paul, the Abraham of the New Testament, was a tentmaker.

e 12:8 Ai means "the heap of ruins." It is often identified as et-Tell about a mile from ancient Bethel. See Josh. 7:2–8:28. The House of God is drawing us in. We must turn our back forever on the old creation life, which is nothing more than a heap of ruins! Bethel is a house; Ai (the world) is a *heap of ruins.*

f 12:8 Or "and he called upon the name of Yahweh," which implies both prayer and offering a sacrifice.

g 12:9 That is, the Negev. Abram had traversed the entire length of Israel from north to south.

h 12:10 Although the promised land was a land flowing (flourishing) with "milk and honey," all three Patriarchs (Abraham, Isaac, Jacob) and Joseph experienced a famine (Gen. 26:1; 41:54; 42:1; 43:1). Faith will always be tested. This famine tested Abram's faith. So often when we set out for our promised land, we encounter a famine. You can be right where God wants you to be, and still be faced with severe trials. It is better to suffer in God's path than to be at ease in Satan's.

i 12:13 In fact, Sarai was his half sister (Gen. 20:12). If the Egyptians were to kill Abram, it would leave Sarai vulnerable to the men of Egypt. This was in fact, a troubling moral dilemma for Abram. By calling her his "sister," it culturally required a negotiation with her "brother" to have any interaction with her.

j 12:14 Sarai was at least sixty-five at this time, ten years younger than Abram.

very well in Egypt and received royal treatment: he was given sheep, cattle, male and female donkeys, camels, and male and female slaves.[a]

[17]But Yahweh struck Pharaoh and his household with terrible diseases because he had taken Abram's wife, Sarai. [18]So Pharaoh sent for Abram and said, "How could you do this to me? Why didn't you tell me she was your wife?[b] [19]And why did you *lie to me* by saying, 'She's my sister,' so that I took her as my wife? Now, here's your wife back; take her and begone!" [20]Then Pharaoh gave strict orders to his men to escort them out of Egypt along with everything they had.[c]

Abram Had a Lot to Lose

13 Abram took his wife and all that he owned, and left Egypt. They returned to the southern desert region, and Lot went with them.

[2]Now Abram had become very rich[d] in livestock, silver, and gold. [3]And he journeyed on from place to place as far as *the hill country region of* Bethel. He returned to the place between Bethel and Ai where he had pitched his tent at the beginning. [4]This was the place he had first built an altar to pray and worship Yahweh.[e]

[5]Now Lot, who accompanied Abram, *was also rich and* had accumulated flocks, herds, family, and servants.[f] [6-7]Arguments erupted between Abram's herdsmen and Lot's herdsmen because the land could not support both living together, for their animals and possessions were too numerous. At that time, Canaanites and Perizzites were also in the land.[g]

[8]So Abram said to Lot, "Let's not quarrel with each other, or between our herdsmen, since we are relatives. [9]Look at the vast land that is in front of you! Let's settle in different regions. If you choose the land on the left, then I'll go right, and if you want land on the right, then I'll go left."

---

a 12:16 All of Pharaoh's gifts were signs of great wealth imparted to Abram by the king. It was the great wealth and many possessions that caused Lot to want to separate from Abram (13:6–7). There were many people who accompanied Abram both into Egypt and back into Canaan. He had the converts he acquired in Haran (v. 5), plus 318 trained soldiers who were born under Abram's care (Gen. 14:14) who also had wives and children. It is possible that Abram had several thousand people who accompanied him.

b 12:18 Somehow, perhaps by a dream, God showed Pharaoh his sin.

c 12:20 Besides great possessions, Abram also acquired servants in Egypt, and Hagar was one of them (Gen. 16:3).

d 13:2 Or "weighty," "heavy."

e 13:4 Or "he called on the name of Yahweh." Abram went back to the first altar he had built to commune with this God who had made promises to him. There are times we, too, need to go back to our beginning in order to recapture our "first love" for Jesus before we can move forward. See Rev. 2:3–4.

f 13:5 Or literally "tents," meaning those who camped with Lot.

g 13:6–7 The implication is that grazing rights were in dispute between all four parties (Abraham, Lot, Canaanites, Perizzites).

¹⁰Lot lifted his eyes and carefully surveyed the land around him*a* all the way to Zoar. He noticed that the Jordan Valley was fertile and well-watered (this was before Yahweh had destroyed Sodom and Gomorrah). It looked *beautiful*, like the garden of Yahweh, or like Egypt. ¹¹So Lot chose to settle in the Jordan Valley. He departed toward the east, and The family split up and separated from each other. ¹²Abram settled in the land of Canaan while Lot settled in the cities of the lowlands, at a place*b* near Sodom. ¹³Now, the people of Sodom were extremely wicked and rebelled against Yahweh.

God Speaks Promises to Abram

¹⁴After Lot separated from him,*c* Yahweh spoke to Abram, "Lift up your eyes and look around you to the north, the south, the east, and the west. ¹⁵As far as you can see in every direction is the land that I will give to you forever—to you and your seed. ¹⁶I will multiply them until they are as numerous as the specks of dust on the earth. If anyone could count the dust of the earth, then your offspring could also be counted. ¹⁷Now, get up and walk through the land— its length and its breadth. *All the land you walk upon* will be my gift to you!"*d*

¹⁸Abram moved his camp and settled by the oaks of Mamre,*e* which are at Hebron,*f* and there he built another altar to Yahweh.

---

a 13:10 Or "Lot lifted up his eyes." When Abram offered the choice to Lot, he should have said, "Uncle, I choose you. God is with you. My choice is your choice." Every young person likes to be separated from the older generation. Lot missed the will of God by separating from the called one, Abram. There is protection, covering, and anointing when we walk with those who walk with God. Our flesh would rather "do it on our own" but God's way is to walk in fellowship with called ones. The meaning of Lot is "covert," "secret," or "concealed." Everything about Lot was hidden away in his heart. Compromise was a way of life for him. The secret tug of the world drew him away from the place of blessing. He had never really left Ur; he was still an idolater at heart. When he chose the rich plains, he was looking for the closest thing that resembled Egypt. He chose what would please him without considering the consequences. Lot's possessions were eventually burned in the fires of judgment, and he ended up living in a cave.

b 13:12 Or "pitched his tent."

c 13:14 Although the New Testament describes Lot as "righteous" (2 Pet. 2:7–8), Scripture portrays him as an object lesson of one who compromised his faith by wanting both to follow Yahweh and to love this present world. See Luke 17:28–32. It appears that God waited until Abram and Lot finally separated before giving Abram further blessings. Through the life of Abram, we learn that separation brings revelation. Abram separated from (1) his country, (2) his relatives, (3) Egypt, (4) Lot, (5) his desire to get wealth (chapter 14), (6) Ishmael (chapter 21), and (7) from his beloved son, Isaac (chapter 22). These seven separations brought revelation, encounters, blessings, miracles, and inheritance.

d 13:17 See Josh. 24:3–4.

e 13:18 Mamre means "fatness." It is a picture of the strength of God's anointing and the weighty glory of the Lord. Mamre is located about three miles north of Hebron. It was the site of a pagan shrine, but Abram reclaimed it for Yahweh and erected an altar to the true God.

f 13:18 *Hebron* means "to unite (in fellowship)." The modern Arabic name for Hebron is *al-Halil er-Rahman*, meaning "friend of the Merciful One," a reference to Abraham, the friend of God.

Abram Rescues Lot

14 During the reign of Amraphel[a] king of Babylon,[b] he allied with three other kings: Arioch[c] king of Ellasar,[d] Kedorlaomer[e] king of Elam,[f] and Tidal[g] king of Goyim.[h] [2]These four kings went to war against five kings: Bera[i] king of Sodom,[j] Birsha[k] king of Gomorrah,[l] Shinab[m] king of Admah,[n] Shemeber[o] king of Zeboiim,[p] and the king of Bela,[q] which is Zoar.[r] [3-4]Kedorlaomer had oppressed these five kings for twelve years until they rebelled against him in the thirteenth year. They all became regional allies in the valley of Siddim,[s] which is now the Dead Sea.

[5]In the fourteenth year, Kedorlaomer went to war with his allied kings. They defeated the Rephaites[t] in Ashteroth-karnaim,[u] the Zuzites[v] in Ham,[w] the Emites[x] in Shavah-kiriathaim,[y] [6]and the Horites[z] in the hill country of

---

a 14:1 Amraphel most likely means "speaker of dark secrets." Some Assyriologists and scholars identify him as the famous King Hammurabi of Babylon.

b 14:1 Or "Shinar," which means "country of two rivers."

c 14:1 Arioch means "fierce lion."

d 14:1 Or "Larsa," a city-state of lower Chaldea. It was the center of the cult of sun-god Utu. It is recognized as modern Tell Senkereh in Iraq. Ellasar means "God is chastener."

e 14:1 Kedorlaomar means "the servant of the goddess Lagamar (no mercy)."

f 14:1 Elam means "hidden" and was an ancient pre-Iranian kingdom in Persia. Susa was its principal city.

g 14:1 Tidal means "great son." He was a chief (king) of various nomadic tribes in Mesopotamia.

h 14:1 Goyim was likely a country called Gutium east of the Tigris in the lowlands of Mesopotamia. Goyim is also the Hebrew word for nations, peoples.

i 14:2 Bera means "with evil."

j 14:2 Sodom means "burning."

k 14:2 Birsha means "with wickedness."

l 14:2 Gomorrah means "submersion."

m 14:2 Although some believe Shinab means "splendor of the father," the *Midrash* (Ber. Rab. 42) explains Shinab as *sho'-ebh mammon*, "one who draws money (wherever he can)."

n 14:2 Admah means "earth fortress."

o 14:2 Shemeber likely means "known for being strong."

p 14:2 *Zeboiim* means "gathering of troops" or "gazelles (beautiful ones)" and is recognized as modern Tsvoyim.

q 14:2 Bela means "destruction."

r 14:2 Zoar means "insignificant" or "small."

s 14:3-4 Siddim means "division" or "demons."

t 14:5 Or "giants." See Deut. 3:11. The Hebrew word Rephaim also means "shades (ghosts)" or "spirits of the dead." See Isa. 26:14, 19; Ps. 88:10.

u 14:5 *Ashteroth* was a Canaanite goddess of fertility and coupled with *karnaim* means "goddess of two horns." Ashteroth-karnaim was the likely capital city of Og, king of Bashan, east of the Sea of Galilee.

v 14:5 Zuzites or "Zuzim" means "roving creatures."

w 14:5 The city of Ham may be the ancient name of the Ammonite capital Rabboth-Ammon.

x 14:5 Emites, or "Emim" means "terrors." Emites is the Moabite name of a giant people who once occupied Moab. See Deut. 2:10–11.

y 14:5 Shavah-kiriathaim means "the plain of the two cities."

z 14:6 Horites means "cave dwellers." Mt. Hor is the location where the first High Priest, Aaron, was buried. Mt. Hor is near Petra in Jordan. See Num. 20:22–28.

Seir,[a] as far as El Paran[b] near the desert.[c] ⁷Then they turned back and attacked En-mishpat[d] (that is, Kadesh) and subdued all the country of the Amalekites[e] and the Amorites[f] who lived in Hazazon-tamar.[g]

⁸Then the king of Sodom, the king of Gomorrah, the king of Admah, the king of Zeboiim, and the king of Bela (that is, Zoar), marched out in battle formation in the valley of Siddim. ⁹There they faced off against Kedorlaomer, king of Elam; Tidal, king of Goyim; Amraphel, king of Babylon;[h] and Arioch, king of Ellasar—four kings against five. ¹⁰Now the valley of Siddim was full of tar pits, and as the kings of Sodom and Gomorrah and their armies retreated from the battle and fled, some of them fell into the tar pits, and the rest fled to the hill country. ¹¹The four victorious kings captured all the possessions and all the food of Sodom and Gomorrah and left. ¹²They captured Lot, Abram's nephew who had been living in Sodom, and took him and all his possessions.

¹³One who escaped came to Abram the Hebrew and told him what had happened to Lot. Abram was living by the oaks of Mamre the Amorite. Mamre had two brothers, Eshcol[i] and Aner, who were allied by treaty with Abram. ¹⁴When Abram heard that his nephew Lot had been taken captive by the four kings, he mobilized all the men in his camp,[j] 318 in all who had been born and trained in his own household, and he pursued the invaders as far as *north* as Dan. ¹⁵Then, during the night, Abram strategically divided his forces and defeated them. His forces attacked them and routed them as far as Hobah,[k] north of Damascus. ¹⁶He recovered all the stolen possessions and brought back his nephew Lot, together with the women and all the prisoners.

Abram Blessed by Melchizedek

¹⁷After Abram returned from defeating Kedorlaomer and the kings who were with him, the king of Sodom went out

---

a 14:6 Seir means "hairy" or "shaggy" and refers to the mountainous area south of the Dead Sea, located in Edom.

b 14:6 El Paran means "beautiful oaks."

c 14:6 The invasion route began east of the Jordan, moved southward, and returned northward toward the Dead Sea, conquering as they went, finally defeating the five kings.

d 14:7 En-mishpat means "the spring of decision" or "spring of judgment," that is, Kadesh meaning "sacred." En-mishpat is identified as modern 'Ayn Qadeis, fifty miles south of Beersheba.

e 14:7 Amalekites means "warlike" or "valley dwellers."

f 14:7 Amorites means "sayers" or "mountain dwellers."

g 14:7 Hazazon-tamar means "dividing the date palm" and is identified in 2 Chron. 20:2 as En-gedi, a town on the western shore of the Dead Sea. The tribes mentioned in verses 5–7 were likely some of the "giants" that were in the land. See Deut. 2:10–11, 20–21; 3:11–13; Josh. 12:4; 13:12; 15:8.

h 14:9 Or "Shinar," a name for ancient Babylon.

i 14:13 Eshcol means "cluster."

j 14:14 These were not only warriors but also disciples (Hebrew *hanikh*, "trained ones") of Abram. It was God who supernaturally won this battle, for Abram was facing fierce and numerous tribal warriors. Abram realized that the battle would be won with God's help. Abram was a noble man, he could have easily left Lot, who chose to live in Sodom, in the hands of his captors.

k 14:15 Hobah means "hiding place."

to meet Abram at the valley of the Shaveh[a] (known as the King's Valley).[b] [18]And Melchizedek,[c] who was both a priest of the Most High God and the king of Salem,[d] brought out to Abram bread and wine.[e] [19]He spoke over him a special blessing, saying,

"Blessed is Abram by God Most High,[f]
Creator[g] of heaven and earth.
[20]And blessed be God Most High, whose *power* delivered your enemies into your hands!"[h]

Abram gave Melchizedek a tenth *of all he possessed.*[i] [21]Then the king of Sodom said to Abram, "Just give me the people you rescued; keep all the spoils for yourself." [22]But Abram said to the king of Sodom, "I raised my hand to Yahweh, God Most High, and I pledged a solemn oath to the Possessor of heaven and earth [23]that I would keep nothing for myself that belongs to you, not even a thread of a garment or sandal strap. That way, you will never be able to say, 'I was the one that made Abram rich.'[j] [24]I will take nothing except what my young men have eaten, and the share of those who went with me—Aner, Eshcol, and Mamre. Let them take their share."

God's Covenant with Abram

15 Afterwards, the word of Yahweh came to Abram in a vision

---

a 14:17 Shaveh means "level" or "equal (equalize)."

b 14:17 The *King's Valley* later became known as the Kidron Valley. All this happened in the "King's Valley," the low place, where we meet the King.

c 14:18 There are varying viewpoints on the identity of Melchizedek; some scholars view Melchizedek as merely a type or picture of Christ or a Canaanite royal priest. Others believe that he was a Christophany, a pre-incarnate appearance of Christ as both a priest of the Most High God and King of Salem (peace). He appeared out of nowhere, with no genealogy or pedigree other than being a king-priest. The Dead Sea scrolls dating back to at least the 1st century BC, found in Cave 11 at Qumran (11Q13, 11QMelch), state that Melchizedek was a divine being, and was given the Hebrew title Elohim. According to this text, Melchizedek proclaims the Day of Atonement as a day coming when one will atone for the sins of the people and will be their supernatural deliverer and their judge [Wise, Abegg, Cook (1996). *The Dead Sea Scrolls: a New Translation*]. See also Ps. 110:4; Heb. 4:14–15; 5:6, 10; 6:19–20; 7:1–21. In John 8:56, Jesus said that "Abraham . . . foresaw me coming and was filled with delight!" Abraham saw the day of Jesus as Melchizedek came out to meet him with bread and wine.

d 14:18 Salem is the name of ancient Jerusalem. See Ps. 76:2. Melchizedek was a priest on behalf of whom? Not the Jews, for Abram was yet to have a son. Rather, it was on behalf of the Gentiles. God established a priesthood over the *Gentiles* before he brought forth a priesthood over the Jews. Melchizedek was a gentile king over a gentile city. Gentiles have been in the heart of God from the beginning.

e 14:18 Bread and wine is the substance of the Lord's Table. Melchizedek is bringing a communion service to Abram.

f 14:19 Or "El Elyon."

g 14:19 Or "Possessor."

h 14:20 Abram was not a warrior; he was a prophet. Yet with God's power behind him, he became a conqueror and won a battle against great odds. Only God gets the glory with every victory we experience.

i 14:20 See Heb. 7:4–10.

j 14:23 Abram resisted the temptation for acquiring wealth apart from a relationship with God. He wanted God to be his boast and his true wealth. See Jer. 9:24; 1 Cor. 1:31; 10:17.

and said,[a] "Abram, don't yield to fear, for I am your Faithful Shield[b] and your Abundant Reward."[c]

[2]But Abram replied, "Lord Yahweh, what good is your reward[d] if I remain childless? *I'm about to die without a son*, and my servant, Eliezer of Damascus, will inherit all my wealth. [3]A servant in my household will end up with everything because you have not given me any children."

[4]Immediately, the word of Yahweh came to him: "*No!* Eliezer will not be your heir.[e] I will give you a son from your own body to be your heir."[f] [5]Then Yahweh brought him outside his tent[g] and said, "Gaze into the night sky. Go ahead and try to count the stars."

He continued, "Your seed will be as numerous as the stars!"[h] [6]And Abram trusted every word Yahweh had spoken! And because of his faith, Yahweh credited it to him as righteousness.[i]

[7]Then he said to him, "I am Yahweh, who brought you out of the Babylonian city of Ur, to give you all this land to possess." [8]But Abram said, "Lord Yahweh, how can I be sure that I can possess this land for myself?"[j]

[9]Yahweh said to him, "Bring me a heifer, a female goat, and a ram, each three years old,[k] also a turtledove and a young pigeon." [10]So, Abram brought the animals to him and killed them. He cut them in two (except the birds) and laid each half opposite the other

---

a 15:1 The phrase "the word of Yahweh came" is found two hundred and forty-five times in the Old Testament. In this instance, the word of Yahweh came *in a vision*. It is possible that Yahweh again appeared before Abram (Acts 7:2).

b 15:1 Yahweh is assuring Abram that now he will be a Shield to protect Abram from any retaliation by the kings he had conquered. He chose to be hidden behind Yahweh's shield rather than to take refuge in what the world could give him. See also Deut. 33:29; Ps. 84:11; 91:1–4; Prov. 30:5. Each of us may claim this promise to have God himself as our Faithful Shield.

c 15:1 Because of what Abram had done by rescuing Lot and refusing to take financial reward for his noble acts, Yahweh himself will become Abram's reward. This new, intimate relationship with God exceeded any financial loss Abram experienced. A new intimacy with God always emerges when we choose him over the world's pleasures.

d 15:2 Or "What can you give me."

e 15:4 Or "This man will not inherit you."

f 15:4 Or "Whoever comes out of your body will inherit you."

g 15:5 God wants to take us "outside" of our tent, our limitations and opinions of how God can do a miracle. Paul, the tentmaker, was taken outside of the natural world and shown the mysteries of God, much like his ancestor Abram. See 2 Cor. 12:2–4.

h 15:5 See Heb. 11:12. The seed of Abraham is now both earthly (as many as the grains of sand) and heavenly (as many as the stars, Dan. 12:3; Matt. 13:43; 1 Cor. 15:41; Rev. 1:20; 2:28). The heavenly stars point to the heaven-born Church of Jesus; the grains of sand point to the earthly seed of Abraham, the Jews who inherit Abram's promises. See Gal. 3:28–29.

i 15:6 That is, Abram found God's acceptance one made righteous by his faith. See Rom. 4:3, 6, 11; 18–22; Gal. 3:6; Heb. 10:38; James 2:23.

j 15:8 Abram is asking God for a sign to assure him that he has legal standing to stake a claim to the land and possess it.

k 15:9 Or possibly, "each three-fold," that is, three of each animal. The pual participial form used here seems rather to indicate the years (though the term for "years" is not included) as there would be other normal ways for saying "three." The number three points to the three years of Jesus's ministry and to his resurrection on the third day. The death of the animals shows that suffering precedes inheritance. See Acts 14:22; Rom. 8:17; Phil. 1:29; Heb. 5:8–9.

in two rows. [11]Vultures[a] swooped down upon the carcasses, but Abram stood there and drove the vultures away.

[12]As the heavy veil of night fell, Abram went into a deep state of sleep,[b] and suddenly a great dreadful darkness surrounded him and he was filled with fear.[c] [13]Then Yahweh said to Abram, "Know this: Your descendants will live as strangers in a foreign country. They will be enslaved and mistreated for four hundred years.[d] [14]Afterward I will punish that nation for enslaving them,[e] and your descendants will come out of slavery with untold wealth.[f] [15]You, however, will go to your ancestors in peace and live a full life.[g] [16]And after the fourth generation, your descendants will return here; for then the sin of the Amorites will be ripe for judgment."[h]

[17]When the sun had set, and it was very dark, there *suddenly* appeared[i] a smoking firepot and a blazing torch that passed between the split carcasses.[j] [18]On that day, Yahweh entered into covenant[k] with Abram: "I have given this land to your descendants, from the Egyptian border[l] to the great river Euphrates, [19]the entire land of the Kenites, the Kenizzites, the Kadmonites, [20]the Hittites, the Perizzites, the Rephaites, [21]the

---

a 15:11 Or "birds of prey." Some expositors see the vultures as symbolic of evil powers attempting to interfere with this covenant ritual. When we step into covenant with God, it is important to stand on the promise and to drive away our own fears and doubts that rise up in our own souls. See Matt. 13:4, 19; Eph. 6:12.

b 15:12 Or "a trance-like state," the same words used in Gen. 2:21.

c 15:12 For those of us with prophetic promises yet to be fulfilled, we must contend with our doubts and wait with faith and patience on God. Even in our dreadful darkness, your Faithful God will not disappoint us.

d 15:13 This was a prophecy of the Israelites being enslaved in Egypt. See Ex. 12:40–41.

e 15:14 Yahweh punished Egypt with ten plagues. See Ex. 7–14.

f 15:14 At the time of their exodus, God will give the Israelites the back wages for four hundred years which they deserved. As they departed, the Egyptians gave great riches to the Israelites (Ex. 12:35–36). It was an extraordinary transfer of wealth. The riches of Egypt funded the building of the tabernacle in the wilderness, including the ark of the covenant and all the golden furnishings.

g 15:15 Abraham lived one hundred and seventy-five years (Gen. 25:7).

h 15:16 One reason why the Israelites were kept in Egypt for four hundred years was the justice of God. He had to wait until the sin of the Amorites was fully deserving of God's judgment, and he could righteously destroy them from the land.

i 15:17 Or "with a flash of fire there appeared . . ." (LXX)

j 15:17 God's manifest presence appeared as a smoking firepot and a blazing torch. The smoking firepot points to the Father (Ex. 19:18; Josh. 8:20–21; Isa. 31:9) and the blazing torch speaks of the Son, the Lord Jesus (2 Sam. 22:9; Isa. 62:1; Nah. 2:3–4; Zech. 12:6). It was the custom in the ancient Near East to light a torch (lamp) when making a covenant, symbolizing the fire of destruction that would come if the covenant were to be broken. See Matt. 25:41–43. God's promise to Abram, spoken that mysterious night, became the "title deed" to the land. Yahweh gave Abram the boundaries of the expanse of the land of promise. Rivers and land will be part of the inheritance—land occupied by the enemy. Powerful princes will be dethroned as the Israelites march into the fullness of their inheritance. The God that walked between the sacrifices will walk in the Land and conquer their foes (Isa. 43:1–7).

k 15:18 Or "cut a covenant."

l 15:18 Or "river of Egypt," possibly the brook (wadi) in eastern Sinai known today as Wadi el-'Arish.

Amorites, the Canaanites, the Girgashites, and the Jebusites."

Hagar and Ishmael

16 Now Sarai had borne no children for Abram. She had an Egyptian slave girl named Hagar,[a] 2so Sarai said to Abram, "Please listen. Since Yahweh has kept me childless, go sleep with my maidservant. Perhaps through her I can build[b] you a family." Abram listened and did what Sarai asked.

3Abram had already lived ten years in the land of Canaan when his wife Sarai took her Egyptian slave girl Hagar and gave her to Abram to be his *second* wife. 4He slept with Hagar, and she conceived. Once Hagar realized she was pregnant, she belittled Sarai and despised her. 5So Sarai went to Abram and said, "*It's totally your fault that Hagar despises me—and you're not standing up for me!*[c] I gave my slave girl to your embrace, and when she found out she was pregnant, she despised me. May Yahweh judge between us *who is in the right!*"

6Abram responded, "She's your slave girl under your authority, so do with her whatever you think best." Then Sarai cruelly mistreated Hagar, who then ran away from her.

7The angel of Yahweh[d] encountered Hagar by a spring in the wilderness, the spring on the way to Shur.[e] 8He asked her, "Hagar, servant of Sarai, where have you come from and what are you doing here?"

She replied, "I'm running away from Sarai, my mistress."

9The angel of Yahweh told her, "You have to go back to your mistress and humbly submit to her." 10The angel added: "I will greatly multiply your descendants until no one can count them."[f]

11Yahweh's angel continued, "You are now pregnant, and soon you will give birth to a son. You will name him Ishmael,[g] for Yahweh has heard your cries of distress. 12Your son will have a wild nature that no one can tame.[h] He will be hostile toward everyone, and everyone will be hostile toward him; and he will live at odds with all his kinsmen."

13After her encounter with Yahweh, Hagar called him by a special

---

a 16:1 There is a Jewish tradition that Hagar was the daughter of Pharaoh, who after seeing the miracles that accompanied Abram and Sarai, gave the Egyptian princess to be Abram's servant (*Midrash; Rashi*). *Hagar* can be translated "ensnaring." It is also related to the word *stranger*. In Arabic, it could mean "fugitive."

b 16:2 That is, give Abram a son. This is an obvious word play in Hebrew. The words for build (*baneh*) and son (*ben*) are quite similar.

c 16:5 In the honor/shame culture of the ancient Near East, barrenness is a disgrace. The shame that Hagar heaped on Sarai was culturally and emotionally more than she could bear.

d 16:7 This is likely a preincarnate appearance of Christ (called a Christophany), for Hagar calls this angel "Yahweh" in verse 13. *The angel of Yahweh* was an appearance of Yahweh in human form. This is the first mention of an angel in Scripture.

e 16:7 Shur means "wall," and is identified with a wilderness near the Egyptian-Israeli border.

f 16:10 This is possibly a Christophany, for only God could multiply Hagar's descendants. We see the kindness of God revealed by his promise to Hagar. God is the guardian of the weak and suffering. See Rom. 2:4; Heb. 4:15.

g 16:11 Ishmael means "God hears" or "May God hear!"

h 16:12 Or "He will be a wild donkey of a man." This was not necessarily a crude insult, but a figure of speech that Ishmael will live a solitary existence. Like a wild donkey left in the desert, he will be wild and untamed. This is the "beast" nature of fallen man, the wild Adam, the flesh.

name, "You are the God of My Seeing,"[a] for she said, "Oh my, did I just see God and live to talk about it?"[b] [14]That is why the well is called Spring of the Living One Who Watches Over Me.[c] The well is still there, between Kadesh and Bered.[d] [15]Hagar *returned and* bore Abram a son, whom Abram named Ishmael. [16]Abram was eighty-six years old when Hagar gave birth to Ishmael.

The Covenant of Circumcision

17 When Abram was ninety-nine years old,[e] Yahweh appeared to him *again* and said, "I am the God who is more than enough.[f] Live your life in my presence[g] and be blameless.[h] [2]I will confirm my covenant between me and you, and I will greatly multiply your descendants."

[3]Then Abram fell on his face *in awe* before God,[i] and God said to him, [4]"I establish my covenant with you:

"You will become a father of many nations.
[5]You will no longer be named Abram *because I am changing* your name to Abraham,[j]

a 16:13 Or "You are the God who sees me" or "You are the God whom I See." This encounter at the "well" reminds us of a later time when Jesus would journey to a well to meet a woman who had a history of running from God. At this well of Jacob the Living One again sees into the heart of a woman and speaks mercy to her. At Jesus' encounter with the woman at Jacob's well, "God saw" into her heart, and she saw into God's. See John 4.

b 16:13 Or "Have I not gone on seeing after he saw me." The exact meaning of the Hebrew is uncertain.

c 16:14 The Hebrew homophone for spring can also be translated "eye."

d 16:14 *Kadesh* means "sacred"; *Bered* means "hail." About four miles north of Petra and situated in a short canyon is a place known as "Little Petra." On maps today it appears as Siq el-Bared. About halfway between Ein Kadesh (also known as Ein Musa) and Siq el-Bared are the ruins of a small Turkish village named Chai, and its spring is called Ein el-Chai. This site seems to match the description of Beer-Lahai-Roi with its spring-fed well.

e 17:1 Thirteen years elapsed between chapters 16 and 17. Abraham and Sarai were incapable of conceiving a child. See Rom. 4:19.

f 17:1 Or "I am El Shaddai." This name of God is found two hundred and eighteen times in the Bible and is the most frequently used name for God prior to the Law being given at Sinai. *El* is one of the words for God. *Shaddai* (*šadday*) is taken from a Hebrew root word that carries multiple expressive meanings. It can mean "God of the Holy Mountain," "God of the Wilderness," "God the Destroyer of Enemies," "God the All-Sufficient One," "God the Nurturer of Babies (the Breasted One)," "God the Almighty," "the Sovereign God," or "the God who is more than enough." The combination of El (Almighty) with Shaddai describes the tender heart of God, one who cares for his beloved ones. To a man ninety-nine years of age, God All-Sufficient is a revelation that will sustain Abraham.

g 17:1 Or "before me." Living consciously before God frees us from the false self that lives only before others.

h 17:1 The Hebrew word *tamim* can also mean "perfect," "complete," "whole," or "full." The more-than-enough God is telling Abram to walk continually in the fullness of God's presence, which will make him perfect and complete. A new revelation of God's goodness (The God of more than enough) will always be followed by a new challenge (walk blameless before God). Because he is Almighty, we can live in holiness, following his ways.

i 17:3 When man bows in the dust, God will speak in grace. Abram's posture is a picture of his humility as he ponders this revelation in the presence of God.

j 17:5 *Abram* means "exalted father"; *Abraham* means "father of a multitude." The church today does not need exalted fathers; we need fathers who will multiply themselves in their sons and daughters. A generational transfer is in the heart of God and is here revealed to Abraham.

for I have made you a father of
many nations.
[6]I will make you abundantly fruitful,
more than you expect.
I will make nations out of you,
and kings will trace their lineage
back to you.[a]
[7]Yes, I will establish my eternal
covenant *of love* between me
and you,
and it will extend to your
descendants throughout their
generations.
I will be your children's[b] God, just
as I am your God.
[8]I will give to you and your seed
the land to which you have migrated.
The entire land of Canaan will be
yours and your descendants'[c]
as an everlasting possession.
And I will be their God *forever!*"

[9]God explained to Abraham, "Your
part of the covenant is to obey its terms,
you and your descendants throughout
the ages. [10]So here is the *sign of the* covenant that you are to keep, so that it will
endure between you and me and your
descendants: Circumcise[d] every male
among you. [11]You must undergo cutting
off the flesh of your foreskin as a special
sign of the covenant between me and
you. [12]Throughout your generations,

each male child must be circumcised
eight days after his birth. This includes
those not of your descendants—those
born in your household and foreign-
born servants whom you have purchased; [13]they must be circumcised,
homeborn and purchased alike. In this
way, you will carry in your flesh the
sign of my everlasting covenant. [14]Any
uncircumcised male who does not have
the foreskin of his flesh cut off, will be
cut off from his people, for he has broken my covenant."

[15]God also said to Abraham:

"Concerning your wife Sarai,
you are not to call her Sarai anymore, but Sarah,[e]
'*My Princess,*' will be her name.
[16]I will *wonderfully* bless her,
and I will certainly give you a son
through her.
Yes, I will bless her *greatly,*
and she will become *a mother of*
nations;
kings of nations will arise among
her children!"

[17]Then Abraham laughed so hard
he fell to the ground, saying to himself, "How *in the world* can a hundred-
year-old man become a father? How
can my wife Sarah get pregnant at

---

a 17:6 David, Solomon, and Hezekiah, for example, are kings and leaders who have come forth
from Abraham's blessed relationship with God. He has likewise made you and me kings and
priests! See Rev. 1:6; 5:10.
b 17:7 Or "descendant's."
c 17:8 Or "seed."
d 17:10 The Hebrew word for circumcision (*muwl*) means "to cut short," "curtail," "to blunt," "to
cut off," or "to destroy." With a new name, Abraham was to perform circumcision on the eighth
(number of new beginning) day. This external sign of circumcision would set the Israelites
apart for God. The New Testament truth of heart-circumcision is the cutting away of our flesh,
our rights to ourselves, in dedication to God (Phil. 3:3; Col. 2:11–12).
e 17:15 The names Sarai and Sarah appear to be dialectical variations of the word for princess
or queen. God is emphasizing to Abraham and Sarah that the past, with its season of waiting,
is over. Their new names signified a new era, a new fulfillment of promises, and a new destiny
calling them forward.

ninety?" ¹⁸And then he spoke out loud: "O, that Ishmael might prosper with your blessing!"ᵃ

¹⁹God said, "Listen to me. I promise that you and Sarah will have a son, and you will call him Isaac.ᵇ I will confirm my everlasting covenant of love with him and his seed. ²⁰And regarding Ishmael, I have heard your cry and I will indeed bless him. I will cause him to have many, many descendants. He will father twelve rulers,ᶜ and I will make him into a great nation. ²¹But my everlasting covenant relationship is with Isaac, who will be born to you and Sarah about this time next year." ²²When he had finished speaking with Abraham, God ascended *up to heaven.*ᵈ

²³So *without delay* Abraham obeyed God and took his son Ishmael and every male in his household (whether born in his house or foreign-born servants) and circumcised them that very same day. ²⁴Abraham was already ninety-nine years old when he was circumcised, ²⁵and his son Ishmael was thirteen. ²⁶They were both circumcised on the same day, ²⁷along with all the men of his household (whether born in his house or foreign-born servants).

Yahweh Appears Again to Abraham

18 Yahweh appeared *once again* to Abraham *while he lived* by the oak grove of Mamre. During the hottest part of the day, as Abraham sat at his tent door, ²he looked up and *suddenly* saw three men standing nearby. As soon as he saw them, he ran from his tent to welcome them. He bowed down to the groundᵉ ³and said, "My Lord,ᶠ if I have found favor in your sight, don't pass me by. *Stay for a while with* your servant. ⁴I'll have some water brought to you all so that you can wash your feet.ᵍ Rest here a while under the tree. ⁵Since you've stopped by your servant's home *and honored me with your presence*, I'll have food prepared for you so that

---

a 17:18 Or "Oh, that Ishmael might live in your sight," a metaphoric way of saying that he longed for Ishmael to prosper and live under God's favor. Ishmael was Abraham's "plan B," and Abraham is still hoping that the promises God had given to him could transfer over to Ishmael. God, however, has no "plan B." He will always accomplish his original, perfect plan.

b 17:19 Isaac means "he laughs." It can mean "he (God) laughs" or "he (Abraham) laughs."

c 17:20 Or "princes." See Gen. 25:12–18; 1 Chron. 1:29–31.

d 17:22 Or "God rose from upon (literal Hebrew)" or "God went up from Abraham." The implication is that God ascended, returning to heaven after coming down to meet with Abraham.

e 18:2 This is the first place the Hebrew word *shachah* is found in the Hebrew Bible. It is most often translated "bow down in worship."

f 18:3 This is the word *'adonai* (Lord), a name used over five hundred times for God. Abraham was waiting for his day of visitation at his tent (tabernacle) door. The tent or tabernacle is a frequent metaphor of our body, our life on this earth. Abraham was prepared and ready for this supernatural day of visitation. We have to get outside of our tent (limitations, flesh life) if we are to believe the promises of God (Gen. 15:5). Jesus said that Abraham saw him (John 8:56). When he saw the men, he knew it was the Lord coming to visit him. Verse 3 makes it clear that it was Yahweh who appeared in human form, a theophany. The two other "men" were angels in human form. See Gen. 19:1.

g 18:4 What sweet intimacy we see in this chapter! Three times Scripture tells us that God made Abraham his friend. In 2 Chron. 20:7, God gave the land to Abraham, his friend. In Isa. 41:8, God calls Abraham his friend. And in James 2:23, because Abraham believed, he was called God's friend. You, too, have been given an inheritance since you believed. You are now his chosen friend.

you can be refreshed; then you can go on your way."

"Very well," they responded, "go ahead and do as you have said."

⁶Abraham hurried back into the tent and said to Sarah, "Quick, *we have guests!* Get three measures*ᵃ* of fine flour, knead it, and bake some bread." ⁷Then Abraham ran to the herd, selected a tender choice calf, and told his servant, "Hurry—prepare this calf *for my guests!*" ⁸Then he brought the meal they had prepared—roasted meat, bread, curds, and milk—and set it before his guests. Abraham stood by them under the tree while they ate.

⁹They asked him, "Where is your wife Sarah?"*ᵇ*

He answered, "Over there—in the tent."

¹⁰Then one spoke up and said, "I will return about this time next year, when your wife Sarah will certainly have a son." Sarah overheard it, for she was at the tent door not far behind him. ¹¹Now, both Abraham and Sarah were already very old, and Sarah was past the age of childbearing.*ᶜ*

¹²Sarah laughed to herself *with disbelief*, saying, "A woman my age—have a baby? After I'm worn out*ᵈ* will I now enjoy marital bliss *and conceive*—and with my aged husband?"

¹³Yahweh *knew her thoughts and* asked Abraham, "Why is Sarah laughing, saying, 'How can a woman my age have a baby?' ¹⁴Do you think there is anything too marvelous*ᵉ* for Yahweh? I will appear to you at the appointed time next year and Sarah will have a son!"

¹⁵Sarah was afraid, so she denied it, saying, "I wasn't laughing."

But he said, "Yes, you were!"

Abraham the Intercessor

¹⁶Afterward, the three men departed and walked toward Sodom,*ᶠ* and Abraham went off with them to see them on their way. ¹⁷*As they walked*, Yahweh said, "Should I really hide from Abraham what I intend to do? ¹⁸After all, he will become a great and powerful nation, and every nation on earth will be blessed through him.*ᵍ* ¹⁹It is true; I have singled him out as my own,*ʰ* so

---

a 18:6 Or "seahs." A *seah* is at least over seven liters of dry measurement. Orthodox Judaism measures a *seah* at over fourteen liters. This would have made a very large batch of bread. Abraham prepared much more food than needed for three hungry men. It is always good to be extravagant when we give to God and others.

b 18:9 This was a statement of revelation knowledge, for how did he know that Abraham was married and that his wife's name was Sarah?

c 18:11 Or "It had ceased to be with Sarah after the manner of women," in other words, she was past menopause.

d 18:12 Or "withered" or "dried up."

e 18:14 This same Hebrew word is used as a title of the Lord Jesus in Isaiah 9:6 (*Wonderful*). Nothing is too extraordinary for God! He is Wonderful! Yahweh's question remained unanswered for 3,000 years until Jeremiah the prophet responded, "There is nothing too hard for You!" (Jer. 32:17). He delights in doing what is impossible to man. See Luke 1:37.

f 18:16 Or "looked toward the face of Sodom."

g 18:18 Or "all nations on earth will (long to) be blessed as he is blessed."

h 18:19 Or "I have known (Hebrew.) *yada'* him." The Hebrew word *yada'* has a universe of meaning that includes "intimacy," "choosing," "knowing fully," "acting justly," "sharing love," "to take someone into your heart," and more.

GENESIS 18 ❧ 57

that he will lead[a] his family and household to follow my ways[b] and live by
what is right and just. I will fulfill all the
promises that I have spoken to him."

²⁰Yahweh explained *to Abraham*,
"The outcry[c] *for justice* against Sodom
and Gomorrah is so great and their sin
so blatant ²¹that I must go down and
see if their wicked actions are as great
as the outrage that has come to me,[d]
and if not, then I will know."[e]

²²As *Yahweh's* two companions went
on toward Sodom, Abraham remained
there, as Yahweh paused before Abraham.[f] ²³So Abraham came forward *to
present his case* before Yahweh, and
said, "Are you really going to sweep
away the righteous while you judge
the wicked? ²⁴What if you find fifty
righteous people in Sodom? *Isn't your
mercy great enough to forgive?* Why

judge the entire city at the cost of the
fifty righteous who live there? ²⁵That's
not who you are—one who would
slay the righteous with the wicked—
treating them both the same way!
Wouldn't the *Merciful* Judge of all the
earth always do what is right?"[g]

²⁶And Yahweh said, "Alright. If I find
fifty righteous in Sodom, I will spare
the whole city for their sake."

²⁷Abraham spoke up again and said,
"I am just a man formed from earth's
dust and ashes but allow me to be so
bold as to ask you, my Lord. ²⁸What if
there are only five lacking, and you only
find forty-five righteous in Sodom? It's
not who you are to destroy the entire
city for lack of five righteous people."

And Yahweh said, "Alright. If I find
forty-five righteous in Sodom, I will
spare the whole city."

---

a 18:19 Or "instruct" or "enjoin after him."

b 18:19 This is the first reference to the "ways of Yahweh," found over fifty times in the Old Testament and twelve times in the New Testament (i.e. "way of the Lord").

c 18:20 Or "the shriek," "lament," "wail," "shout," or "outrage." The Septuagint reads "their outcry," i.e. the outcry against the people of Sodom and their indictment against them. The sin of Sodom was blatant and outrageous. See Jer. 23:14; Ezek. 16:49. The voices that cry out would literally include those suffering the abuses of those in power in their homes and cities. Sin has a voice that cries out for justice, but the blood of Jesus has a greater voice!

d 18:21 Or "according to the outrage that has come to me they have completed." The Hebrew word for completed is *kalah*, meaning "finished" or "completed." God already knows the extent of their wickedness. He is searching to see if there is still a reason to withhold judgment.

e 18:21 This is the word *yada'*, the same word God used "to know Abraham (fully, intimately, firsthand knowledge)" in verse 19. The "if" God used in this verse sparked hope in Abraham that God might relent of his judgment.

f 18:22 This verse is listed as a rare instance of Masoretic interference with the text known as *Tiqqun soferim* or "scribal corrections." The implication is that the text needed to be amended to read, "Abraham still stood before the Lord." The translator has left this in its original state, as translated from the oldest manuscripts and ancient external sources. God paused before Abraham, giving him time to ponder and ask for mercy for the city. God waits for our interces-sion. God wants us to plead for mercy even when judgment is imminent.

g 18:25 Or "act justly." Abraham appeals to Yahweh not only to spare the righteous but for his merciful heart to be expressed. Yahweh's character, not the character of the people of Sodom, is what is on the line. Abraham stands alone before Yahweh and pleads for the lives of wicked people to be spared. This moved God's heart, and he granted each request Abraham made—until Abraham stopped asking. Abraham asked six times. What would have happened if Abraham had asked the seventh time? Abraham did not change the mind of God; he demonstrated what was already on God's heart.

²⁹"But what if there are only forty?" Abraham asked further.

Yahweh answered, "Alright. If I only find forty, I will spare the city."

³⁰Abraham *paused*—then he said, "Lord, please don't be offended with me, and let me speak . . . What if there are only thirty?"

Yahweh answered, "Alright. If I find only thirty, I will spare the city."

³¹Abraham ventured even further, asking, "Allow me to dare speak this way to you, my Lord. But what if you find there only twenty righteous?"

Yahweh answered, "Alright. For the sake of the twenty I will not destroy the city."

³²Then Abraham *took a deep breath* and asked, "Once more, please don't let my Lord be angry with me if I make but one more request. What if you find only ten righteous?"

And Yahweh answered, "Alright. I will *extend my mercy* and not destroy the city for the sake of ten righteous."

³³Yahweh finished speaking with Abraham. He immediately went on his way, and Abraham returned home.

The Wickedness of Sodom

19 That evening, the two angels came to Sodom[a] while Lot was sitting at the city's gateway.[b] When Lot saw them, he got up to meet them and bowed with his face to the ground. ²He said, "Please, my lords, come to your servant's house to spend the night and wash your feet; then you can rise early and go on your way."

"No," they answered. "We will *be fine to* spend the night in the town square."

³But Lot was so insistent they finally agreed to go to his house. Lot had unleavened bread baked for them and prepared a feast, and they ate. ⁴But before they retired for the night, the men of the city, men young and old, from every part of the city of Sodom, to the last man, surrounded the house. ⁵They shouted out to Lot, "Where are the men who came to your house tonight? Bring them out to us so that we can have sex with them!"[c]

⁶Lot went outside, shutting the door behind him, ⁷and said to them, "No! My brothers, *I beg you,* don't sink to such depravity! ⁸Look, I have two virgin daughters; I'll bring them out to you, and you can do with them as you please. Only don't do anything to these men, for they are guests in my house."[d]

⁹"Get out of our way," they replied. "This guy comes as a foreigner to live among us, and now he dares to judge us! We'll inflict more harm on you than on them!" Just then they lunged at Lot and tried to break down the door, ¹⁰but the two angels reached out and pulled Lot safely back into the house and bolted the door. ¹¹They struck the men

---

a 19:1 Sodom means "scorched" or "burnt region."

b 19:1 A city gateway usually consisted of towers, guardrooms, and a meeting area where people could sit. Often, the city leadership would conduct meetings there (Ruth 4:1–11). Recent archeological discoveries at Tel-Dan revealed a stone bench that was fifteen feet long connected to the wall of one of its towers.

c 19:5 Or "that we may know (*yada*') them." This word is used frequently for sexual relations. They surrounded the house, not simply to introduce themselves to the men, but to sexually abuse them. See Gen 13:13; Lev. 18:22; 20:13; Deut. 23:18; Judg. 19:22; Rom. 1:18–32; 1 Cor. 6:9–10.

d 19:8 Or "they have come under the shadow of my roof."

outside the house, young and old, with one blazing flash of light[a] so that they could not find the door!

[12]Then the visitors said to Lot, "Who else lives here? Do you have any other family here—sons or daughters, sons-in-law or *daughters-in-law* who live in Sodom? Get them all out of the city, [13]because we are about to destroy this place. A tremendous outcry against the people has come before Yahweh, and he has sent us here to destroy it!"

[14]So Lot went out to find the two men who were pledged to marry his daughters and told them, "Hurry, leave the city, for Yahweh is about to destroy it!" But they thought he was only joking *and paid him no attention.*

[15]At dawn, the angels urged Lot, saying, "Go! Take your wife and your two daughters and leave or you will be consumed in the judgment about to come to the city!" [16]But Lot hesitated, so the angels grabbed his hands and the hands of his wife and daughters and brought them outside the city, because Yahweh was merciful to them. [17]Once they were safely outside the city, the angels said to them, "Run for your lives! Don't stop anywhere in the plain until you've reached the mountains. And don't even look back, or you'll die!"

[18]Lot replied, "Oh no, my lords. [19]You've been so gracious to your servant, and you've been so kind to save our lives, but I can't make it to the mountains. It's so far from here; disaster will overtake me, and I'll die! [20]Look, over there is a village close enough to run to, and it's a small one. Let me escape there instead. You can see that it's such a small village.[b] Let my life be spared!"

[21]"All right," he replied. "I will grant this request too.[c] I will not destroy that village. [22]Now, you must hurry. Run to that village, for I can't do anything until you are there." (That is why the village was called Zoar.)

The Destruction of Sodom and Gomorrah

[23]By mid-morning,[d] Lot arrived at *the small village of* Zoar. [24]And Yahweh's fire from heaven fell upon Sodom and Gomorrah. [25]He completely destroyed the cities of the plain, and all their inhabitants and whatever grew in the valley.[e] [26]But Lot's wife turned and gazed *longingly on the city* and turned into a pillar of salt.[f]

---

a 19:11 The Hebrew word *sanverim* is found only here and in 2 Kings 6:18. The word indicates more than sightlessness (Hebrew *invaron*), but a sudden immobilizing and dazzling flash of light. See also the Aramaic Targums; Yoma 22b. H. M. Orlinsky, *Notes on the New Translation of the Torah* (Philadelphia: Jewish Publication Society, 1969), 93f.; E. A. Speiser, "The 'elative' in West-Semitic and Akkadian," *JCS* 6 (1952): 81ff.

b 19:20 Or "Zoar," a word play in Hebrew. The word for small sounds like Zoar.

c 19:21 Or "I have lifted up your face," a figure of speech for showing favor.

d 19:23 Or "When the sun had risen upon the earth."

e 19:25 Jesus made it clear that if the miracles he did in Israel had been seen in Sodom, the people of Sodom would have repented. Therefore, it will be more tolerable for them in the Day of Judgment than for the cities of the Galilee (Matt. 11:20–24). Knowing how God will soon judge the corrupt world, it is vital that we live holy lives (2 Pet. 3:11–15).

f 19:26 See Luke 9:62; 17:32. Perhaps there really was a salt-pillar that resembled a human. In the book *The Wisdom of Solomon* (10:7), which was included in the Septuagint, it says, "A pillar of salt stands as a memorial to an unbelieving soul," and Josephus (Ant. 1.203) claims to have seen it in his day.

[27]That morning,[a] Abraham hurried back to the place where he had stood before Yahweh.[b] [28]Looking down toward all the land of the plain, he saw columns of smoke billowing up from Sodom and Gomorrah[c]—like the smoke of a furnace!

[29]So before God destroyed the cities of the plain where Lot had settled, he remembered *his affection for* Abraham[d] and spared Lot from all the destruction.

Lot and His Daughters

[30]Afraid to remain in Zoar, Lot left there and settled in the hill country and lived in a cave with his two daughters. [31]*One day*, his firstborn suggested to the younger, "Our father is getting old, and there isn't a man anywhere who could impregnate us in the normal way. [32]Come, let's get our father drunk with wine and have sex with him. That way we can *at least* have children through our father."

[33]That night, they got their father drunk with wine, and the firstborn went in and slept with him. Lot *was so drunk* he didn't have a clue about what had happened.[e] [34]The next day, the firstborn said to the younger, "I slept with my father last night. Tonight, it's your turn. We'll get him drunk with wine, and you can sleep with him and we can preserve our family line through our father."

[35]So they got their father drunk the second time; and the younger went in and slept with him. He *was once again so drunk* he had no clue what had happened. [36]As a result, both Lot's daughters became pregnant by their father. [37]The older daughter had a son named Moab,[f] who is the ancestor of the Moabites of today.[g] [38]The younger also had a son named Ben-Ammi,[h] the ancestor of the Ammonites of today.

---

a 19:27 Or "The next morning." It is unclear whether Abraham saw the moment of destruction of the cities or if he viewed the smoke rising the next day.

b 19:27 See Gen. 18:22. The implication from Gen. 18:16 and 18:33 is that this high point may have been some distance from Abraham's camp.

c 19:28 Gomorrah means "a ruined heap" or "to chastise."

d 19:29 That is, he honored Abraham's request. God had not forgotten Abraham and then suddenly remembered him, but rather showed his affection for Abraham by fulfilling his request to spare the righteous.

e 19:33 Or "he did not know when she lay down and when she arose." See also verse 35. This chapter opens with Lot sitting at the gate of Sodom, the seat of authority, and ends with him drunk in a cave—from councilman to caveman! Lot could have returned to his uncle, Abraham, but instead he fled to a cave.

f 19:37 Or "from my father," a word play which in Hebrew sounds like "(conceived) from my father."

g 19:37 Jewish tradition views these two daughters as righteous women whose motives were noble. Perhaps they presumed the entire world had been destroyed and that Zoar was spared only while they were there, leaving no other living male except their father. Regardless, there would one day come a descendant of Moab, Ruth, who would be included in the roots of the Jewish monarchy as David's great-grandmother (Ruth 4:17–22) and listed in the genealogy of Jesus Christ (Matt. 1:5). There is no sin or evil that can hinder God's grace from shining through even the darkest cloud of human failure.

h 19:38 Or "son of my relative," a word play which in Hebrew sounds like "son of my (paternal) relative."

Sarah Taken into the King's Harem

20 Abraham journeyed from *the oaks of Mamre* to the southern region of Canaan[a] and settled between Kadesh and Shur, to live as a temporary resident in Gerar.[b] [2]Now Abraham had said about his wife Sarah, "She's my sister." So Abimelech,[c] king of Gerar, sent for her and took her *into his harem.*[d] [3]One night, God appeared to Abimelech in a dream[e] and said to him, "You're as good as dead, for you have taken *into your harem* a married woman!"

[4]Now Abimelech had not touched Sarah, so he said to the Lord, "Would you really destroy people who are innocent?[f] [5]Didn't the man tell me, 'She is my sister'? And didn't she agree and say, 'Yes, he's my brother'? I've done this with clean hands and a clear conscience."

[6]Then God answered him in the dream, "Yes, I know you did this with a clear conscience. Furthermore, it was I who kept you from sinning and kept you from touching her. [7]Now return the man's wife, and because he is a prophet,[g] he will intercede on your behalf that you may live. But if you don't give her back—you will certainly die, you and your entire household."[h]

[8]So Abimelech rose early in the morning and gathered all his servants. When he told them about his dream, they were terrified! [9]Abimelech summoned Abraham and asked him, "What is this trick you have played on us? I did nothing wrong to you. Why would you bring such great guilt upon me and my kingdom? You have done to me what no one should ever do to another." [10]Then Abimelech asked, "What is your purpose in doing this?"

---

a 20:1 Or "the land of the Negev."

b 20:1 Abraham was a very wealthy man with hundreds of servants and many flocks and herds of livestock. *Gerar* means "lodging place" and was a Philistine city-kingdom south of Gaza.

c 20:2 Abimelech has two possible meanings, "Melech (Molech) is my father" or "my father is king."

d 20:2 Sarah was ninety years old. God had supernaturally rejuvenated her and made her attractive to a king. See Heb. 11:11. According to Jewish tradition, "her flesh was rejuvenated, her wrinkles smoothed out, and her original beauty was restored" (Beva Metzia 87a). The Dead Sea scrolls likewise comment on Sarah's miraculous restoration due to her faith in the promise of God with these words: "fair indeed are her eyes . . . and all the radiance of her face . . . and her hands how perfect. Her legs how beautiful and without blemish her thighs . . . And when the king heard the words of [his three officials], he desired her exceedingly, and he sent [them] at once to bring her to him, and he looked upon her and marveled at all her loveliness . . . and he (God) sought to slay her." See *The Message of the Dead Sea Scrolls*, Simon & Schuster, 1957.

e 20:3 We see from this that God speaks in dreams not only to the righteous, but that he will also come to the lost and share his heart with them (Prov. 21:1). Dreams are powerful avenues into the human spirit. God may speak to you in dreams, if you will listen.

f 20:4 Or "Would you really slaughter an innocent nation?"

g 20:7 This is the first time the word prophet is found in the Bible. The Hebrew word *navi'* means "to bubble up," referring to the stirring of the Holy Spirit that bubbles up through the prophet with divine utterance. *Navi'* is the most common word used for a prophet and can also be translated, "to declare (one who declares)." However, some etymologists connect it with Akkadian *nabû*, "to call." Assyrian kings had the title of "the one called," that is, called by the gods. The form *navi'* in Hebrew could also signify "one who receives the (divine) call."

h 20:7 See Ps. 105:15

[11]Abraham answered, "Because I thought, 'There's no one here that fears God. They will kill me to get to my wife.'[a] [12]Besides, she really is my half sister. She's my father's daughter, but not my mother's, so I married her. [13]When God sent me out to wander from my father's house, I said to her, 'Here is how you can show your love for me. Everywhere we go, you must say about me, "He's my brother."'"

[14]Then Abimelech gave Abraham's wife Sarah back to him. In addition, he gave him sheep, cattle, and both male and female servants. [15]Abimelech told him, "Look, my land is now before you; feel free to settle wherever you please." [16]Then he turned to Sarah and said, "I am giving your brother a thousand pieces of silver[b] as compensation to settle any claim against me, to exonerate you in the eyes of all who are with you,[c] and to clear your reputation."

[17]Then Abraham prayed to God; and God healed Abimelech! He also healed Abimelech's wife and female servants *of their infertility* and they began to have babies again.[d] [18]For Yahweh had shut all the wombs of the women of Abimelech's household because he took Sarah, Abraham's wife.

Birth of Isaac

21 Yahweh visited Sarah,[e] just as he said he would, and fulfilled his promise to her. [2]And Sarah conceived and bore Abraham a son in his old age, at the exact time God had promised them. [3]Abraham named his son Isaac, the *miracle* son, whom Sarah bore him. [4]When Isaac was eight days old, Abraham circumcised him, as God had commanded him. [5]Abraham was one hundred years old when his son Isaac was born. [6]Sarah said, "God has brought me laughter, and everyone who hears about this will laugh[f] with me." [7]And she added,

"Who would ever have told Abraham
that Sarah would one day nurse
children!

---

a 20:11 Or "over the matter of my wife."

b 20:16 Or "a thousand shekels," which would amount to about twenty-five pounds of silver.

c 20:16 Or "a covering of eyes," with uncertain meaning.

d 20:17 Considering that Abraham's wife had never given him a child, it was an amazing miracle for Abraham to pray for someone else to give birth! The very first healing in the Bible was through the prayer of a childless man, Abraham. He had no confidence in himself as he prayed this prayer of faith. He could pray in total confidence that it had to be God doing the miracle. He prayed for the very thing he had not yet received. When the last two verses of Genesis 20 are read together with the first two verses of Genesis 21, we see that Isaac's conception occurred as a result of Abraham's prayer for another person with an identical need.

e 21:1 We are not told if the Lord appeared to Sarah or visited her in a dream, but it is clear that Yahweh came to her to confirm his promise.

f 21:6 This verse contains a double allusion to the name *Isaac*, which means "he laughed." Every time they speak Isaac's name, they are acknowledging the miracle of God. The name *Yitzhak* is the word for "laughter" but in the past tense. It could be translated "delayed laughter." If you had a baby after turning one hundred, you might laugh too! Notice the details of Isaac's birth and how they foreshadow the birth of our Lord Jesus: (1) Both were the promised seed—Gen. 17:6; Isa. 7:14. (2) Both were long awaited—Gen. 12:5–6; 21:1–3; Gal. 4:4. (3) Both had mothers who asked questions—Gen. 18:13–14; Lk. 1:34–37. (4) Both had names given before birth—Gen. 17:19; Matt. 1:21. (5) Both births were miraculous—Gen. 21:2; Matt. 1:18. (6) Both were a delight to their father—Gen. 21:3; Matt. 3:17.

Even though Abraham is an old man,
look—I have given him a son!"

Hagar and Ishmael Sent Away

[8]Isaac grew and was weaned; and on the day Sarah weaned him, Abraham prepared a great feast. [9]But Sarah noticed the son of Hagar, the Egyptian, was mocking[a] *her son Isaac.*[b] [10]So she said to Abraham, "Get rid of this slave woman and her son. Banish them, for the son of that slave woman must not become a coheir with my son Isaac!"

[11]Abraham was very upset over Sarah's demand, for Ishmael was his son too. [12]God spoke to Abraham,[c] "Don't be distressed over the slave woman and her son. And whatever Sarah says to you, do it, for it will be through Isaac your promise of descendants will be fulfilled.[d] [13]Rest assured, I will make the son of your slave woman into a nation too, because he is your son."

[14]Abraham rose up early the next morning, bundled up some food and a skin of water, and strapped them to Hagar's shoulders. Then he gave her his son and sent them away. So, Hagar and her son Ishmael departed and wandered off into the wilderness of Beersheba. [15]When the water was gone, she grew desperate, so she left her son[e] under a bush. [16]Then she walked about the distance of a bowshot and sat down, for she thought, "I can't bear to watch my son die." As she sat nearby, she broke into tears and sobbed uncontrollably.

[17]And God heard the voice of the boy. The angel[f] of God called out to Hagar from the heavenly realm and said, "What's the matter, Hagar? Don't be afraid, for God has heard the voice of your son crying as he lies there. [18]Get up! Help the boy up and hold him by the hand, for I will make him into a great nation." [19]Then God opened her eyes to reveal a well of water. She went over to the well and filled the skin with water and gave the boy a *long, cool* drink.

[20]God was with Ishmael as he grew up in the wilderness of Paran. He became an expert archer, [21]and his mother, Hagar, arranged a marriage for him with an Egyptian woman.

Abraham's Oath to Abimelech

[22]At that time, King Abimelech and Phicol,[g] his army commander, came to Abraham and said, "*It is obvious that* God is with you *and blesses* everything you do.[h] [23]Now swear to me here before God that you will not deceive me, my children, or my descendants, but as I have shown you loyal friendship, so you will treat

---

a 21:9 The Hebrew word used here is built on the root stem from the name "Isaac." It is possible to translate it "jesting," "playing," or "making fun of (Isaac)." Regardless, Sarah saw it as a threat to her son. See Gal. 4:21–31.

b 21:9 The italicized words are found both in the Septuagint and the Latin Vulgate.

c 21:12 Perhaps, God spoke to Abraham in a night vision or dream. God still speaks to his prophets today, as he spoke to Abraham.

d 21:12 Or "through Isaac, your seed will be counted." See Rom. 9:7; Gal. 3:16; Heb. 11:18.

e 21:15 Ishmael was not an infant, for he had been circumcised at thirteen (Gen. 17:25), and Isaac was born a year afterwards. It was common to wean children at the age of four or five, so Ishmael was at least a teenager when Hagar was sent away.

f 21:17 Both Ishmael and Isaac were saved by a voice from heaven (Gen. 22:11).

g 21:22 Phicol means "strong."

h 21:22 It was not simply the wealth of Abraham that impressed them; it was the supernatural healings that took place when Abraham prayed.

me—and the land in which you live as a foreigner—with loyal friendship."

²⁴"I give you my oath," Abraham answered.

²⁵But Abraham voiced a complaint about a well of water which Abimelech's servants had seized by force. ²⁶Abimelech responded, "This is the first time I've heard about this; you never told me before now. I don't know who has done this." ²⁷So Abraham took sheep and cattle, gave them to Abimelech, and the two men made a covenant.

²⁸Then Abraham set apart from his flock seven ewe lambs, ²⁹and Abimelech asked him, "What are you doing with these seven ewe lambs you have set apart?"

³⁰He replied, "*I am giving them to you*, and by accepting these seven ewe lambs, you acknowledge the proof that I dug this well *and it belongs to me*." ³¹That place was called Beersheba,ᵃ because it was there that both men swore an oath to one another.

³²After completing their pact at Beersheba, King Abimelech and Phicol, his army commander, departed and returned to Philistine country. ³³Abraham planted a tamarisk treeᵇ in Beersheba, and there he worshiped Yahweh, the everlasting God.ᶜ ³⁴And Abraham lived many years *in peace* as a foreigner in Philistine country.

God Tests Abraham's Faith

22 Some time later, God tested Abraham.ᵈ

He said, "Abraham!"ᵉ

"Yes, I'm here," Abraham answered.

²God said, "Pleaseᶠ take your son, your only son, Isaac, whom *I know*

---

a 21:31 *Beersheba* can be translated either "well of seven (lambs)" or "well of oath."

b 21:33 A tamarisk tree is a type of evergreen that can grow up to fifty feet. Abraham did not plant the tamarisk tree for landscaping; it was a statement proclaiming his faith. Planting the tree revealed Abraham's faith for endurance until the time of fruitfulness (Isa. 65:21–22).

c 21:33 Or *El Olam*, which means "God Eternal," "the Hidden God," or "the Always God" (Ps. 90:2). This name proclaims that he is God over Eternity, God over eternal things. Abraham's heart and focus were turning to the God of Eternity. The things of the earth were growing meaningless to him (1 John 2:15–17). *El Olam* was preparing Abraham to yield his greatest treasure, his son. Only one whose heart is fixed on eternity can ever make sacrifices pleasing to God (Rom. 12:1; Heb. 13:16). When we see the Eternal One, we can let go of temporary things. Abraham touched eternal life as he dwelt by the tamarisk tree and the well. This was his true preparation for giving up Isaac.

d 22:1 See Heb. 11:17–19. A new revelation (seeing God as El Olam) will always bring a new test (ch. 22). There is no indication that Abraham knew he was being tested. The word for "tested" is most commonly translated "proved." The purpose of God's tests are not so that you would fail, but that he would prove that you are faithful. The *Midrash* shows the word for "tested" is derived etymologically from a word that means "(elevated) banner," like a flag flying high above a ship or a victory banner elevated over an army. This means that God elevated Abraham and made him great by testing—test upon test, greatness after greatness. He does the same thing today with the spiritual "seed" of Abraham. We all want Abraham's faith, but do we want Abraham's trial to perfect our faith? Tests are God's vote of confidence in our future. The budding qualities of Christ-likeness are brought forth in every test of our faith. Someday, you may call a "blessing" what you once called a "burden."

e 22:1 God had spoken many, many times to Abraham. Perhaps this time he spoke by an audible voice or by a dream.

f 22:2 "Please (Hebrew *na'*) take your son." God's merciful, understanding heart is seen by the word "please."

you dearly love,[a] and go to the land of Moriah.[b] Offer him up to me as a burnt offering on one of the mountains which I will show you." [3]Early the next morning, Abraham cut the wood for the burnt offering, loaded it on his donkey, and set out for the distant place God had shown him. He took with him two of his servants, and his son Isaac.

[4]On the third day,[c] Abraham looked up and saw the place in the distance. [5]"Stay here with the donkey," Abraham told the young men. "Isaac[d] and I will go up and worship;[e] then we[f] will return to you." [6]So Abraham took the wood for the burnt offering and placed it on Isaac's back.[g] Abraham carried the knife and the fire,[h] and the two of them walked up the mountain together.

[7]"Father?" Isaac broke the silence. "Yes, my son," Abraham replied.

"We have the wood and the fire," Isaac said, "but where is the lamb for the burnt offering?"

[8]Abraham answered, "My son, God himself will provide[i] the lamb for an offering." So they went on together.

[9]When they arrived at the place *on Mount Moriah* that God had shown him, Abraham built an altar and stacked the wood on it. He tied up his son Isaac and laid him on top of the wood on the altar. [10]Then Abraham took the knife in his hand to plunge it into his son, [11]but the angel of Yahweh called to him from heaven, saying, "Abraham—Abraham!"

"Yes, I'm here," he answered.

---

a 22:2 Every detail of God's instruction became more challenging. Ishmael was his only son with Hagar, but when God spoke Isaac's name, Abraham's heart sank. Then, God added, "whom you dearly love." What a test this was of our father of faith, Abraham! Early Jewish tradition holds that Abraham concealed this encounter with God from Sarah so that she would not hinder him from doing as God commanded. See Josephus, Ant. 1.12.2.

b 22:2 Moriah means "chosen by Yahweh" and comes from a root word meaning "sight," or "vision." Abraham was told to go to the mountain of Clear Vision. Moriah is inside the city walls of modern Jerusalem and is part of the historic site of the Temple Mount. The Temple of the Lord will always be built at the place of sacrifice.

c 22:4 So many wonderful things happen "on the third day." See Hos. 6:2; Matt. 12:40; Luke 18:33; John 2:1; 1 Cor. 15:4. Keep in mind, a journey like this would be difficult for an aged man. Think about what heart-breaking agony he must have endured for these three days. Truly, Abraham is the father of faith (Rom. 4:11–24).

d 22:5 Or "The boy," a noun which encompasses a wide age range, from a baby to a young man. Scholars speculate Isaac's age at this time as around twenty; however, Josephus, the Jewish historian has his age at twenty-five (Josephus, *Ant.* 1.13.2), while others calculate he was thirty-seven.

e 22:5 This is the first instance of worship in the Bible. Abraham freely offered his beloved son to God and called it worship. True worship always involves a sacrifice. The first reference of the New Testament to worship is found with men bowing down before a child and offering sacrificial gifts to Jesus—gold, frankincense, and myrrh. The Biblical concept of worship includes freely bowing down before God bringing our gifts (sacrifices of praise) to honor and adore him.

f 22:5 Notice the faith of Abraham. He knew that God, if he had to, would resurrect Isaac so that both Isaac and his father would return to where they left the servants. See Rom. 4:20–21; Heb. 11:17–19.

g 22:6 Isaac carrying the wood foreshadowed Christ carrying his cross. See John 19:17; Phil. 2:5–8.

h 22:6 That is a "fire (stone)," most likely a flint rock to strike and build a fire.

i 22:8 Or "God will see for himself."

¹²"Do not lay a hand on the boy or harm him," he said, "for now, I know you are fully dedicated to me,ᵃ since you did not withhold your son, your beloved son,ᵇ from me."

¹³As Abraham looked up, his eyes fell upon a ram caught by its horns in a nearby thicket. Abraham took the ram and sacrificed it on the altar as a burnt offering in Isaac's place.ᶜ ¹⁴So Abraham named that place Yahweh Appears.ᵈ Even to this day, it is said, "On Yahweh's Mountain there is vision."ᵉ

¹⁵Yahweh's angel spoke a second time from heaven:

¹⁶⁻¹⁷"'I solemnly promise you,
    by *the glory* of my own name,'
    decrees Yahweh,

'because you have obeyed my
    voice
and did not withhold from me
    your son—your beloved son,ᶠ
I will greatly bless you!
I will make sure your seed
    becomes as numerous
as the stars of heaven and as the
    sand of the seashore.
Your offspring will take possession
    of the city gates of their enemies.ᵍ
¹⁸Because you have obeyed me,
    the entire world will be blessed
    through your seed.'"ʰ

¹⁹So Abraham *and Isaac* returned to the waiting servants, and they departed for Beersheba, where Abraham had settled.ᶦ

---

a 22:12 Or "that you fear God."

b 22:12 As translated from the Septuagint. The Hebrew is "your only son."

c 22:13 The ram caught in the thicket becomes a picture of Christ who was "caught in the thicket" of our sins. Here we have the doctrine of substitution. Christ became our Substitute as the ram became a substitute for Isaac. See Isa. 52:13–53:12; Matt. 20:28; John 6:51; 10:11–18; 11:50–52; 15:13; Rom. 4:25; 5:6–8; 14:15; 1 Cor. 15:3; 2 Cor. 5:14–21; Heb. 2:9–18.

d 22:14 Or "Yahweh sees (to it)" or "Yahweh provides." However, the verb in the descriptive clause is pointed as a passive, "Yahweh appears." Also, the Septuagint renders it, "On the mount the Lord appears."

e 22:14 Or "On Yahweh's mountain there is vision." On Yahweh's mountain (Golgotha) we see clearly the vision of God placing our sins upon his Son. Our salvation is already provided for us through the blood of Jesus' cross. Solomon's Temple was built on Moriah (2 Chron. 3:1). This was also the site where David purchased Araunah's threshing floor (2 Sam. 24; 1 Chron. 21).

f 22:16–17 There is a hint in the test of Abraham offering his sons, that one day God would require a human sacrifice to take away the sin of the world. See Rom. 8:32.

g 22:16–17 Possessing the city gates of their enemies is a figurative expression that refers to conquering, defeating, and taking possession of the enemy's city. It means simply, the seed of Abraham will have great authority to conquer cities.

h 22:18 The "seed" has his life, his life of faith.

i 22:19 Behind the testing of Abraham lies the wisdom of God. Notice these four divine principles of God's tests: (1) When God tests us, his requirements of us often make no sense at the time. Therefore, faith is needed. Faith yields to God, even when it does not make sense. (2) Faith is never brought to maturity without a measure of suffering attached. Even Jesus was made perfect through sufferings (Acts 14:22; Heb. 2:10; 5:8). Faith will carry you through even the most severe trial. (3) We must obey the Holy Spirit even before we know all the details of what is involved. We must be willing not to know where God is taking us. Obedience is always one moment, one step at a time. (4) Others may not be permitted to know what God is doing with us. Abraham left the two servants behind, he left Sarah behind, and only he and God would see this test. Often, God will bring you to the lonely place where others cannot intrude; they wouldn't understand anyway!

The Children of Nahor

[20-23]Some time later Abraham heard the news, "*You're an uncle!* Milcah and your brother Nahor have eight sons! Uz, their firstborn, Buz[a] his brother, and Kemuel the father of Aram,[b] Chesed,[c] Hazo,[d] Phildash, Jidlaph, and Bethuel the father of Rebekah."[e] [24]Moreover, Nahor had another wife,[f] Reumah, who also had four sons: Tebah, Gaham, Tahash, and Maacah.

The Death of Sarah

23 Sarah lived to be one hundred and twenty-seven.[g] [2]She died in the land of Canaan at Kiriath Arba,[h] now known as Hebron. There Abraham mourned and wept for her. [3]*After his time of mourning was over,* Abraham got up from where her body lay, and went to speak with the Hittites. He said to them, [4]"I live as an alien and stranger among you. Sell me some of your property so I can use it as a burial site *for my wife.*"

[5-6]"Hear us, my lord," the Hittites answered, "you are a mighty prince *of God[i]* among us. You may bury your dead in the choicest of our tombs. None of us would withhold our burial ground from you."

[7]Then Abraham bowed respectfully before the Hittites, the people of the land [8]and he said to them, "If you are willing to allow my wife a proper burial, then please hear me out. On my behalf please persuade *your countryman,* Ephron the son of Zohar, [9]to sell

---

a 22:20–23 Buz means "contempt" and is mentioned in Jer. 25:23. Elihu, Job's fourth friend, was called a "Buzite" (Job 32:2).

b 22:20–23 Aram was the ancestor of the Syrians.

c 22:20–23 Chesed means "increase" and is thought to be the name from which his eponymous ancestors, the Chaldeans (Hebrew *kasdim*), got their name.

d 22:20–23 The name Hazo means "vision" and was found in an ancient inscription. Hazo possibly represents the Hazu region in northern Arabia, known from the records of Esarhaddon's campaigns. Uz, Buz, and Hazo likely settled in the land north of Edom.

e 22:20–23 Rebekah is the wife-to-be of Isaac. Her name is derived from a Hebrew root meaning "to loop a cord over the head of a lamb or kid"; thus, some etymologists define the meaning of her name as "captivating (beauty)" or "beauty that ensnares."

f 22:24 Or "concubine," a term referring to a wife with secondary status in the family. She may have been either taken as a captive in war or purchased. Wives taken as captives in war were given certain protection from exploitation (Deut. 21:10–17). This list contains the names of twelve Aramaean tribes traced to Nahor, the same number associated with Ishmael (Gen. 25:13) and Jacob. See Gen. 49.

g 23:1 This reference to Sarah is the only time that Scripture mentions a woman's age at death.

h 23:2 Kiriath Arba means "the city of the four (giants)." See Joshua 14:15. Some Jewish scholars believe "the city of the four" refers to the four couples buried there: Adam and Eve, Abraham and Sarah, Isaac and Rebekah, Jacob and Leah. See also the first footnote on v. 9 for Machpelah.

i 23:5–6 Or "king of God" (LXX). The Hebrew reads "a mighty chief among us," with the generic term for "god" being likely used as the superlative for "mighty."

me the cave he owns at Machpelah*a* on the edge of his land. Let him sell it to me publicly*b* and at the full price, so that I may own it for a burial site." ¹⁰Now Ephron the Hittite was sitting there among his countrymen. He spoke up so all the Hittites who sat at the gate as elders of the city could hear him,*c* and said, ¹¹"No, my lord, listen. I will give you not only the cave but also the entire field! In the presence of my people, I will give it to you to bury your dead."

¹²Then Abraham bowed low before the people of the land, ¹³and he said to Ephron in the hearing of all the people, "No, please listen, *kind sir*. I will pay whatever the field is worth. Take my money so that I can bury my dead there."

¹⁴⁻¹⁵"If you insist, my lord," answered Ephron. "But what is a piece of land worth only four hundred silver shekels to men of our standing? Go ahead and bury your dead." ¹⁶So Abraham agreed to the amount, weighed out the four

hundred silver shekels according to the merchant's standard of weight, and in the presence of the Hittites he gave the money to Ephron.*d*

¹⁷So Ephron's field of Machpelah, east of Mamre, along with the cave and all the trees within its borders, passed ¹⁸to Abraham as his legal possession. The complete transaction was carried out in the presence of the Hittites—those who sat as elders at the city gates. ¹⁹After this, Abraham buried his wife Sarah in the cave there in the field of Machpelah near Mamre (now Hebron) in the land of Canaan. ²⁰Both the field and the cave passed from the Hittites to Abraham's possession to be his family burial ground.

Abraham Seeks a Wife for Isaac

24 Now, Yahweh had wonderfully blessed Abraham in every way, and he became a very old man, well advanced in years.*e* ²One day, Abraham *called for* his *trusted* head servant,*f* who was in charge of all that he had,

---

a 23:9 Machpelah means "double" or "doubling." Everyone buried in this cave would be as one of a couple: Abraham and Sarah, Isaac and Rebekah, Jacob and Leah (Gen. 23:19; 25:9; 49:29–32; 50:13). Death for the patriarchs was a gateway into the resurrection. This cave was more like a bedroom to rest than a tomb, more an altar than a grave. It was an altar to the God of Abraham, Isaac, and Jacob, who is not a God of the dead but of the living (Matt. 22:31–32). According to Jewish tradition, Adam and Eve were also buried in this cave. See Jerusalem Talmud, *Taanith* 4:2; Babylonian Talmud, *Erubin* 53a; *Pirke Rebbe Eliezer*, ch. 20; *Midrash* Rabba (*Genesis Rabba*), 28:3. According to the *Midrash*, the patriarchs were buried in the cave because the cave is the threshold to the garden of Eden. Some New Testament scholars believe that it could have been the patriarchs who were raised from the dead at the resurrection of Christ and were seen in Jerusalem. See Matt. 27:52–53.

b 23:9 Or "in your presence" or "among you."

c 23:10 Or "who came in at the gate of his city," a figure of speech for stating they had leadership in the city. See Ruth 4:1–12.

d 23:16 The price was undoubtedly high. Jeremiah gave only seventeen shekels for land that was probably no less spacious than the field of Machpelah (Jer. 32:9). Although difficult to estimate the cost, some have calculated four hundred shekels of silver to be approximately ten pounds of silver.

e 24:1 Or "gone in days," a figure of speech for saying Abraham was very old and had little time left.

f 24:2 Or "oldest servant." Many scholars conclude this was Eliezer. See Gen. 15:2. He becomes a type or prefigure of the Holy Spirit, who finds and draws a bride for the Son of God by revealing him as Savior.

and said "Please, put your hand here under my thigh,[a] ³and I will make you swear by Yahweh, the God of heaven and earth, that you will not acquire a wife for my son among the daughters of the Canaanites among whom I am living. ⁴Promise me you will go instead to my relatives in my native land and find a wife among them for my son Isaac."

⁵The servant asked him, "Suppose the woman is not willing to come back with me to this land. Should I then take your son back to your native land?"

⁶"Absolutely not," Abraham answered, "make sure that you do not take my son back there. ⁷For Yahweh, the God of heaven, took me from my father's house and from the land of my birth. He spoke to me and solemnly promised that he would give this land to my descendants. *I know* he will send his angel before you[b] so that you can find a wife for my son from there. ⁸And if for any reason the woman is unwilling to come back with you, then you are released from this oath that you swear to me. But *no matter what*, do not take my son back there!" ⁹So, the servant put his hand under the thigh of his master Abraham and swore an oath to carry out his wishes.[c]

The Woman at the Well

¹⁰So the servant took ten of his master's camels, loaded them with all sorts of gifts, some of the best things his master owned, and journeyed toward the *distant* land of Mesopotamia[d] until he got to the village where *Abraham's brother Nahor had lived.*[e] ¹¹He had his camels kneel by a well outside the village. It was evening, the time when the women came out to draw water. ¹²He prayed: "Yahweh, God of my master Abraham, let my journey here be a success and show your gracious love to my master Abraham. ¹³I am standing here by this well, and the young women of the village are coming out

---

a 24:2 Abraham is euphemistically referring to his private parts, his "family jewels." The servant touching his private parts while making this oath was acknowledging that if he broke his solemn promise, Abraham's seed (offspring) had the right to avenge him of this sin. In Western society, we raise our right hand and swear, but in this episode, the servant put his hand on Abraham's reproductive power to give life.

b 24:7 That is, the angel of God would lead Abraham's servant to the right woman for his son. See Ex. 23:20; 32:34; Num. 20:16.

c 24:9 We can see a picture here of the Father releasing the Holy Spirit to seek out a bride for his Son, Jesus Christ. It is the Father that brings the Bride to Jesus as his love gift to the Son (John 17:24). In picture form, the details of this chapter point us to the heavenly scene of gathering a Bridal-partner for Jesus from the nations of the earth. The Church is the Bride, the Lamb's wife (Rev. 21:9). His ministers are *"friends of the Bridegroom"* who are sent to awaken bridal love in the nations as they persuade souls to espouse their heart to him (Matt. 9:15; John 3:29; 2 Cor. 11:2). Only the trusted Servant, the Holy Spirit, is capable of drawing hearts to the Son, imparting endless love for him. Although unnamed here, the servant is elsewhere named Eliezer (Gen. 15:2), which means "the God of help" or "the God of comfort." Is not the Holy Spirit our helper, the Comforter (2 Cor. 1:3)? He desires a willing bride for the heavenly Isaac. She will be willing to leave all to follow this Prince. She will be willing to follow the Holy Spirit as he leads us back to our Bridegroom.

d 24:10 Or "Aram Naharaim," which means "two rivers" and refers to the Tigris and Euphrates rivers in modern Iraq.

e 24:10 From Canaan to Mesopotamia was a journey of at least five hundred miles (eight hundred kilometers).

to draw water. *Give me a sign.* [14]I will say to one of the girls,[a] 'Please, lower your jar and give me a drink.' And if she is the right one, the girl whom you have chosen to be a wife for your servant Isaac, then let her say to me 'Drink, and I will also draw water for your camels.' By this *sign* I will know that you have shown your gracious love to my master."[b]

[15]Suddenly, before he had finished praying, there was Rebekah approaching the well with her jar on her shoulder. She was the daughter of Bethuel and the granddaughter of Milcah and Abraham's brother Nahor. [16]The young woman was strikingly beautiful, unmarried, and still a virgin. She walked down to the well, filled her jar, and came back up. [17]Abraham's servant hurried over to meet her and said, "Please, lower your jar and give me a little drink." [18]She responded, "Drink, my lord." She then quickly lowered her jar to give him a drink. [19]Then, after she had finished giving him a drink, she added, "I will also draw water for your camels until they have finished drinking." [20]She quickly emptied her jar into the watering trough and ran back to the well to draw more water, until she had watered all the camels.[c]

[21]Meanwhile, the servant stared at her, silently pondering whether Yahweh had indeed made his journey successful. [22]After the camels had finished drinking, he took a costly gold nose ring weighing a half shekel[d] and two solid gold bracelets weighing ten shekels,[e] and gave them to Rebekah. [23]Then he asked her, "Tell me, who is your father? Is there room in your father's house for me *and my men* to stay tonight?"

[24]She replied, "My father's name is Bethuel, and my grandparents are Milcah and Nahor."[f] [25]She went on, "There is room for you to spend the night at our home, and plenty of straw and food for the camels." [26]Upon hearing this, the servant bowed down and worshiped Yahweh, [27]saying, "Praised be Yahweh, the God of Abraham, for you have faithfully kept your promise to my master and displayed your wonderful kindness and love. Yahweh, you led me straight to the very place of my master's relatives!"

Rebekah's Family Agrees to the Marriage Arrangement

[28]Then the girl quickly ran[g] to inform her mother and family about all that had happened. [29-30]Now Rebekah had

---

a 24:14 Or "virgins" (LXX).

b 24:14 Would the girl be willing to give ten thirsty camels water from the well? The woman's willingness to serve water showed that she had a true servant-spirit. What work to draw water for these thirsty camels! She would have to lower her bucket down the well MANY times, for one camel can drink twenty gallons—all for a stranger! It was evening, and it would be dark after she was done. Only an exceptional woman would do something like this. She is a picture of the servant-bride of Jesus Christ.

c 24:20 This one act of service qualified Rebekah to be Isaac's bride and to be brought into the line of Christ and his inheritance. We do not realize how one act of humble service will affect the world and bring promotion to our own life (Matt. 10:42).

d 24:22 That is, approx. 6 grams or ¼ ounce.

e 24:22 That is, approx. 110 grams or 5 ounces.

f 24:24 Rebekah was Isaac's second cousin.

g 24:28 What energy Rebekah had! After filling many buckets of water, she now runs home to tell her household what had taken place.

an older brother named Laban,[a] and when he heard everything the man had told his sister and saw her gold nose ring and the costly bracelets dangling on her wrists, Laban ran out to meet the man waiting at the well— and there he was standing beside his camels. [31]Then Laban said to the man, "Friend, Yahweh has wonderfully blessed you; please, come to my home. Why are you standing out here when I have prepared the house for you and a place for your camels?" [32]So the man came into the house, and his camels were unloaded and given straw and feed. The servants brought water to wash the man's feet and the feet of the men with him. [33]But when they set food before him, he said, "I won't eat until I tell you why I'm here."

"Please, tell us," Laban said.

[34]"I am Abraham's servant," he began. [35]"Yahweh has wonderfully blessed my master, and he has become extremely wealthy.[b] Yahweh has given him flocks and herds, camels and donkeys, a fortune in silver and gold, and many male and female servants. [36]And my master's wife, Sarah, has *miraculously* borne him a son in her old age, and my master's son is the *sole* heir of his fortune. [37]My master has put me under an oath saying, 'Do not get a wife for my son from among the daughters of the Canaanites among whom I am living. [38]Instead, go to my relatives in my native land and find a wife among them for my son.' [39]In reply I said to my master, 'Suppose the woman refuses to return with me.' [40]He answered me, 'Yahweh, in whose presence I have walked *all these years*, will send his angel with you and will make your mission successful. You will find a wife for my son from among my relatives, my father's family. [41]If you go to my relatives, and they will not give her to you, then and only then will you be released from this oath.'[c] [42]So, when I arrived at the well today, I prayed, 'O Yahweh, God of my master Abraham, make my mission a success. [43]I'm here standing at this well. May the right girl for my master's son come out to draw water. And when she does, I will say to her "Please give me a little drink from your jar." [44]And if she replies, saying, "Drink, and I will also draw water for your camels," then I might know that she is the young woman Yahweh has chosen for my master's son.'

[45]"Before I had even finished my heartfelt prayer, there was Rebekah coming out with her water jar on her shoulder! After she went down to the well and filled her jar, I said to her, 'Please give me a drink.' [46]She quickly lowered her jar and said, 'Drink, and I will also draw water for your camels.' So, I drank, and she also watered the camels. [47]Then I asked her, 'Tell me, who is your father?' She said, 'I'm the daughter of Bethuel, son of Nahor, whom Milcah bore to him.' *When I learned she was of my master's family*, I put a gold ring in her nose and gold bracelets on her wrists,[48]and I bowed before Yahweh and worshiped him. I

---

a 24:29–30 Rebekah's brother, Laban, saw her running home wearing gold jewelry and knew something good must have happened (Prov. 18:16). Laban means "white." It is also used poetically for the moon. See Song. 6:10; Isa. 24:23; 30:26.

b 24:35 Or "great" or "powerful."

c 24:41 Or "from my adjuration." The Hebrew implies that only if the girl's family refused to release her would the servant be absolved from the curse and penalty for breaking his oath.

praised Yahweh, the God of my master Abraham, who led me perfectly on the right path to find the very daughter of my master's brother to *marry* his son. ⁴⁹Now, if you will show faithful love to my master and do what is right, *then give me permission to take Rebekah back to his land.* If not, tell me, and I will go on my way."*ᵃ*

⁵⁰*After hearing this*, Laban and Bethuel said, "This was all planned by Yahweh!*ᵇ* If this is his plan, what can we say?*ᶜ* ⁵¹Here stands our Rebekah before you. You may take her and go and let her marry your master's son and fulfill Yahweh's plan for her."

⁵²When Abraham's servant heard their words, he bowed his face down to the ground and worshiped Yahweh. ⁵³Then he brought expensive jewelry of silver and gold and *exquisitely embroidered* garments, and gave them all to Rebekah, and he gave *costly* gifts to her brother and her mother.*ᵈ* ⁵⁴Afterward, the servant and his men ate and drank, and they spent the night *in Laban's home.*

First thing in the morning, he said to them, "Allow me now to return to my master." ⁵⁵Her brother and mother replied, "Please let Rebekah remain with us a while—for ten days or so, then she may go with you."

⁵⁶He responded, "Please, Yahweh has made my mission successful. Send me off *with her* to my master, don't make me wait."

⁵⁷They answered him, "We will call for Rebekah and see what she wants to do." ⁵⁸So they called for Rebekah and asked her, "Will you go with this man?"

"I will *gladly* go with him," she answered. ⁵⁹So they sent their sister Rebekah away with her servant girls to go with Abraham's servant and his men. ⁶⁰*As she departed*, they blessed her with these words:

"Our dear sister,
may you become thousands of ten
    thousands!*ᵉ*
May your descendants gain
    possession
of the city gates of their foes!"*ᶠ*

⁶¹Then Rebekah and her servant girls mounted the camels and followed the servant and his men.*ᵍ*

---

a 24:49 Or "I will turn to the right or to the left," which suggests going elsewhere to look for a wife for his master's son.

b 24:50 So many times we think the events of our life are happenstance, but they may be a 'Divine setup' to release the next phase of destiny in our lives.

c 24:50 Or "We are not able to speak to you bad or good." It didn't matter to Laban and Bethuel what they could add, for they viewed all that happened as God's will.

d 24:53 These costly gifts would likely serve as the "bride price" required by the culture of that day.

e 24:60 Or "may you be (grow into) thousands of myriads!"

f 24:60 Destiny hung over them that moment as the Spirit of Prophecy fell. The prophetic blessing is this: The seed (descendants) of Rebekah received the same blessing as the seed of Abraham; they would possess the gates of their enemies. They would take cities! They would possess the places once held by God's enemies. This is a prophetic promise of a coming anointing that would reach cities. This city-reaching power comes when God's people walk with a heart like Rebekah. We must become Rebekah's 'spiritual seed,' so that we may enter into the gate-taking anointing for our cities.

g 24:61 Their journey to Isaac's home would have lasted at least a month.

Isaac Meets Rebekah

[62]Meanwhile, Isaac, who was living in the southern desert of Canaan,[a] had just come back *to his camp* from the Well of the Living One Who Watches Over Me.[b] [63]Isaac went out in the evening into the field to meditate.[c] He looked up, and saw camels coming *in the distance.* [64]As Rebekah got closer, she raised her eyes, and when she saw Isaac, she nearly fell off her camel![d] [65]She whispered to the servant, "Who is that man walking in the field toward us?"

"Why, he's *the one about whom I told you*, that's my young master!" the servant said. So Rebekah quickly took her veil and covered her face. [66]Then the servant began to explain to Isaac *in detail* all the amazing things that had happened. [67]Isaac fell in love[e] with Rebekah. He took her to be his wife, and they were married, and he brought her into his mother Sarah's tent.[f] In this way, Isaac was greatly comforted after his mother's death.

Abraham and Keturah's Descendants

25 Now Abraham had taken another wife, whose name was Keturah.[g] [2]She and Abraham had sons[h] named Zimran, Jokshan, Medan, Midian, Ishbak, and Shuah. [3]Jokshan was the father of Sheba and Dedan. [4]Dedan's sons were the Ashurites, the Letushites, and the Leummites. Midian's sons were Ephah, Epher, Hanoch,[i] Abida, and Eldaah. All these were the descendants of Keturah.

[5]Abraham gave all that he possessed to Isaac, [6]but to his sons by his concubines he gave gifts while he

---

a 24:62 Or "the land of the Negev."

b 24:62 Or "Beer-Lahai-Roi." See Gen 16:14.

c 24:63 Or possibly "to mourn (the loss of his mother)." The Hebrew is uncertain. Some translations have "Isaac went out into the field to take a walk."

d 24:64 The Hebrew phrase is literally "she fell off her camel" or "she collapsed." One can imagine their eyes met, they locked eyes with each other, and something sparked between them. Some interpretations suggest that Isaac was simply glowing with God's light and shining with God's glory from spending time with God. Rashi (a well-known Torah commentator) writes about Rebekah and this initial meeting: "She saw his [Isaac's] majestic appearance, and she was astounded by him."

e 24:67 Isaac's love for Rebekah is the second time in the Bible that love is mentioned between people. The first is Abraham's love for his son, Isaac. And now we have a man who loves his wife. This speaks of the two most loving bonds among humanity: the love of parents for their children and the love bond between husband and wife.

f 24:67 With Rebekah coming into Sarah's tent, we have the matriarchal continuity from Sarah to Rebekah, a fitting successor.

g 25:1 It is not clear when Abraham took Keturah to be his wife. It is possible this happened after the death of Sarah. This would mean that he married her when he was more than one hundred and thirty-seven years old. (Sarah died at age one hundred and twenty-seven, and Abraham was ten years older than Sarah.) The six sons would have been born when Abraham was between the ages of one hundred and thirty-seven and one hundred and seventy-five. Another possibility is that Abraham had taken Keturah while Sarah was still living. The name Keturah may be a variant of a word referring to the smoke from a sacrifice or from incense ("sweet smelling smoke" or "sweet incense").

h 25:2 See 1 Chron. 1:32–33.

i 25:4 Or "Enoch."

was still living.[a] He sent them all away eastward, *separating them* from his son Isaac.

The Death of Abraham

[7]Abraham lived a total of one hundred and seventy-five years. [8]Abraham took his final breath, dying at a good old age. After having lived a full, content life, he joined his ancestors. [9]His sons, Isaac and Ishmael, buried him in the cave of Machpelah, in the field which had belonged to Ephron, the son of Zohar the Hittite, east of Mamre. [10]They buried him next to his wife Sarah, in the same field that Abraham purchased from the Hittites. [11]After Abraham had passed, God greatly blessed his son Isaac, and Isaac settled near the well named the Well of the Living One Who Watches Over Me.[b]

The Descendants of Ishmael

[12]This is the account of the descendants of Abraham's son Ishmael,[c] whom Sarah's servant, Hagar the Egyptian, bore to Abraham.

[13]The names of Ishmael's sons in their birth order are: Nebaioth the firstborn; and Kedar, Adbeel, Mibsam, [14]Mishma, Dumah, Massa, [15]Hadad, Tema, Jetur, Naphish, and Kedemah. [16]These twelve sons of Ishmael became princes[d] of twelve tribes that were named after them, listed by the places they settled and camped. [17-18]They occupied the land from Havilah to Shur, which is east of Egypt, in the direction of Assyria. And Ishmael lived in hostility toward all of his people. At the age of one hundred and thirty-seven, Ishmael breathed his last and died[e] and was joined to his ancestors.

The Birth of Jacob and Esau

[19]This is how the story of Isaac begins. He was the *beloved* son of Abraham[f] *and the successor of Abraham's blessing.*

[20]When he was forty, he married Rebekah. She was the daughter of Bethuel and the sister of Laban. Both her father and brother were Arameans from Paddan-Aram.[g] [21]Now, Rebekah

---

a 25:6 These gifts may have included jewels, precious metals, animals, slaves, or combinations of these. It was unlikely that he gave them land, for he wanted them to have a legal settlement that would enable these sons to begin life on their own, away from Isaac.

b 25:11 Isaac was a man of the well (Gen. 26:18–25). Isaac lived near *Beer-Lahai-Roi*, which means "The Well of the Living One who sees me." This is where Hagar once cried out for deliverance and God heard her. In a time of desperation Ishmael drank from this well of grace. It is the place where God sees our problems and provides a "well" of mercy and satisfaction. Isaac did not visit there; he lived there, making the all-seeing God his source of supply. He saw a realm where the Living One sees all things. It is a well of perpetual revelation and grace.

c 25:12 See 1 Chron. 1:29–31.

d 25:16 Or "tribal chieftains."

e 25:17–18 The Hebrew word for "died" is *gava'*, the word commonly used for the death of a righteous person. The Semitic origin of the word *gava'* is "to hunger or be empty," "to have a longing to be filled with something." The famed Jewish sage, Rashi, translated this as "Ishmael died (as a righteous man) still hungering for righteousness."

f 25:19 Or "Abraham became the father of Isaac." The redundancy of Abraham in this verse is a literary device for showing the promise given to Abraham was passed on to his son.

g 25:20 Paddan-Aram is also called *Aram-Naharaim*, "Aram of the two rivers" (Gen. 24:10). It is another name for Mesopotamia, the area between the Tigris and Euphrates rivers in modern Iraq.

was unable to have children, but Isaac pleaded with Yahweh on behalf of his wife because she was barren—and she did get pregnant, for Yahweh responded to Isaac's prayer.[a] [22]*During her pregnancy*, Rebekah could feel twins thrashing and struggling[b] with each other inside her womb. So she went to inquire of Yahweh, saying, "Why do I have to live with this?" [23]And Yahweh answered her, saying:[c]

"The two sons in your womb will
    become two nations,
and the two peoples within you
    will become rivals.[d]
One people will become stronger
    than the other,
and the older will serve the
    younger."

[24]And when the time came for Rebekah to give birth, sure enough, she had twins! [25]The first one came out reddish and covered with hair like a hairy garment;[e] so they named him Esau.[f] [26]And his brother came out with his hand grasping Esau's heel; so, they named him Jacob.[g] Isaac was sixty when the twins were born.[h]

Esau Sells His Birthright

[27]When the boys grew up, Esau became a rugged outdoorsman and a hardy hunter, but Jacob was more contemplative,[i] content to stay close to home. [28]Isaac loved Esau because he was fond of eating wild game, but Rebekah *dearly* loved Jacob.

[29]One day, when Jacob was cooking a stew,[j] Esau returned from hunting,[k] and he was famished. [30]*Smelling the aroma of food*, Esau said to Jacob, "I'm starving! Let me eat some of that red stuff you're cooking." (This is why he is also called Edom.)[l]

---

a 25:21 During their twenty-year wait for children, there is no mention that Isaac fathered children with his handmaiden, as his father Abraham did. Isaac loved Rebekah and was patient and prayerful until the miracle happened.

b 25:22 The Hebrew is literally "they crushed each other." It was an intense struggle going on inside of Rebekah.

c 25:23 We do not know how God answered her. It could have been by an audible voice or by a dream.

d 25:23 Or "divided," a Hebrew word used for a river dividing into branches (Gen. 2:10).

e 25:25 Or "a mantle."

f 25:25 Esau is a wordplay on the Hebrew word *se'ar* meaning "hairy."

g 25:26 The Hebrew word for Jacob sounds like "heel" and sounds like "cheat" (see Gen. 27:36). Jacob can be translated "heel grabber" or "supplanter." Even in the womb, Jacob was jostling for the right of the firstborn.

h 25:26 Isaac waited twenty years for God to fulfill the promise of a child. God's promises are worth waiting for.

i 25:27 Although the Hebrew word *tam* can mean "blameless" (Job 1:1), it is better translated "meditative," "tranquil," "quiet," or "contemplative."

j 25:29 Jewish sages state that Abraham, Jacob and Esau's grandfather, had just died, and the stew Jacob was cooking was fulfilling a cultural obligation to cook and was related to the prescribed season of mourning. See *Bava Basra* 16b.

k 25:29 Or "from the field."

l 25:30 Edom in Hebrew sounds like "red."

³¹"Yes, but first you must trade me your birthright,"ᵃ Jacob replied.

³²"Can't you see I'm dying of hunger," Esau said, "What good is the birthright if I'm dead?"

³³But Jacob insisted, "First, swear to me that you'll give it to me." So, Esau swore an oath and surrendered his birthright to Jacob.

³⁴Then Jacob gave Esau some lentil stew and bread. When Esau had finished eating and drinking, he just got up and walked away. Esau cared nothing about his own birthright.ᵇ

The Adventures of Isaac in Gerar

26 Now, another famine struck the land, like the one in Abraham's time. Isaac traveled to Gerar where Abimelech was the Philistine king. ²Yahweh appeared before Isaac and said, "Do not go down to Egypt. Stay in the land that I will reveal to you.ᶜ ³Live there as a foreigner, and my presence will be with you. I promise to bless you,ᵈ for I will give all these lands to you and your descendants. I will fulfill the oath I swore to your father Abraham. ⁴I will make your descendants as numerous as the stars of heaven, and I will *one day* give them all these lands. I will bless all the nations of the earth through your offspring ⁵because Abraham was faithful to me. He listened to my voice and yielded his heart to follow my direction. He kept my commandments, my instructions, and my teachings."ᵉ

⁶So Isaac settled in Gerar. ⁷The men of the land *noticed Rebekah's beauty* and asked Isaac about her. "Oh, she's just my sister," he replied. Rebekah was indeed very beautiful, and he was afraid to tell them, "She's my wife," for he thought that the men of the land would kill him and take his wife.

⁸One day, after Isaac had lived there awhile, the Philistine king Abimelech looked out his window and saw Isaac affectionately caressingᶠ his wife Rebekah. ⁹So Abimelech summoned Isaac and said, "So, this woman is

---

a 25:31 The birthright refers to the right of the firstborn to inherit from the father a double portion—twice as much as the younger siblings inherit. Jacob now rightfully possesses the rights and blessings of the firstborn, which included authority, headship, double portion inheritance, and the right to be the priest of the family. God identifies himself as the "God of Abraham, Isaac, and Jacob" (Ex. 3:6). The God of Abraham is God of Promises Fulfilled. The God of Isaac is the God of Inheritance and Miracles. The God of Jacob is the God of Transformation, for Jacob will become Israel, a prince with God. God gives us the promise, but the promise requires a miracle to perform it. This "miracle-promise" releases true transformation within the heart of man. This is the revelation of the God of Abraham, Isaac, and Jacob.

b 25:34 See Heb. 12:16.

c 26:2 Gerar means "lodging place" and was directly on the route to Egypt. Isaac and Rebekah were apparently on their way down to Egypt.

d 26:3 God blesses Isaac even in a time of famine. See verses 12–14.

e 26:5 Or "my laws." The laws of Moses for Israel had not yet been given. Abraham had no Bible; therefore, he depended on hearing Yahweh's voice and following his revelation in all its forms. Yahweh commends Abraham for his faithfulness. The Hebrew word for teachings is a plural form of *torah*. Many years later, Yahweh revealed the Torah to Moses, who set it down in the books we know as Genesis, Exodus, Leviticus, Numbers, and Deuteronomy (see Ex. 34:27). The universe of meaning for the Hebrew word torah includes direction, instruction, rules, etc.

f 26:8 Or "fondling." Perhaps we could say, "They were making out." This Hebrew word in its consonantal form is a play on words with the name Isaac.

your wife! Why did you say that she was your sister?"

"Because I thought the men of the land would kill me *and take her*," Isaac said.

[10]"Don't you realize what you've done to us?" Abimelech asked. "One of our men might have slept with your wife, and you would have brought guilt *and punishment* upon us!" [11]So Abimelech issued a stern warning to all the people, saying, "Whoever lays a hand on this man or his wife shall be put to death!"

Isaac Becomes Very Wealthy

[12]Isaac planted crops in that land, and in the same year[a] reaped a hundred-fold harvest, for Yahweh greatly blessed him![b] [13]Isaac grew richer and richer[c] until he was extremely wealthy. [14]He acquired so many flocks and herds and so many servants that the Philistines grew jealous, [15]so the Philistines stopped up all of Isaac's wells and filled them with dirt—the same wells his father's servants had dug in the time of Abraham.[d] [16]*Eventually Abimelech's jealousy got the better of him,* and he said to Isaac, "You must leave us! You have become too rich and powerful for us!" [17]So Isaac departed from Abimelech's domain and camped near the Wadi of Gerar, where he settled.

Isaac Digs New Wells

[18]Isaac reopened and restored the wells his father Abraham had originally dug—the wells the Philistines had stopped up after Abraham's death. And Isaac gave these wells the same names that his father had given them.

[19]One day, when Isaac's servants dug in the valley, they uncovered a spring-fed well.[e] [20]But the herdsmen of Gerar picked a fight[f] with Isaac's herdsmen, saying, "That's our well!" So Isaac named the well Argument[g] because of the sharp contention. [21]They dug a second well, and it also caused a quarrel, so Isaac named that well Hostility.[h] [22]Then he pulled up stakes from there and dug a third well, but this one was dug without any quarreling, so Isaac named it Spacious,[i] saying, "Finally, Yahweh has made ample room for us

---

a 26:12 Isaac did not hoard his seed in a time of famine but sowed it in the enemy's land and reaped great blessing. See Deut. 28:1–14.

b 26:12 God transformed a land of famine into a land of abundant harvest. If you sow your seed in the day of famine, watch God multiply it into an abundant harvest. See 2 Cor. 8:1–5; 9:6–11.

c 26:13 Or "greater and greater."

d 26:15 In the culture of the day, to dig a well on unclaimed land was a proof of title to the land. To stop the wells of someone else was considered an act of war. Isaac refused to war against the people and chose instead to move away.

e 26:19 Or "living water," that is, an unfailing spring of water flowing beneath the surface. Isaac not only reopened ancient wells but also went on to open his own. God's spiritual "Isaacs" will always be those who not only respect the wisdom of the elders but also will go on to dig their own wells.

f 26:20 There is an implication of physical violence over the well, for the same Hebrew word is found in Ex. 21:18 concerning a fistfight.

g 26:20 Or *Esek*, which means "contention," "dispute," "quarrel," or "argument."

h 26:21 Or "Sitnah," which means "accusation," "hostility," or "enmity."

i 26:22 Or "Rehoboth," which means "broad places," "room (roomy)," or "spacious places." This place was later known as Wadi Ruhebe located about twenty miles (thirty kilometers) southwest of Beersheba.

and we will become prosperous[a] in the land!"

[23]From there, Isaac moved his camp to Beersheba. [24]That very night, Yahweh appeared before him[b] and said:

"I am the God of Abraham your father.
You will never need to fear a thing for I am with you
and I will greatly bless you.
Your children will flourish and succeed
because *of the promises I gave* my servant Abraham."

[25]So Isaac built an altar,[c] prayed, and worshiped Yahweh there. He pitched his tent there, and his servants started digging another well.[d] [26]Then King Abimelech came to Isaac from Gerar with his adviser[e] Ahuzzath and his army commander Phicol. [27]Isaac asked them, "Why have you come to me now, since you hated me and sent me away?"

[28]They answered, "We have witnessed firsthand how *powerfully* Yahweh's favor has been with you, so we say, let there by a peace treaty among us. Let us make a covenant [29]to do each other no harm. Swear to us that you will not trouble us, just as we have not troubled you and have always treated you well and sent you away in peace. Now look at how Yahweh has blessed you!" [30]So Isaac prepared a *wonderful* feast for them, and they all ate and drank together. [31]Then the next morning, they got up early and exchanged oaths. Isaac said goodbye to them, and they left Isaac in peace.

[32]Later that same day, Isaac's servants came with wonderful news about the well they had dug, saying, "We've just found water!"[f] [33]So he named it Oath.[g] This is why the city where they dug the well is called Beersheba[h] to this day.

The Hittite Wives of Esau

[34]When Esau was forty, he married two Hittite women, Judith[i] the daughter of

---

a 26:22 Or "fruitful."

b 26:24 In Beersheba, God dug a well in Isaac. The strife with others had taken its toll on Isaac, leaving him hungry for a fresh encounter with God. When others were jealous, continually harassing him, faithful Isaac was visited by God.

c 26:25 Building an altar implies that Isaac offered sacrifices upon this altar, remembering the altar he once was placed upon by his father (Gen. 22).

d 26:25 The altar, the tent, and the well—each one points to an aspect of the lives of the patriarchs. The altar of worship, the tent of temporary sojourn, and the deep well of our satisfaction in God.

e 26:26 Although the Hebrew word can be translated "friend," Ahuzzah was a counselor who had the ear of the king. The names Abimelech and Abraham are both found seven times in this chapter.

f 26:32 Yahweh truly smiled on what Isaac had done, in forgiving and feeding his enemies, for on the same day he made this covenant with Abimelech, his servants brought him the news of a fresh well of water they found. Since Isaac had remained silent over the offense of losing wells, God honored him with a new one.

g 26:33 Or *Shibah*, which means "oath" or "seven." The triliteral Hebrew root can also be interpreted as "abundance" and is translated in this way by Syriac, Vulgate, Aquila, and Symmachus. The preferred translation is "oath" (LXX) or "vow."

h 26:33 Or "Well of the Oath." Isaac's name is associated with wells seven times in Genesis.

i 26:34 Judith means "praised."

Beeri[a] and Basemath[b] the daughter of Elon. [35]They made life miserable for Isaac and Rebekah.[c]

Jacob Defrauds Esau

27 When Isaac was very old and blind, he called for his oldest son, Esau, and asked him, "My son?"

"*I am here, father,*" Esau answered.

[2]"As you can see, I am now an old man," Isaac said. "And I may die any day now. [3]So please take your hunting gear—your bow and arrows—and go out into the field and hunt some wild game for me. [4]Then prepare me a savory meal, the food I love, and bring it to me. After I eat it, I will bless you from my innermost being before I die."[d]

[5]Now, Rebekah was eavesdropping on their conversation. So, when Esau left for the field to hunt for game to cook for Isaac, [6]she found Jacob and said to him, "I just overheard your father say to your brother Esau, [7]'Bring me some wild game and prepare a savory meal for me. Afterward I will bless you in the presence of Yahweh before I die.' [8]Listen carefully my son and do everything I tell you. [9]Go out to the flock and bring me two of the best young goats. I'll cook them for your father and prepare a delicious meal, the way he loves it. [10]Then, you take it to him to eat and your father will bless you before he dies."[e]

[11]Jacob objected, "But my brother Esau is covered with hair, and I'm smooth skinned. [12]If my father feels my hairless skin, *he'll know I'm not Esau.* He'll think I'm a trickster, and I'll end up bringing a curse upon myself rather than a blessing!"

[13]"My son," his mother said, "let any curse against you fall on me alone! Just do what I say and go and get the goats for me."

[14]So he went and got the goats and brought them to his mother. She prepared a delicious meal, just the way his father loved it. [15]Then Rebekah picked out the best clothes[f] of her older son Esau, and put them on her younger son Jacob.[g] [16]She covered

---

a 26:34 Beeri means "my well."

b 26:34 Basemath means "fragrance," "spice."

c 26:35 Isaac failed to deal with Esau concerning his Hittite wives. Remember how much care Abraham gave to finding a wife for Isaac (Gen. 24)? Why wouldn't Isaac now give great attention to finding the proper wife for his son? The Targums say that Esau and his wives rebelled against Isaac and Rebekah's instruction.

d 27:4 Or "After I eat, my soul will bless you before I die." The repeated mention of this meal (vv. 19, 25, 31, 33) implies that it is a ceremonial meal closely connected with the act of blessing.

e 27:10 Rebekah thought she was pursuing the best course, for she remembered Yahweh's promise of the older son serving the younger. She could not stand to see Esau, who had broken her heart by taking foreign wives (Gen. 26:34), receive Isaac's blessing. This entire episode attests to the conniving nature of man and the overriding purposes of God that cannot be thwarted by our sin.

f 27:15 These were probably Esau's dress-up clothes reserved for celebrating feasts or ceremonial occasions. The Hebrew word for clothes is *beged*, which can also be translated "treachery" or "deceit." This is a play on words, for Jacob used Esau's clothes to deceive. The *Midrash* Rabbah teaches that Esau ambushed Nimrod in the field, killed him, and took his garments. Jacob wore Nimrod's garments and deceived his father. According to the apocryphal Book of Jasher, the clothing that God robed Adam with was passed down to Noah who gave it to his son Ham and were eventually acquired by Nimrod.

g 27:15 Jacob is about to "pull the wool over the eyes" of his father. Jacob would do anything just to get his father's blessing!

Jacob's hands and the soft part of his neck with goatskins. [17]Then she handed Jacob the tasty dish and the bread that she had prepared [18]and he took them to Isaac.

"Father?" Jacob said.

Isaac replied, "Which one of my sons are you?"

[19]Jacob answered, "It's I—Esau—your firstborn. I have done as you asked. Please, sit up. Eat some of this *delicious* game *you love* so that you may give me your innermost blessing."[a]

[20]Isaac asked his son, "How in the world did you find game so quickly, my son?"

"Yahweh, your God, caused it to come right to me," he replied.

[21]Then Isaac said to Jacob, "Please, please, come closer that I may touch you, my son. I need to really know for certain that you are Esau." [22]So Jacob inched closer to his father Isaac, who felt his skin and said, "You sound like Jacob, but your hands are Esau's." [23]Because his hands were hairy like his brother Esau's, Isaac was *tricked and* did not recognize that it was really Jacob. As he was about to give him his blessing, [24]Isaac asked him again, "Are you really my son Esau?"

Jacob answered, "I am."

[25]"Then bring the food to me," Isaac said, "and let me eat my son's game. Then I will give you my blessing." So, Jacob gave his father the food and he ate it. He brought him wine and he drank it. [26]Then Isaac said to him, "My son, come near and kiss me." [27]So he came near and kissed him. Isaac recognized the smell of his son's clothes and blessed him, saying,

"Ah, the smell of my son
　is like the smell of a lush field that
　　Yahweh has blessed!
[28]May God give you heaven's dew,[b]
　the fatness of earth,
　and an abundance of grain and
　　new wine![c]
[29]Let peoples serve you
　and nations bow down to you!
May you be master[d] over your
　brothers
and may your mother's sons bow
　down to you!
Those who curse you will be cursed
and those who bless you will be
　blessed!"[e]

---

a　27:19 Or "so that your soul may bless me."

b　27:28 Dew is a frequent biblical metaphor of God's anointing, favor, abundance, revelation-truth, renewal, and unity. In Judges 6:36–40, Gideon's fleece, saturated with dew, was a sign to him that God was with him. He wrung out a "bowl full" of dew. We are bowls, vessels of honor, full of heaven's dew. See Num. 11:9; Deut. 33:13; Ps. 110:3; 133:3; Zech. 8:12.

c　27:28 The fatness of the earth means not only its finest produce (grain and wine) but also abundant prosperity. The earth's finest blessings are given to Jacob and his seed.

d　27:29 The Hebrew word for master is *gebir,* used here for the first time in Genesis. The word is closely related to *gibbor,* which means "strong," "mighty," "valiant," or "one who does acts of bravery."

e　27:29 The "Faith Chapter" (Hebrews 11) reveals a remarkable insight into this account. God commends Isaac in Hebrews 11:20, saying, "The power of faith prompted Isaac to impart a blessing to his sons, Jacob and Esau, concerning their prophetic destinies." At first glance, it does not appear to be an act of faith but rather a blunder for Isaac to bless Jacob instead of Esau. But God called it faith. All of this was contrary to Isaac's natural inclination. Instead of doubt or unbelief, he acted by faith. It is the nature of faith to give priority to God's will rather than our own. This is what Abraham had to do in giving up his son Isaac. Now Isaac had to give up Esau and his opinion of how God was to accomplish his purposes.

Esau's Lost Blessing

[30]No sooner had Jacob left from receiving the blessing of his father Isaac, than his brother Esau arrived home from hunting. [31]He too prepared a savory meal for his father and took it to him. He said to Isaac, "Sit up my father; eat some of your son's wild game so that you can give me your innermost blessing."[a]

[32]His father Isaac asked him, "Who are you?"

"I'm Esau, your firstborn son," he answered.

[33]When Isaac *realized what had happened*, he began to tremble and shake violently. He asked, "Who was it then that hunted wild game and brought it to me? I've already eaten it all before you came, and I gave him the blessing—yes, and he will be blessed indeed!"

[34]When Esau heard his father's words, he burst into bitter weeping and uncontrollable sobbing. He said to his father, "*Bless me!* Bless me too, father!"

[35]Isaac answered, "Your brother was here and deceived me. He has taken away your blessing."

[36]Esau exclaimed, "Jacob, *that heel grabber*[b]—the name fits him perfectly!

Now he has tricked me twice! He stole my birthright, and now he's robbed me of my blessing!" Then he asked, "*Father*, haven't you reserved a blessing for me?"

[37]Isaac replied, "*You don't understand*. My blessing will empower him to be master over you.[c] I have already given him all his brothers and relatives as servants. My blessing will richly provide him with grain and new wine. What more is left for me to do for you, my son?"

[38]Esau pleaded with his father, "Is that the only blessing you have to give? Bless me too, my father!"[d] Esau could not hold back his tears and he wept loudly. [39]Then Isaac his father spoke these words:

"You will live far from earth's
  bounty
and far from heaven's dew on
  high.
[40]You will live by the sword and
  serve your brother;
but when you grow restless,
you will break free from his
  control."[e]

[41]Esau hated Jacob because he stole his blessing. He said to himself, "In a

---

a 27:31 Or "that your soul may bless me."

b 27:36 Jacob's name comes from the word "heel" and can be translated "trickster," "heel grabber," or "cheater."

c 27:37 This demonstrates the power of a father's prophetic blessing. It can shape the future of our children. The words we speak over our children can make them or mar them. Be sure to speak life and blessing over your children!

d 27:38 The Septuagint adds, "But Isaac remained silent."

e 27:40 Esau would be given all the provisions he would need in life. Notice that Isaac reverses the order, the fatness of the earth is given first because Esau would be a man with his heart attached to the world. He would live by the sword-principle, always retaliating and unable to forgive. How many believers today have enough of God to get by, but live with unresolved anger and unforgiveness like Esau? Hebrews describes Esau as somewhat *careless about God's blessing* (Heb. 12:17). The descendants of Esau were known as Edomites. They were a violent people who raided caravans and pillaged cities. During David's reign, the united monarchy dominated the Edomites, but they later revolted under the reign of Jehoram (849–842 BC).

short time my father will be gone. After the time for mourning his death has passed, I will kill my brother Jacob!"[a]

[42]But when Rebekah found out about her older son Esau's plan, she quickly sent for her younger son Jacob,[b] and said to him, "Listen, your brother Esau is planning to exact revenge by killing you.[c] [43]My son, you must do what I say. Run away at once to my brother Laban in Haran. [44]You can live with him for a while until your brother calms down. [45]After your brother's anger has died down and he has forgotten what you've done to him, I will send a messenger to bring you back from there. Why should I lose both my sons in one day?"[d]

[46]Later, Rebekah said to Isaac, "I'm so disgusted with our Hittite daughters-in-law. I'd rather die than see Jacob marry one of these local girls—these Hittite women!"

Jacob Flees to Laban

28 Before Jacob left, Isaac called for him, blessed him, and gave him these instructions: "I forbid you to marry any Canaanite woman. [2]Leave at once for the land of your grandfather Bethuel in Paddan-Aram and find one of the young women there to marry, one of your uncle Laban's daughters.[e]

[3]May the God who is always more than enough[f] bless you *abundantly*. May he make you fruitful and multiply your descendants until you become many tribes! [4]May he impart to you and your seed the blessing of Abraham so that you may possess the land where you now live as a foreigner—the land God gave to Abraham."

[5]Then Isaac sent Jacob on his way[g] to Paddan-Aram, the land of his grandfather Bethuel the Aramean, to the home of Laban, Bethuel's son and the brother of Rebekah, the mother of Jacob and Esau.

Esau Takes Another Wife

[6]Esau had learned that Isaac had blessed Jacob and had sent him away to Paddan-Aram to find a wife there, and that while blessing him, Isaac had instructed him, "Don't marry a Canaanite woman." [7]Furthermore, Esau found out that Jacob had obeyed his parents and fled to Paddan-Aram. [8]Esau, knowing that his father Isaac disapproved of Canaanite women, [9]went to Ishmael's clan and chose a woman named Mahalath to be one of his wives. She was the daughter of Ishmael, Abraham's son, and sister of Nebaioth.[h]

---

a 27:41 Isaac sealed Jacob's blessing with a kiss but not Esau's. All of this caused Esau to hate his brother. Following in the way of Cain, Esau made an inner vow to murder his brother as soon as his father died. His jealousy turned to hatred and hatred to murder, all because his younger brother received a blessing that he did not.

b 27:42 Jacob may have been in hiding for fear of Esau.

c 27:42 Or "is consoling himself [over what you did to him] by planning to kill you."

d 27:45 This would be the last time Rebekah saw her son before she died.

e 28:2 Marriage with a cousin was acceptable in that day and continues to be common among people in the Near East today.

f 28:3 Or "El Shaddai." See footnote for Gen. 17:1.

g 28:5 Jacob was in his seventies when he fled from his brother Esau, and the journey was about 500 miles.

h 28:9 Nebaioth was the firstborn of Ishmael (Gen. 25:13) and is identified with Nabaiti, possibly the ancestor of the later Nabateans.

The Escalator of Eternity

[10]Jacob left Beersheba and journeyed toward Haran. [11]He encountered a certain[a] place at sunset and camped there for the night. He took a stone[b] from there, made it his pillow, and lay down to sleep. [12]He had a dream[c] of a stairway securely fixed on the earth and reaching into heaven. In his dream, messengers of God were ascending and descending on the stairway.[d] [13]And Yahweh stood beside him[e] and said to him, "I am Yahweh, the God of your father Abraham and the God of Isaac. You are lying on the very ground that I will give to you and your descendants. [14]They will become as numerous as the specks of dust on the earth, and they will extend their territory in all directions. Through you and your descendants, I will bless the whole world.[f] [15]Never forget—I am always with you and will protect you wherever you go. And one day I will bring you back to this land, for I will neither leave you nor fail

---

a 28:11 In the twilight, Jacob set up camp at Bethel. The Hebrew implies that it is "the Place," a special place, or holy place. Indeed, it was, for God had also manifested there to Abraham (Gen. 12:8). In Jacob's helpless, lonely condition, a new revelation would be given to him.

b 28:11 Perhaps this was one of the stones of the altar erected by Jacob's grandfather, Abraham. Jesus is the anointed Stone on whom we lay our head. To lay your head (thoughts and dreams) on him is to discover the beauty of God (Isa. 33:17–22). When the anointing of Jesus fills our head (mind), we will see heaven opened with fresh revelation and perceive the visions of God. Jesus is the Chief Corner Stone, the Stone that killed Goliath, and the Stone of Daniel Chapter 2:34 and 45 that conquers kingdoms.

c 28:12 Dreams in the Bible are a valid form of divine communication. God frequently speaks to people through dreams. See Gen. 41:1–7; Judg. 7:13–15; 1 Kings 3:5–14; Dan. 2:28; Matt. 2:12–13; 27:19. It is also the promise of Joel that Peter quotes on the Day of Pentecost that those who received the Spirit would "dream dreams." See Joel 2:28; Acts 2:17.

d 28:12 The steps of this stairway go up into the heavenly realm where our true riches are found. Each step is a progressive revelation of God's purpose for our lives found in Jesus Christ. The stairway goes both ways, touching heaven and touching earth. Jesus Christ can be thought of as the Stairway that reaches from earth (his human nature) to heaven (his heavenly nature). Jesus spoke to Nathaniel using the same terminology (John 1:51). Jesus is the only valid entry into the spirit realm, the true way into the heavenly realm. By him, we ascend and leave our lower life. This Jesus-Ladder was filled with messengers ascending and descending. Who are these messengers? Note the order: they ascended first. It does not say they were descending and ascending which would be true if they were the angels in heaven. If you ascend first, you are leaving earth to go to heaven. These messengers may be people or divine beings. If people, they are intercessors and promise-claimers. The Hebrew word translated "angel" is malak, which can also be translated "ambassador," "deputy," "messenger," or "prophet." The Greek word used in the New Testament for angel is angelos or "messenger." It can refer to either people or to a heavenly being. Paul wrote to the Galatians that they had welcomed him in their midst as if he were an angel (messenger) from God (Gal. 4:14). In Rev. 2–3, John is instructed to write to the seven churches and to the seven angelos of those churches. The angels were the human overseers of those churches. In Gen. 18:2, three angels come to Abraham and are described as "three men" (cf. Gen. 19:1). We are like angelic-ambassadors who ascend and descend upon the Jesus-Stairway. See Isa. 35:8–9; 57:14–15; 62:10; Eph. 2:6; Heb. 12:22–24.

e 28:13 Or "above it (the stairway)."

f 28:14 See Gen. 12:3; Matt. 8:11; 28:19–20; Acts 15:17–18.

to fulfill every word I have promised you."*a*

[16]When Jacob awoke from his dream, he said, "Yahweh is here! He is in this place and I didn't realize it!"*b* [17]Terrified and overwhelmed he said, "How awesome is this place! I have stumbled right into the house of God! This place is *a portal*, the very gate of heaven!"

[18]Early in the morning, Jacob took the stone he had under his head, set it up as a pillar and anointed it by pouring oil over the top of it.*c* [19]He named that place Bethel;*d* though the city was once called Luz.*e*

[20]Then Jacob committed himself to God, saying, "If you will always be with me and protect me on this long journey, and if you give me bread to eat and clothing to wear, [21]and if I return safely to my father's house, then Yahweh, you will be my God! [22]See! I have set up this sacred stone pillar and it will be your house, God. I promise to set aside a tenth of all that you give me as my gift to you."

Jacob Meets a Woman at the Well

29 Jacob resumed his journey*f* and entered the land east *of*

---

a 28:15 What did God tell Jacob? Did he scold him for being a crafty deceiver? Did he rebuke him for his lack of faith? Not at all. He revealed himself to Jacob as the one who would never leave or forsake him. This revelation of grace was a steady stream of assurances that washed over wayward Jacob! The Lord gave these promises to Jacob while he still was unbroken, unreliable, and a deceiver. Our God is a confident, capable God who can subdue and conquer the most difficult of men. Our future blessing and usefulness depend on God's strength, not ours. When God brought Jacob back to Bethel twenty years later, he was changed. God will change you. Your transformation may take more than a year, even more than ten or twenty, but your God will finish the work of changing you into the image of his Son (Phil. 1:6). You will be his look-alike. You will carry the blessings of God to the next generation!

b 28:16 How many times have we been led to an uncomfortable place in life, only to encounter the Lord? Have you said, looking back over your life: "Truly, the Lord really was in all I went through, and I didn't even know it!" We often discover that he is where we did not think he would be. You may have a divine visitation anywhere! Ordinary places can become holy places.

c 28:18 He builds a pillar from his pillow. The church is described by Paul as the "pillar and firm foundation of the truth" (1 Tim. 3:15). By pouring oil on the stone, Jacob consecrates the pillar as a memorial to God. See Lev. 8:10–11.

d 28:19 Bethel means "House of God." Jacob could see in a heap of stones the House of God that would arise. This is the first mention of God's house in the Scriptures. The House of God was filled with his presence, a gateway to heaven, a stairway with angels, and revelation. One day, *the House of God* would be born among us, born of a virgin. Jesus came to be an example of the House of God, the dwelling place of God and men under one roof, living in one body. Jesus is the God-Man, the House of God. As the House, he invites us to dwell as one with the Father. But Jesus was the initial fulfillment of the House of God, not the ultimate fulfillment which would include others incorporated into Jesus. Today, the House of God, the gate to heaven, is also a description of the *church*. We are God's house (1 Cor. 3:16), for the Lord dwells among us as his people. And we become a gateway for others to come to God through our message of new life in Christ.

e 28:19 Luz means "separation." God calls us to separate ourselves to himself, and when we do, we become the House of God.

f 29:1 Or "Jacob lifted up his feet." This unusual Hebrew expression could be double entendre, telling us that Jacob lifted up his feet not only to go on his journey but also to go up that Stairway he had just seen in his dream. To move forward is always to move higher with God.

Canaan.ᵃ ²One day, Jacob came to a well out in the open country where the shepherds watered their animals. Three flocks of sheep and goats were lying near the well, which had a large, heavy stone covering the opening. ³Whenever all the flocks gathered there, the shepherds would roll away the stone from the mouth of the well, water their sheep, and then roll the stone back over the top of the well.

⁴Jacob approached them and said, "Good day, friends; where are you from?"

"We're from Haran," they answered.

⁵"Do you happen to know Laban, a grandsonᵇ of Nahor?" Jacob said.

"We do." they replied.

⁶Jacob asked, "How's he doing?"

"He's doing well." they answered. "As a matter of fact, here comes his daughter Rachelᶜ right now with her flock."ᵈ

⁷Jacob said to them, "Look, it's not time for the animals to gather together here; it's now the hottest hour of the day. Let's go ahead and water the sheep, then you can go and pasture them."

⁸They replied, "First, we have to wait until all the flocks are gathered. After that, the stone needs to be rolled away from the mouth of the well, then we'll water the animals."

⁹While they were still speaking, Rachel, the shepherdess, drew near to the well with her father's sheep. ¹⁰As soon as Jacob took one good look at Rachel, the *beautiful* daughter of his uncle Laban, he quickly went over to the mouth of the well and *single-handedly* rolled away the stone and watered all the flock of his uncle Laban!ᵉ ¹¹Immediately, he walked up to Rachel and kissed her! *Unable to hold back his tears*, Jacob wept aloud.ᶠ ¹²*After he composed himself*, he explained to Rachel, "I'm your father's nephew, your aunt Rebekah's son." Upon hearing this, Rachel ran to tell her father. ¹³When Laban heard the news that his nephew Jacob had arrived at the well, he ran to greet him. Laban hugged and kissed Jacob and welcomed him into his home. After Jacob told him the story of all that happened, ¹⁴Laban said to him,

---

a 29:1 Or "the land of the sons of the east," that is, east of Canaan. Jacob arrived at Paddan-Aram in Mesopotamia.

b 29:5 Laban was the son of Bethuel and the grandson of Nahor, Abraham's brother.

c 29:6 Rachel means "ewe lamb."

d 29:6 It is obvious that God led Jacob supernaturally to the very well where Rachel would appear, and she came at an unusual time of day to water her father's flocks. This was a divine appointment for Jacob. And you can be assured that God has his hands of guidance upon you also.

e 29:10 At the sight of the lovely Rachel, Jacob's soul is so moved that he gains the strength to roll away the stone all by himself. One flash of her eyes (Song. 4:9) made him a momentary "superman." After he moved the heavy stone, Jacob drew gallons and gallons of water for her flocks.

f 29:11 This entire scene is filled with emotion. Jacob sees the girl of his dreams, becomes supercharged to move the heavy stone and water her flock. Then he kisses her and lifts up his voice with passionate tears. You can almost hear the tender music playing in the background as this "guy meets girl" scene unfolds. As you read it over again, think of Jesus who also rolled away a heavy stone so that he could come meet you to "romance" your soul (see Song of Songs). He drew you to faith in him, then offered you a drink from the well of life.

"Certainly, you are my own flesh and blood!" Jacob stayed with him for an entire month *and worked for him.*

Jacob Marries Leah and Rachel

[15]Afterward, Laban said to Jacob, "Just because you're my relative doesn't mean I expect you to work for nothing. Tell me, what do you want your wages to be?" [16](Now, Laban had two daughters; the older was Leah,[a] and the younger was Rachel. [17]Rachel had a lovely figure and was gorgeous,[b] but Leah's eyes were weak.[c])

[18]Jacob had fallen in love with Rachel, so he answered Laban, "I will serve you for seven years for the hand of your younger daughter, Rachel!"

[19]Laban replied, "I'd rather give her to you than to some other man. Stay and work for me." [20]So Jacob served Laban for seven years in exchange for Rachel, but because he loved her so deeply, the seven years seemed like only a few days.[d]

[21]After the seven years, Jacob said to Laban, "My time is fulfilled; give me your daughter so that I may marry her and sleep with her." [22]So Laban prepared a *wedding* feast[e] and invited all the people of the surrounding area. [23]That night, Laban *tricked Jacob* by bringing his older daughter Leah to Jacob's tent, and he slept with her *on his wedding night!*[f] [24](Laban assigned Zilpah[g] to be Leah's servant.)

[25]When Jacob woke up the next morning, he was shocked to find Leah lying next to him! So he confronted Laban and said, "What have you done to me? Didn't I serve you these seven years for Rachel? Why have you tricked me?"

[26]Laban answered, "It's not our custom here to give the younger daughter in marriage before the older daughter is married. [27]Wait until this bridal week

---

a 29:16 The etymology of the name Leah is somewhat ambiguous. Some Hebrew scholars equate the name Leah with "weak," "sluggish," or "weary." Tradition has it that Leah was cross-eyed, or perhaps partly blind. Her vision was impaired; seeing dimly. A "Leah" church does not function with clear vision. She represents those with limited vision that cannot discern the timing and ways of God. Like the lukewarm Laodiceans, the church is instructed to "purchase eye salve" so that they could see clearly (Rev. 3:18). A vision impaired church will live by principles, laws, traditions, and customs. It was the "custom" for Leah to marry Jacob. Like many today, she was unable to see clearly, felt unloved, and was unable to perceive God's greater purpose. The fruit of Leah (and her handmaiden, called "the slave girl" in Gal. 4:21–22) was only bondage. Jacob had to "work" after getting her!

b 29:17 Or "Rachel was beautiful of form and beautiful in appearance." Rachel becomes a picture of the radiant bride of the last days who makes herself ready for her bridegroom. See Eph. 5:27; Rev. 19:7.

c 29:17 Or "her eyes were sickly." (LXX) The Hebrew is uncertain.

d 29:20 Love can make long, hard service short and easy. This is why the Scriptures speak of a "labor of love" (I Thess.1:3; Heb. 6:10). In Hosea 12:12, we learn that Jacob tended sheep for those seven years in order to get the bride he loved. There is Another who has waited now for nearly seven thousand years for his Bride that he dearly loves! And what has he been doing for these years? He has been carrying his lambs close to his heart and tending his flock like a Shepherd (Isa. 40:11).

e 29:22 Or "drinking party."

f 29:23 Perhaps Jacob was drunk on wine, and Leah was wearing a bridal veil.

g 29:24 Zilpah means "small" or "a trickling."

of festivities is over, then I'll give you Rachel, but you must serve me for another seven years."[a]

28–30 Jacob complied with Laban's request. After he completed the prescribed week of Leah's wedding feast, Laban gave his daughter Rachel to be his wife, and he slept with her. Rachel was his true love, not Leah. (Laban assigned Bilhah[b] as his daughter Rachel's servant.) And Jacob remained there serving Laban for another seven years.

Leah's Four Sons

31 When Yahweh saw that Leah was unloved, he opened her womb, but Rachel remained childless. 32 Leah conceived, gave birth to a son, and named him Reuben,[c] saying, "Because Yahweh looked upon me with compassion in my misery, surely, my husband will love me now!" 33 She conceived again, gave birth to a son, and named him Simeon,[d] saying, "Yahweh has heard that I am despised, and in his mercy, he has given me this son also." 34 Leah conceived the third time, gave birth to a son, and named him Levi,[e] saying, "This time my husband will be joined to me, because now I've given him three sons!" 35 Once again, Leah conceived and gave birth to a son. She named him Judah,[f] saying, "This time I will praise the Lord!" Then she stopped bearing children *for a while.*

Battle of the Brides

30 When Rachel saw that she could not give Jacob children,

---

a 29:27 For those seven years, God was teaching Jacob submission to the rights of the firstborn. It was not right to marry the younger before the *firstborn.* All that Jacob circumvented in stealing the blessing from Esau, he now must learn by serving another for seven years and learn the timing of God. After the seven years were over, Laban tricked Jacob by giving him Leah, not Rachel on his wedding night. Jacob was fooled by the veil over the bride thinking it was Rachel, even as he had fooled his father with a hairy skin over his arms, confusing him with Esau. Every "Jacob" will one day meet his "Laban."

b 29:28–30 The name Bilhah may come from an Arabic word for "stupid," "unconcerned," or if Hebrew, "troubled."

c 29:32 Reuben means "See! A son!" Leah's definition of fulfillment would only come through Jacob's love. Envy can often be traced back to an inward struggle to gain identity. Leah and Rachel competed for Jacob's heart. Leah called her firstborn Reuben, which in Hebrew sounds like "He has seen my misery."

d 29:33 Simeon's name comes from the verb "to hear." God saw Leah's pain and heard her cry. She named her first two children after God's mercy and compassion for the downcast and rejected. There is a mercy-chord in God's heart that is touched by the broken, poor, and rejected. God gives greater honor to the dishonored ones (I Cor. 12:24). It is the nature of God to be drawn to those who hurt. God saw her pain, her loneliness, and her heartache. If only she understood how greatly the Lord loved her.

e 29:34 The name Levi sounds like the Hebrew word meaning "to join," "bind," or "attach."

f 29:35 The name Judah sounds like the verb "to praise." Over the years of struggling with the pain of being unloved, Leah finally opened her heart to the Lord, and grace touched her. God was tenderly wooing her to himself through her disappointment in her marriage. At last, she gives birth to her fourth son and resolves to praise the Lord no matter what. Leah has now become a worshipper of the Almighty. She found her fulfillment in God, so she names her son Judah (praise) and declares, "This time I will praise the Lord!" Leah, not Rachel, became the mother of Judah and ancestor of Jesus.

her jealousy toward her sister simmered. So, she said to Jacob, "Give me sons, or I'll die!"[a]

[2]Jacob became furious with Rachel and said, "Am I God? He's the one keeping you from bearing children!" [3]She replied, "Here's my servant Bilhah. Sleep with her. She can be my surrogate; then I can have children through her[b] and build a family."[c]

[4]So Rachel gave her servant Bilhah to Jacob as another wife, and Jacob slept with her. [5]And Bilhah conceived and bore Jacob a son, [6]and Rachel named him Dan, saying, "God has vindicated me.[d] He heard my voice and gave me a son." [7]Then her servant Bilhah conceived again and bore Jacob a second son. [8]Rachel named him Naphtali, saying, "I have wrestled mightily[e] with my sister, and I won!"

[9]Meanwhile, when Leah saw that she had ceased bearing children, she took her servant Zilpah and gave her to Jacob as another wife. [10-11]Zilpah bore Jacob a son, and Leah named him Gad, saying, "What good fortune!"[f] [12]Zilpah bore Jacob a second son, [13]and Leah named him Asher, saying, "Oh happy day![g] All the women will say, 'She's happy now!'"

[14]One day, during wheat harvest, Reuben found some mandrake plants[h] in the field and brought them to his mother Leah. Rachel said to Leah, "Please give me some of your son's mandrakes."

[15]Leah replied, "You already took away *the affection of* my husband, so now you're going to take my son's mandrakes, too?"

Rachel said, "All right then, I'll let him sleep with you tonight in exchange for some of your son's mandrakes."

[16]That evening, when Jacob was coming home from the field, Leah went out to meet him and said, "You must sleep with me tonight, for I've paid for your services with my son's mandrakes." So Jacob slept with Leah that night. [17]God listened compassionately to Leah's cry, she became pregnant, and bore Jacob a fifth son, [18]whom she named Issachar, saying,

---

a 30:1 Ironically, Rachel dies while giving birth to her second son (Gen. 35:16–19).

b 30:3 Literally, "that she may bear upon my knees," a Hebrew figurative expression that refers to the practice of obtaining children through the service of another woman and legally adopting the child as one's own. See Gen. 50:23 (and footnote); Job 3:12.

c 30:3 Or "I will be built up through her."

d 30:6 Or "judged me (decided in my favor)." The name Dan sounds like the verb "to judge." The Hebrew contains a word play on his name—"God has vindicated (*dananni*) me."

e 30:8 The name Naphtali means "wrestle," "contest," "struggle," or "fight." The Hebrew is "with wrestling of 'elohim," posing both a translation and an interpretive problem. There are three ways to understand this phrase: (1) Many scholars see 'elohim as a descriptive term of intensity meaning "great" or "might." (2) Some interpret this statement as Rachel wrestling with God for his favor. (3) Some see it as a mysterious struggle or "fateful contest (of God)" or "playing a trick on her sister." Nonetheless, this was one troubled home. As Jacob struggled with his older brother, Rachel now struggled with her older sister.

f 30:10–11 The name Gad means "good fortune" or "good luck has come."

g 30:13 The name Asher means "happy."

h 30:14 Mandrakes, or "love apples," had an erotic connotation and were considered in that culture to have aphrodisiac properties. Aphrodite, the Greek goddess of love, beauty, and sex, was known as "Lady of the Mandrake." The Hebrew root for mandrake is similar to the word for "love."

"God rewarded[a] me for giving my maidservant to my husband."

[19]Once again, Leah conceived and bore Jacob a sixth son, [20]whom she named Zebulun, saying, "God has given me good gifts for my husband! Now he will accept[b] me, for I've given him six sons." [21]Lastly, Leah gave birth to a daughter and named her Dinah.[c]

[22]God listened to Rachel's heart-cry, and had compassion[d] on her, and made her fertile.

[23-24]She conceived, and bore a son, and named him Joseph, saying, "God has taken away my disgrace. May Yahweh add[e] to me another son."

Jacob Makes a Deal with Laban

[25]After Rachel gave birth to Joseph, Jacob said to Laban, "Release me to go back home to my homeland. [26]You know how hard I've worked for you these many years to finish paying for my two wives. Give them to me along with my children, and I'll be on my way."

[27]Laban countered, "If you please, I have learned by divine inquiry[f] that I have become prosperous because of you and the blessing of Yahweh that's on your life. [28]Just name your price, and I'll give it to you."

[29]Jacob replied, "You know how hard I've worked for you and how your livestock has increased under my care. [30]The little you had before I came

has multiplied greatly, for Yahweh has blessed you wonderfully because I am here.[g] But now, I need to provide for my own family, too."

[31]So Laban asked, "What should I give you?"

"Nothing," Jacob replied, "You don't need to give me a thing. If you will do but one thing for me, I will continue to care for your flocks: [32]Just let me pass through all your flocks today and take out every speckled and spotted sheep or goat, and every black lamb. That's all the payment I ask. [33]And in the future, when you review my wages, the integrity of my dealings with you will be obvious. If you find any animal among mine that is not speckled, spotted, or black, then you will know that I stole it."

[34]"Agreed!" Laban said, "We'll do what you've suggested." [35]But that same day, Laban secretly removed all the male and female goats that were speckled or spotted (all that had white on them) and all the black lambs and left them under the care of his sons. [36]He set a distance of a three-day journey between himself and Jacob; while Jacob continued to tend the rest of Laban's flocks.

[37]Jacob, however, cut green branches of poplar, almond, and plane trees and peeled back part of their bark, to expose the white inner wood of the branches. [38]Then he set the partially peeled branches inside the water

---

a 30:18 The name Issachar comes from the word "reward."
b 30:20 The name Zebulun sounds like the word "honor," "raise up," or "accept."
c 30:21 Dinah means "judgment" or "vindication."
d 30:22 Or "God remembered."
e 30:23–24 The name Joseph means "he adds (another)."
f 30:27 Or "by divination (omens, astrology, fortune-tellers)." God forbids divination among his people (Lev. 19:26; Deut. 18:10, 14.)
g 30:30 Literally, "according to my foot," a figure of speech for "because I am here (working for you)."

troughs where the goats would see them when they came to drink. ³⁹For they mated when they came to the water troughs, and *as they lowered their heads to drink*, they saw the stripped branches in front of their eyes. *Miraculously*[a] they gave birth to streaked, speckled, and spotted young. ⁴⁰But with the mating ewes, on the other hand, he made them face the streaked or completely black animals in Laban's flock. By doing this, he produced his own special flocks, which he didn't allow to mingle with Laban's. ⁴¹Moreover, every time the stronger females were in heat, Jacob laid the partially peeled branches in the water troughs in front of the flock, so that they would mate among the branches. ⁴²But he didn't place the branches in front of the scrawny goats when they mated, leaving the feeble animals for Laban and the stronger for himself. ⁴³In this way, Jacob quickly grew very wealthy and owned large flocks, a great number of camels and donkeys, and many male and female servants.

Jacob Escapes from Laban

31 Now Jacob heard that the sons of Laban were complaining, "Everything Jacob owns he has taken from our father! He gained all his wealth from what our father owned." ²And Jacob saw that Laban no longer viewed him favorably as he once did. ³Then Yahweh said to Jacob, "Return to the land of your ancestors where you were born; and *remember*, I will be with you." ⁴So Jacob sent a message for Leah and Rachel to meet him in the field where his flocks were *grazing*. ⁵When they arrived, he said to them, "I can see that your father's attitude toward me has changed, but the God of my father has been with me. ⁶You both know I have worked for your father as hard as I could; ⁷although he has cheated me and reduced[b] my wages over and over. Yet God has not allowed him to harm me. ⁸If he said, 'The speckled ones will be your wages,' then all the flock bore speckled. If he said, 'The striped ones will be your wages,' then all the flock bore striped. ⁹Because of these *miracles*, God has taken away your father's livestock and given them to me!"

¹⁰*Jacob continued*, "Once during the breeding season, I had a dream. I saw that the male goats who were mating were all speckled, streaked, or spotted. ¹¹In the dream, the angel of God called me by my name, 'Jacob.'"

"I am here," I answered.

¹²"Then he said, 'Observe and note that all the male goats that are mating are speckled, streaked, or spotted, for I have seen all that Laban is doing to you. ¹³I am the God who appeared

---

a 30:39 This was not simply principles of animal husbandry, but a divine miracle revealed to Jacob through a dream. God always has unique and puzzling methods to perform a miracle. He may require bathing seven times in the Jordan River (2 Kings 5:10), parting the Red Sea (Ex. 14), or having the sun stand still (Josh. 10:13–14). God displayed his creative power through the birth of these multi-colored young goats. Perhaps the miracle teaches us that what we see or gaze upon can impregnate us with the object of our vision, for you can determine what you conceive by what you behold. What you set your gaze upon is what you will give birth to.

b 31:7 Or "changed." The implication is that Laban obviously did not give him raises, but reduced his salary ten times, a term not meant to define how many times, but a figure of speech for "many, many times."

to you at Bethel,^{a} where you anointed a pillar and made a vow to me. Now leave this land at once and return to the land of your birth.'"

¹⁴Then Rachel and Leah answered him, "Our father doesn't want us to inherit a portion from his estate. ¹⁵Hasn't he treated us as outsiders *and not as members of his family*? Not only did he sell us *like property*, but he has also spent our purchase price! ¹⁶Our father's wealth that God has given you was legally ours and our children to begin with! So, go ahead and do whatever God has told you."

¹⁷Jacob immediately put his wives and children on camels ¹⁸and took with him all the livestock and everything he had amassed in Paddan-Aram. He set out to return to his father Isaac in the land of Canaan.

¹⁹One day, when Laban had gone *to his fields* to shear his sheep,^{b} Rachel stole her father's household idols.^{c} ²⁰Jacob had outwitted Laban the Aramean by secretly departing without telling him. ²¹He fled with all that he had, and after crossing the Euphrates,^{d} he headed for the hill country of Gilead.

²²And it wasn't until three days later that Laban discovered Jacob had left.

Laban Pursues Jacob

²³Laban, along with some of his relatives, took off in pursuit and chased after Jacob for seven days. He had almost caught up with him in the hill country of Gilead, ²⁴when God appeared to Laban the Aramean in a dream and warned him, "Be careful that you neither *harm nor* threaten Jacob."^{e}

²⁵Now Jacob had set up his camp with his flocks on a hill, and Laban had him in his sights. Laban and his companions set up their camp nearby. ²⁶Laban *approached* Jacob and said, "*Nephew*, what have you done? You've deceived me and carried away my daughters like captives on a battlefield. ²⁷Why did you trick me and run away in secret without telling me? I would have sent you off joyously, celebrating with singing and dancing to the tambourine and stringed instruments. ²⁸And why did you not even let me kiss my daughters and grandchildren goodbye? What you have done is foolish! ²⁹I could harm you, but the God of your father spoke

---

a 31:13 As translated from the Septuagint and ancient Targums. The Hebrew is "I am the God of Bethel."

b 31:19 Sheep shearing was done in the spring, and it was a time of celebration and festivities that could have lasted a week (1 Sam 25:2, 8, 11; 2 Sam. 13:23). Laban was preoccupied with the festivities and didn't realize that his household gods had been stolen and that Jacob was secretly taking off with his daughters.

c 31:19 This is the Hebrew word *teraphim* and can be described as small, carved figurines passed down within the family or clan. *Teraphim* is taken from an Aramaic root word meaning "to inquire." Apparently, Laban used these images for guidance by divination. Taking her father's gods would be taking his ability to discover where they had gone (Judg. 17:5; I Sam. 19:13; Ezek. 21:21). Other scholars believe that the teraphim guaranteed the right of inheritance to whoever possessed them. According to ancient Akkadian writings, the possession of these family idols (gods) could verify legal title to the family estate. This was perhaps the reason for Laban's angry accusation of Jacob (v. 30).

d 31:21 The Euphrates was known to the Hebrews simply as "The River." It was about fifty miles from Laban's home to the Euphrates.

e 31:24 Or "that you speak not to Jacob a word either good or evil." This is a merism, for God was not telling Laban to remain silent, but rather neither to harm nor threaten Jacob with his words.

to me *in a dream* last night, saying, 'Be careful that you neither *harm nor* threaten Jacob.' ³⁰Now I realize you ran away because you desperately long to return to your father's house, but why did you steal my gods?"

³¹"*I left in a hurry* because I was afraid," Jacob answered, "and I thought you would take your daughters from me by force. ³²Whoever has taken your gods will be put to death! So here, in the presence of our relatives, if you can find among our possessions anything that is yours, take it." Now Jacob had no clue that Rachel had stolen the gods.

³³Laban went immediately into Jacob's tent to search. Then he went into the tents of Zilpah and Bilhah but found nothing. After searching Leah's tent, he went into Rachel's. ³⁴Now Rachel had taken the family gods and put them in her camel's cushion and sat on them. ³⁵She said to her father, "Please my father,ᵃ don't be angry if I don't rise before you, for I'm having my period." When he rummaged through her tent, he did not find them.

³⁶Then Jacob became angry and complained to Laban, "What have I done wrong? What sin have I committed that you would hotly pursue me *as if you were chasing a criminal*? ³⁷You have rummaged through all my things, and did you find anything of your own property? If you did, set them here in front of your relatives and mine. Let them decide between the two of us."

³⁸*Jacob continued*, "For the last twenty years I have served you, and the whole time your sheep and goats did not miscarry, nor did I feast on any of your rams. ³⁹If one from your flock was mauled by a wild beast, I didn't bring it to you; I absorbed the loss myself. And you always made me pay for any missing animal, whether snatched by day or by night. ⁴⁰Many times, scorching heat consumed me by day and hard frost by night; I endured sleepless nights. ⁴¹For these twenty years that I've lived among you, I slaved away fourteen years for your two daughters, and six years for your flocks. And *besides all that*, you've reduced my wages over and over. ⁴²If the God of my father, the God of Abraham, and the Awesome Oneᵇ of Isaac, had not been on my side, you certainly would have sent me away empty-handed! But God *in his mercy* took notice of how much I've suffered and how hard I've worked—and that's why he rebuked you last night *in your dream!*"

Laban and Jacob Make a Covenant

⁴³Laban replied to Jacob, "These women are my daughters, these children are my grandchildren; and the flocks are mine. In fact, everything you see belongs to me. But from today I will not be able to do anything more for my daughters and grandchildren.ᶜ ⁴⁴Come now, let's form a covenant between you and me. Let it endure as a witness between us."ᵈ ⁴⁵So Jacob took a stone, set it up as a pillar, ⁴⁶and in the presence of his relatives, he said to them, "Everyone gather stones, and place them here in a pile." And

---

ᵃ 31:35 Or "my lord."

ᵇ 31:42 Or "the One whom Isaac worships" or "the Fear of Isaac." The Hebrew is uncertain.

ᶜ 31:43 Or "What can I do today about these daughters of mine and these children they have borne?"

ᵈ 31:44 This covenant (treaty), memorialized by the heap of stones and their covenant meal, would be an agreement to never harm each other.

they did so, and afterward, they ate together next to the heap of stones. [47]Laban and Jacob named the place *in both languages, Aramaic*[a] *and Hebrew,*[b] calling it Witness Heap. [48]And Laban said, "Today, this heap of stones will be a witness between you and me *of our enduring friendship.*" He called it Witness Heap [49]and Watchpost,[c] for Laban declared, "May Yahweh keep his eyes on us when we are absent from each other. [50]If you mistreat my daughters or marry other women besides my daughters, remember that even though no one else is with us, God is watching us. [51]Here is the heap of stones and here is the memorial pillar that stands between us.[d] [52]This heap and this pillar stand as witnesses that I will never pass beyond them to harm you and that you will never pass beyond them to harm me. [53]Now may the God of Abraham and the god of Nahor judge between us!"[e]

Jacob made his vow by the Awesome One of his father Isaac.[f] [54]Then Jacob offered a sacrifice on the mountain and called everyone together for a meal, and they remained there all night on the mountain.

[55]Early the next morning, Laban kissed his daughters and grandchildren, blessed them, and then he returned home.

A Divine Encounter

32 As Jacob continued *toward Canaan*, the angels of God came to meet him! [2]When he saw them, he exclaimed, "This is God's military camp!"[g] So he named that place Two Camps *of Angels.*

[3]Jacob sent messengers ahead to his brother Esau *who was living* in the land of Seir, the country of Edom. [4]He instructed them, "Give this message from me to my master Esau, 'I am your servant. I have lived with our uncle Laban all these years [5]and have acquired sheep, cattle, donkeys, and both male and female servants. I send this message to you, my master, in the hope of finding favor in your eyes.'"

[6]When the messengers returned to Jacob, they informed him, "We gave your brother Esau your message, and he himself is coming here to meet you. In fact, he's on his way now with four hundred men!"

[7]Gripped with fear to the point of panic,[h] Jacob split all the people who were with him into two camps, and also the flocks, herds, and camels. [8]He said to himself, "If Esau attacks the first camp and destroys them, at least the other camp will escape."

[9]Then Jacob prayed, "Yahweh, God of my father Abraham and God of my father Isaac, you said to me, 'Return

---

a 31:47 *Jegar Sahadutha*, Aramaic for "Heap of Witness."

b 31:47 *Galeed*, Hebrew for "Heap of Witness."

c 31:49 Or "Mizpah," which means "Watchpost (Lookout)." Jesus is our Mizpah. Ephesians 2:14 states that Jesus made Jew and Gentile one, breaking down the middle wall between them. Jacob, the father of the Israelites, and Laban, a Gentile, find peace at Mizpah.

d 31:51 Or "that I have set up between us."

e 31:53 As translated from some manuscripts and the Septuagint. Other Hebrew manuscripts add, "the gods of their father." Yahweh, the God of Abraham, is not the god of Nahor. Yahweh called Abraham out of Haran (Gen. 12:4) and away from idol worship (Josh. 24:2).

f 31:53 Or "by (in the name of) the Fear of Isaac (the One whom Isaac feared)."

g 32:2 Or "This is God's camp," "This is God's army," or "Mahanaim."

h 32:7 Or "bound," "tied-up," "restricted," implying that Jacob was immobilized by his anxiety.

to your country and to your family, and I will make you prosper.' ¹⁰I am so unworthy of all the loving-kindness and faithfulness that you have showered upon me, your servant. When I crossed this river Jordan *years ago*, all I had to my name was a staff in my hand, and now I have increased to become two camps! ¹¹Save me, I pray, from the hand of my brother Esau, for I'm afraid he will come and kill all of us, including the women and children. ¹²You said to me, 'I will certainly prosper you and make your offspring as innumerable as the sand of the sea.'" ¹³So he spent the night there.

From what he had with him, Jacob sent a gift*ᵃ* to his brother Esau: ¹⁴two hundred female goats and twenty male goats, two hundred ewes and twenty rams, ¹⁵thirty female camels and their calves, forty cows and ten bulls, twenty female donkeys and ten male donkeys.*ᵇ* ¹⁶He placed them in the care of his servants, each herd by itself. He told them, "Go on ahead of me, and put some space between each herd." ¹⁷He gave these instructions to the one in the lead, "When my brother Esau meets you, and asks, 'Who is your master?*ᶜ* Where are you going? Who owns these herds you are driving?'*ᵈ* ¹⁸then you are to say, 'They belong to your servant Jacob. He's sent them as a gift to you, my lord Esau, and he is coming behind us.'"

¹⁹He likewise instructed the leaders of the second and the third herds and all those following them, "You must say the same thing when you meet Esau. ²⁰And be sure to say, 'Your servant Jacob is coming behind us,'" because he reasoned, "If I can appease Esau with these gifts before I have to meet him face-to-face, he may accept me." ²¹So he sent the gifts on ahead of him, while he spent that night in the camp.

A Midnight Wrestling Match

²²During the night, Jacob arose, woke up his two wives, his two maidservants, and eleven sons, and had them cross the ford of the Jabbok River.*ᵉ* ²³He sent them across along with everything he had, ²⁴and Jacob was left all alone.*ᶠ* Suddenly, *out of nowhere*, a man appeared and wrestled*ᵍ* with him until daybreak. ²⁵When the man saw that he was not winning the match,

---

a 32:13 Or "Jacob sent from what he had in his hand."

b 32:15 This was at least five hundred and fifty animals, a substantial gift indeed. Perhaps, Jacob was attempting to return a portion of the stolen birthright.

c 32:17 Or "To whom are you?"

d 32:17 Or "Whose are these ahead of you?"

e 32:22 The name of this river was a prophecy of what God was doing in his servant. Jabbok means "emptying." The Jabbok is known today in Arabic as the Wadi Zerga, which empties into the Jordan twenty-five miles north of the Dead Sea.

f 32:24 To be left alone with God is the only true way of coming to self-discovery. This was the turning point for Jacob. His schemes have all failed, and now he faces God alone.

g 32:24 The Hebrew word for wrestle is related to a word for "dust," "get dusty," as two people do when wrestling on the ground. There is an amazing play on words in the Hebrew between he wrestled (*ye'abeq*), Jabbok (*yabboq*), and Jacob (*yàaqob*). The eyes of Jacob could not discern who was coming out of the shadows, in the same way as Jacob's father, Isaac, could not discern who it was that received his blessing. It was not Jacob wrestling a man, but a Man wrestling with Jacob. The One whom Jacob saw at the top of the stairway at Bethel had come down to wrestle with him—and roll in the mud of Jacob's mistakes.

he struck Jacob's hip and knocked it out of joint, leaving it wrenched as he continued to wrestle with him.ª

²⁶Eventually, the man said to him, "Let me go, for the day is breaking."

But Jacob refused, "No! Not until you bless me!"ᵇ

²⁷"What is your name?" asked the man.ᶜ

"Jacob" he replied.

²⁸"Not anymore," the man said to him. "Your new name is Israel,ᵈ for you have struggled both with God and with people and have overcome."

²⁹Jacob said, "Please, tell me your name."

"Why ask my name?"ᵉ the man replied, then he spoke a blessingᶠ over Jacob.

³⁰So Jacob named the place Penuel,ᵍ saying, "I have seen God face-to-face, yet my life has been spared!"ʰ ³¹The sun rose upon him as he crossed the Jabbok River from Penuel, limping because of his hip. To this day, the Israelites do not eat the thigh muscle attached to the hip socket, because the man struck Jacob's hip socket at the thigh muscle.

Brothers Reconcile

33 When Jacobⁱ looked up, he saw Esau approaching with four

---

a 32:25 Jacob grabbed a heel; God grabbed his thigh! Through these private encounters with the Lord, we become those whose names have been changed (Gen. 17:5; Isa. 62:2, 4; Rev. 2:17; 3:12) into humbled, transformed ones who are subdued by the power of God (Phil. 3:21). Jacob had at least two night encounters with the Lord. One while he rested (Gen. 28), and the other while he wrestled. When he wrestled he got a new name. When he rested, the region got a new name—from Luz to Bethel.

b 32:26 Jacob initially may have thought it was Esau who came at midnight to wrestle him. But as the night wore on, he realized the Man was a divine being (Hos. 12:4). Perceiving this was a supernatural Man who would have the power to bless or to curse, Jacob refused to release him until he pronounced a blessing over him.

c 32:27 This was a strange question because God knew his name. God touched not only his thigh but also his slumbering conscience. In asking this question, Jacob's imagination took him back over twenty years to the dark tent where his blind, aged father had faced him with the same question . . . *"I am Esau"*—and he got away with it! Now the Lord had come to Jacob insisting he acknowledge that he was the one who took advantage of his father and his brother. Jacob means heel grabber, supplanter. The Lord was insisting that his blessings would only begin when Jacob realized the true need of his heart. By speaking out his name, Jacob confessed his true nature. "I am a deceiver, a cheat. My name is heel grabber." This confession liberated Jacob and opened the way for inner transformation (Ps. 119:116; 2 Cor. 4:16). Jacob was forgiven.

d 32:28 Israel means "one who struggled with God and prevailed," "may God (El) preserve," or "prince with God."

e 32:29 If a rhetorical question, it may mean "You should not ask my name."

f 32:29 This blessing empowered Jacob to succeed and prosper.

g 32:30 Or "Peniel (face of God)." Eight times in the Old Testament it is spelled "Penuel," and only once "Peniel." Since they are both the same location in verses 30 and 31, the translator has chosen to leave both spellings identical.

h 32:30 Once you have seen the face of God, the face of those who oppose you will no longer intimidate you. Jacob can now look Esau in the eyes.

i 33:1 Jacob's name had been changed, but like us, he was slow to realize his new identity. It was not until Rachel died that Israel journeyed onward (Gen. 35:19–21). Jacob entered his promised inheritance with a limp. When he walked toward Esau, and bowed down, he was limping. Esau did not see a whole Jacob; he saw a crippled Jacob.

hundred men.*a* So he *quickly* divided the children among Leah, Rachel, and the two maidservants. ²He lined up the maidservants and their children in front, then Leah and her children, then Rachel and Joseph last of all. ³Then Jacob went ahead of them *to face Esau*. As he approached his brother, he bowed down to the ground seven times*b* before reaching him.

⁴But Esau ran to Jacob and hugged him! He threw his arms around Jacob's neck, he kissed him, and they wept in each other's arms.*c* ⁵When Esau looked up and saw the women and the children, he said to Jacob, "Who are all these coming behind you?"

Jacob replied, "These are the children, *your niece and nephews*, whom God has so graciously given*d* your servant." ⁶Then the maidservants came forward with their children and bowed low before Esau. ⁷Leah likewise came forward with her children and bowed down. Finally, Rachel *and Joseph* came forward and they bowed down to the ground before Esau.

⁸Esau asked Jacob, "Why did you send all these animals to me?"

"I was hoping to find favor with you, my lord." Jacob replied.

⁹"But my brother," Esau laughed, "I have plenty. Keep what you have for yourself."

¹⁰Jacob replied, "No, please. If I have found favor in your eyes, please take the gifts. For truly, seeing your face *after all these years*, it's like looking upon the face of God!*e* Since you have received me so warmly, ¹¹please accept the blessing I have brought to you, for God has poured his grace over me, and I have everything I want!"*f* So with these words Jacob urged him, and Esau accepted the gifts.

¹²Then Esau said, "Let's start out on our journey, and I'll walk alongside you."

---

a 33:1 Esau came with four hundred men; Jacob came with four women and his children. Jacob divided his children by their mothers and sent them to Esau one group at a time. The most loved of all to Jacob were Rachel and Joseph, those he reserved for last, just in case the anger of Esau broke out against him and his family. Jacob was a clever, thoughtful man, but he still is walking in man's wisdom. Because he anticipated vengeance from the hand of Esau, he exposed those whom he cared about the least to the first stroke of that vengeance.

b 33:3 It is hard to miss the irony here, for Isaac's prophecy was that Esau would be ruled by Jacob and bow down to him (Gen. 27:29), but here we see Jacob bowing down before his estranged brother.

c 33:4 Imagine the sense of emotional release Jacob (Israel) felt as he stood there hugging Esau. Jacob had deceitfully kissed his father, pretending to be Esau (Gen. 27:26). Now the kiss of restoration comes to the two brothers. Their tears released and washed away the emotional pain of their past! Reconciliation between brothers always pleases God (Ps. 133). Remember that, in a moment, God can turn enemies into friends. Remember that God turned Saul into Paul (Acts 13:9)! Our hearts must always be postured to reconcile with others who have distanced themselves from us.

d 33:5 This comes from a verb meaning to "be gracious," "show favor," or "be kind to." Indeed, children are a gracious gift from God. See Ps. 127:3.

e 33:10 Jacob sees again that same glorious face of God (Gen. 32:30) through the mending of his relationship with his brother. How sweet is forgiveness, how pleasant to the soul when we are made one again with those we love! It is like gazing on the face of God. We see God most clearly as we touch mercy and forgiveness. Are there some in your life that need to see the face of God in your countenance?

f 33:11 Jacob is offering to share the blessing he took away from Esau many years earlier.

¹³But Jacob replied, "My lord, you can see how tired the children are, and all our flocks and herds are nursing their young. If we drive them too hard for even a day, they will die. ¹⁴Please, my lord, go ahead of your servant. Let me move along slowly with my flocks and herds, *to give them a chance to graze*. I must think of my children, too, so go ahead of me, my lord, until I catch up with you in Seir."

¹⁵Esau said, "Well, at least let me leave you with some of my men."

"You're so kind," Jacob replied, "but there's no need to do so."

¹⁶So that very day Esau *and his men* left to return to Seir, ¹⁷but Jacob went *the opposite direction* to Succoth instead,ᵈ and built himself a house there. He also built shelters for his livestock, and that is why Jacob named the place Succoth.

Jacob Builds an Altar at Shechem

¹⁸Jacob's journey home from Paddan-Aram finally brought him safe and sound to the Canaanite city of Shechem,ᵇ where he camped just outside of the city. ¹⁹He purchased the field where he pitched his tent from the clan of Hamor,ᶜ Shechem's father, for one hundred pieces of silver.ᵈ ²⁰There he set up an altarᵉ and named it To the *True* God, the God of Israel.ᶠ

Dinah Raped by Shechem

34 One day, Jacob and Leah's daughter, Dinah, went out to visit the neighborhood girls.ᵍ ²Now Hamor, the tribal chief of the Hivites, had a son named Shechem, who was the prince. When he saw *how attractive Dinah was*, he seized her and sexually assaulted her. ³His heart was drawn to Dinah, Jacob's daughter, so he sought to win her affection and spoke tenderly to her. ⁴Shechem went to his father Hamor and said, "Get me this girl to be my wife."

⁵Now Jacob heard that Shechem had violated his daughter Dinah; but his sons were in the fields with his livestock, so he waited to act until his sons returned home. ⁶Shechem's father Hamor *brought his son*ʰ to speak with Jacob *about marriage arrangements*. ⁷During their conversation, Jacob's sons came in from the field,

---

a 33:17 Succoth means "booths," "shelter," "huts," or "stalls." There is a large tell, or archeological mound called Deir 'Allah, located in the center of the Jordan Valley, which is now identified as Succoth.

b 33:18 Shechem lies about forty miles north of Jerusalem, the site where Abram first built an altar in the promised land (Gen. 12:7). Joseph was eventually buried on this parcel of land (Josh. 24:32). In John 4 Jesus encountered a woman of Samaria in the vicinity of Sychar (Shechem). The well was on a piece of land which was bought by Jacob and given to his son, Joseph (John 4:5–8). The well mentioned in John 4 was Jacob's well. Jesus sat on top of the very place where Jacob dwelt at Shechem. At that time, Jacob had no clue that his "seed" would indeed sit upon that well someday. There, the long-awaited Messiah patiently won the soul of a sinful woman at Shechem. The Mighty God of Israel visited Jacob's well at Shechem!

c 33:19 Hamor means "donkey."

d 33:19 Some ancient manuscripts have "one hundred sheep" as the purchase price.

e 33:20 Or "pillar."

f 33:20 Or "El-Elohe-Israel" or "Mighty is the God of Israel."

g 34:1 Perhaps the local women introduced her to Shechem, the prince of the city named for him. Dinah was likely fifteen or sixteen years old.

h 34:6 From verse 11 we learn that Shechem was present during this conversation.

and they heard the report of what Shechem had done to *their sister* Dinah.*a* They were shocked and furious over the shameful act Shechem committed against Israel*b*—a criminal act of sexual assault that never should have happened.

⁸But Hamor tried to defuse the situation, saying, "Listen, my son Shechem is in love with your daughter. Please, give her to him in marriage. ⁹Let's allow our people to intermarry.*c* Let your daughters marry our sons, and we will let our daughters marry your sons. ¹⁰You may settle here among us, live anywhere you wish,*d* move about freely,*e* and acquire*f* property."

¹¹Then Shechem spoke up and said to Dinah's family, "Please, let me find favor in your eyes. Whatever you require of me, I'll pay. ¹²Set the bride-price as high as you wish, no matter how expensive it is, I'll pay whatever you ask. Only give me the young woman to be my wife."

Jacob's Sons Exact Revenge

¹³*The sons of Jacob concocted a devious plan.* Because of the rape of their sister Dinah, they answered Shechem and Hamor deceitfully, ¹⁴saying, "Our culture will not allow us to consent to our sister Dinah marrying someone who is uncircumcised, for that would be a disgrace to us. ¹⁵We would only approve of the marriage on one condition: you must circumcise every male among you and become as we are. ¹⁶Then we will allow our daughters to marry your sons and your daughters to marry our sons. And we will live among you and become one people. ¹⁷But if you refuse to be circumcised, then we will take our sister*g* and be gone." ¹⁸The offer pleased Hamor and his son Shechem. ¹⁹And the young man lost no time in doing what they asked, because Shechem really wanted to marry Jacob's daughter!

Now Shechem was the most honored*h* in all his family, ²⁰so Hamor and his son went to the gate of the city and spoke to the men, saying, ²¹"These people are our friends. Let them settle in our land and make themselves at home; there's plenty of room in the country for them. And, let's agree to exchange our daughters in marriage and unite with us as one people. ²²They only have one condition in order to live among us and to unite with us as one people: every male among us must be circumcised as they are circumcised. ²³Won't all of their livestock and property become ours? Let us agree to their request, so they will live among us." ²⁴So all the townsmen agreed with Hamor and his son Shechem, and every male of the city was circumcised.

²⁵Three days later, while all the men were still suffering in pain, two

---

a 34:7 Apparently, Dinah is still being held in Hamor's house within the city (vv. 17, 26).
b 34:7 Or "in Israel."
c 34:9 Or "partner (with us)," that is, become our brothers-in-law.
d 34:10 Or "the land is before your faces." This could be an idiom meaning "make yourselves at home here."
e 34:10 Or "trade" (LXX, Vulgate, Targums).
f 34:10 The basic meaning of the Hebrew verb used here is "take possession of land."
g 34:17 Or "daughter."
h 34:19 Or possibly, "the most important."

of Jacob's sons, Simeon and Levi, Dinah's brothers, took their swords and attacked the unsuspecting city. They slaughtered every male of the city. ²⁶They even killed Hamor and his son Shechem, and took Dinah from Shechem's house, and left. ²⁷Later, Jacob's *other* sons came upon the dead bodies, and they looted the city as retribution for the violation of their sister. ²⁸They seized the flocks, herds, and donkeys, and all that was in the city and in the field. ²⁹They plundered all their wealth and their household goods and took their wives and children as captives.

³⁰When Jacob found out, he said to Simeon and Levi, "*What have you done?* You have ruined my name,ᵃ and now the Canaanites and Perizzites and all the people of this land will hate me! My men are so few that if they unite against me and attack, I and all my household will be destroyed!"

³¹But they answered him, "Why should they treat our sister like a whore?"

Jacob Returns to Bethel

35 God said to Jacob, "Arise, go at once to Bethel, and settle there. Build an altar there to God, who appeared to you when you were fleeing from your brother Esau."ᵇ

²So Jacob said to his household and to all who were with him,ᶜ "Get rid of every foreign god you have, purify yourselves, and change your clothes.ᵈ ³Then come with me; let us go up to Bethel. I will build an altar there to God who answered my prayer when I was in distressᵉ and whose presence has been with me wherever I have gone." ⁴Then they surrendered all the foreign gods they had as well as their earrings.ᶠ Jacob buried them under the oak tree near Shechem.

⁵As they made their way *to Bethel*, a tremendous fear of God fell upon all the cities around them, and no one dared pursue them. ⁶Jacob and all the people who were with him arrived in the land of Canaan at Luz,ᵍ now known as Bethel. ⁷He built an altar there and named it El-Bethel,ʰ because it was the place that God had unveiled himself when Jacob was running from his brother. ⁸During that time, Rebekah's nurse Deborah died. They buried her under an oak tree nearⁱ Bethel, and they named the place Weeping Oak.ʲ

⁹After Jacob returned from Paddan-Aram, God appeared to him once

---

ᵃ 34:30 Or "You have muddied the waters" or "made a stink." That is, they have brought trouble upon Jacob.

ᵇ 35:1 Jacob fulfilled the vow he had made to God thirty years previously. See Gen. 28:20–22.

ᶜ 35:2 Those "with him" would include the captives he took at Shechem.

ᵈ 35:2 Our old clothes speak of our old life that must be laid aside as we put on Christ (Isa. 64:6; Rev. 3:18). Changing our garments is to change our manner of life and put on a new man (Rom. 13:14).

ᵉ 35:3 See Ps. 20:1.

ᶠ 35:4 Most scholars consider these earrings to have been certain religious objects, perhaps amulets or magical charms.

ᵍ 35:6 Luz means "departure" or "almond tree."

ʰ 35:7 That is, "God of the House of God."

ⁱ 35:8 Or "below."

ʲ 35:8 Or "Allon-Bacuth."

again[a] and blessed him, [10]saying, "Your name was once Jacob, but no longer. Your new name is Israel!"[b] God named him Israel [11]and said to him, "I am the God who is more than enough.[c] Go and have many children, and they will multiply. A nation and a *gathering of* many nations will come from you; and you will be the ancestor of kings. [12]I will give you the land which I gave to Abraham and to Isaac, and after you are gone, to your descendants."

[13]Then God ascended *into heaven*[d] from the place where he had spoken to him. [14]Jacob set up a stone pillar *to memorialize* the place where he had met[e] with God. He poured over it a drink offering[f] and anointed the pillar with oil. [15]Jacob called the place where God had spoken with him Bethel.

Rachel Dies in Childbirth

[16]From Bethel, they journeyed on, and as they were approaching Ephrath, Rachel went into very hard and painful labor. [17]As she was having great difficulty in giving birth, the midwife said to her, "Don't be afraid, for you're having another son!" [18]With her dying breath, Rachel said, "His name is Son of My Sorrow,"[g] but his father called him Son of My Right Hand.[h] [19]Rachel died and was buried on the road to Ephrath (now Bethlehem).[i] [20]Jacob set up a pillar to mark her burial site, and it is known as The Marker of Rachel's Tomb to this day.[j]

---

a 35:9 "Once again" may refer to Jacob's earlier encounter with God either at Mahanaim (Gen. 32:1–2) or Penuel (Gen. 32:29–30), but more likely it refers to a new experience. God revealed himself many times to Abraham, Isaac, and Jacob, and he will reveal himself to this generation also.

b 35:10 See Gen. 32:28.

c 35:11 Or "El Shaddai." Some translate *El Shaddai* as "Almighty God" or "Sovereign God." However, in this context, God blessed Jacob and gave him the power of life and multiplication. See Gen. 17:1–4; 28:3; and T. N. D. Mettinger, *In Search of God*, 69–72; R. Gordis, "The Biblical Root sdy-sd," *Journal of Biblical Studies*, 54 (1935): 173–210.

d 35:13 Or "Elohim ascended from upon him *into heaven*."

e 35:14 Or "where God had spoken to him (Jacob)."

f 35:14 Lit. "he poured a pouring." One may assume that it was a drink offering of wine. Jacob poured wine and oil over the pillar at "the House of God (Bethel)." See Ex. 29:40–41; Num. 6:17; 15:1–5; 28:7–10; 2 Sam. 23:16. The drink offering was a unique offering that was offered by a priest in gratitude for the firstfruits of harvest (Lev. 23:10–13). Often, it was poured out upon other offerings. Jacob himself is the drink offering that is poured out to God. The pillar becomes a picture of the overcoming life (Rev. 3:12).

g 35:18 Or in Hebrew *Ben-oni*, which means "son of my sorrow" or possibly "son of my strength."

h 35:18 Or in Hebrew *Ben-yamin* (Benjamin), which means "son of the right hand" or possibly "son of the south." In the entire universe, there is only one Son that is both *Son of Sorrow* and *Son of the Right Hand!* Jesus is his name! Christ is a wonderful person with these two aspects to his name. Isaiah 53:3 describes him as the "Man of deep Sorrows," and Acts 2:33 tells us that "God exalted him to his right hand." Mary, the mother of Jesus, also experienced pain as Simeon prophesied: "a painful sword will one day pierce your inner being" (Luke 2:34–35). When her Son was raised from the dead, he rose to be at God's right hand (Eph. 1:20).

i 35:19 See Gen. 48:7.

j 35:20 This was the fourth pillar Jacob set up. The first was at Bethel to symbolize the end of his fleshly self-confidence, replaced with a new revelation of God and his faithfulness (Gen. 28:1, 5, 10–22). The second was a pillar at Mizpah to symbolize that God was watching over Jacob and could be trusted (Gen. 31:49). The third was at Bethel and a pillar of his confidence in the Living God (Gen. 35:1–15).

²¹Israel journeyed on and pitched his tent beyond Migdal Eder.ª ²²While Israel was living in that land, Reuben went and slept with Bilhah,ᵇ his father's concubine, and Israel found out.

Jacob had twelve sons.

²³Leah's sons were Reuben (Jacob's firstborn), Simeon, Levi, Judah, Issachar, and Zebulun.

²⁴Rachel's sons were Joseph and Benjamin.

²⁵The sons of Rachel's maidservant Bilhah were Dan and Naphtali.

²⁶The sons of Leah's maidservant Zilpah were Gad and Asher.

These were the sons of Jacob born to him in Paddan-Aram.

The Death of Isaac

²⁷Jacob came home to his father Isaac in Mamre, near Kiriath Arba (that is, Hebron), where Abraham and Isaac had lived as foreigners. ²⁸Isaac was one hundred and eighty when he breathed his last and died.ᶜ ²⁹He died an old man and had lived a full life when he joined his ancestors. And his sons Esau and Jacob buried him there.

The Descendants of Esau

36 Here are the descendants of Esau, also known as Edom:

²⁻³Esau chose three wives from among Canaanite women: Adah (daughter of Elon the Hittite), Oholibamahᵈ (daughter of Anah son of Zibeon the Hivite),ᵉ and Basemath (Ishmael's daughter, sister of Nebaioth).

⁴Adah bore Eliphaz to Esau; Basemath bore Reuel; ⁵and Oholibamah bore Jeush, Jalam, and Korah. These are the sons who were born to Esau in the land of Canaan.

⁶Esau took his wives, his sons, his daughters, and his entire household, and the cattle, livestock, and possessions he had acquired in the land of Canaan, and migrated to the land of Seirᶠ some distance from his brother Jacob. ⁷Since the land where Jacob was living could not support their combined possessions and livestock, ⁸Esau (also known as Edom), settled in the hill country of Seir.

⁹This is the account of Esau, ancestor of the Edomites in the hill country of Seir:

¹⁰⁻¹³Esau's wife Adah bore him one son Eliphaz, and Eliphaz had five sons: Teman, Omar, Zepho, Gatam, and Kenaz. Eliphaz also had a son with his concubine Timna, named Amelek.

Esau's wife Basemath bore him one son Reuel, and Reuel had four

---

ª 35:21 Or "Watchtower of the Flock." This was the place where shepherds watched over the sacred flocks meant for Temple sacrifice and where the Passover lamb was selected. Migdal Eder is mentioned in Micah 4:8 as the possible birthplace of Jesus, Israel's Messiah. See also Mic. 5:2.

ᵇ 35:22 Why would Reuben have slept with Rachel's servant girl, his father's concubine? Since Rachel had been Jacob's favorite wife before her death, Reuben hoped that by having sex with Bilhah, he would prevent her from taking Rachel's place. Reuben wanted his mother Leah to be the favored wife of Jacob and take over the leadership of his clan. Immediately following Rachel's death, this episode seems to imply that this was at least part of Reuben's motivation in lying with Bilhah.

ᶜ 35:28 Isaac died years after Joseph was sold into Egypt as a slave. Isaac lived the longest of all the patriarchs.

ᵈ 36:2–3 Oholibamah means "a tent-shrine (cultic)."

ᵉ 36:2–3 Or "Horite" (v. 20–21).

ᶠ 36:6 As translated from the Syriac and explicitly stated in verse 8. The Hebrew is "to a land." The Septuagint is "from the land of Canaan." See also Deut. 2:5; Josh. 24:4.

sons: Nahath, Zerah, Shammah, and Mizzah.

[14]Esau's wife Oholibamah, the daughter of Anah and granddaughter of Zibeon, bore Esau three sons: Jeush, Jalam, and Korah.

[15-16]These are the tribes[a] descended from Esau's firstborn son Eliphaz whom Adah bore, and who lived in Edom: Teman, Omar, Zepho, Kenaz, Korah, Gatam, and Amalek.

[17]These are the tribes descended from Esau and Basemath's son Reuel, who lived in Edom: Nahath, Zerah, Shammah, and Mizzah.

[18]These are the tribes descended from Esau's wife Oholibamah, the daughter of Anah: Jeush, Jalam, and Korah. [19]This concludes the list of the descendants of Esau (also known as Edom) and their respective tribes.

The Descendants of Seir

[20-21]These are the tribes descended from Seir the Horite, of the original inhabitants of Edom: Lotan, Shobal, Zibeon, Anah, Dishon, Ezer, and Dishan. All of these were the descendants of Seir.

[22]Lotan's sons were Hori and Heman, and Lotan's sister was Timna.

[23]Shobal's sons were Alvan, Manahath, Ebal, Shepho, and Onam.

[24]Zibeon's sons were Aiah and Anah. This is the Anah who discovered the springs in the wilderness while he was grazing the donkeys of his father Zibeon.

[25]Anah's son was Dishon, and Anah's daughter was Oholibamah.

[26]Dishon's sons were Hemdan, Eshban, Ithran, and Keran.

[27]Ezer's sons were Bilhan, Zaavan, and Akan.

[28]Dishan's sons were Uz and Aran.

[29-30]This concludes the list of the Horite tribes in the land of Seir: Lotan, Shobal, Zibeon, Anah, Dishon, Ezer, and Dishan.

The Kings of Edom

[31]Long before the Israelites had kings, these are the *eight* kings who reigned in Edom:

[32]Bela[b] son of Beor[c] from the city of Dinhabah.[d] [33]When Bela died, Jobab[e] son of Zerah from *the city of* Bozrah[f] succeeded.

[34]When Jobab died, Husham from the land of Teman succeeded him.

[35]When Husham died, Hadad from the city of Avith, who was the son of Bedad, succeeded him. Hadad defeated the Midianites in the land of Moab.

[36]When Hadad died, Samlah of Masrekah succeeded him.

[37]When Samlah died, Shaul of Rehoboth-on-the-River[g] succeeded him.

[38]When Shaul died, Baal-Hanan son of Achbor succeeded him.

[39]When Baal-Hanan son of Achbor died, Hadar[h] from the city of Pau,

---

a 36:15–16 Or "clans" or "chiefs," a Hebrew word related to "thousand."

b 36:32 Some etymologists link Bela to Balaam, whose father was Beor. Bela means "swallowing up" or "gluttony."

c 36:32 *Beor* means "stupid," "dull-hearted," "unreceptive," "cruel," "inhuman," and "barbarous."

d 36:32 Dinhabah means "given over to judgment."

e 36:33 There is an ancient Jewish tradition that equates Jobab with the biblical figure of Job.

f 36:33 Bozrah is identified as modern Buseirah. See Isa. 63:1; Amos 1:12.

g 36:37 The river is possibly Wadi el-Hesa, which formed the boundary of Edom and Moab, or possibly the Euphrates.

h 36:39 Or "Hadad."

whose wife was Mehetabel the daughter of Matred, Me-Zahab's granddaughter, succeeded him.

⁴⁰⁻⁴²These are the tribes of Esau according to their clans and regions: Timna, Alvah, Jetheth, Oholibamah, Elah, Pinon, Kenaz, Teman, Mibzar, ⁴³Magdiel, and Iram. This concludes the list of the Edomite tribes who settled and possessed land in different regions of their country. All the Edomites descended from Esau.

The Story of Joseph

37 ¹⁻²This is the story of the family of Jacob, who had settled in the land of Canaan, where his father *Isaac* had lived as an immigrant.ᵃ

Jacob's son Joseph was seventeen, and he served his older half brothers, the sons of his father's wives Bilhah and Zilpah, helping them watch over the flocks. One day Joseph went to his father with a bad report about their behavior.ᵇ

³Now Israel's love for Joseph surpassed that for his other sons because he was born to him in his old age.ᶜ So Israel had made him a richly ornamented robe.ᵈ ⁴When Joseph's brothers saw that their father loved him more than he loved them, they hated him and would not speak a kind word to him.ᵉ

⁵One night Joseph had a dream, and when he shared it with his brothers, they hated him even more! ⁶"Listen to this dream I had," he told them. ⁷"There we were, binding sheaves of grain in the field. Suddenly, my sheaf rose up and stood upright. Then your sheaves gathered around mine and bowed down to mine!" ⁸His brothers asked him, "Oh, so you think you're going to be our king? Do you actually think you're destined to rule over us?" So, the dream that he told them about made them hate him even more.

⁹Then another night he had a dream, and he shared it with his brothers,ᶠ saying, "Listen, I had another dream. This time, the sun and moon and eleven stars were bowing down to

---

a 37:1–2 According to the Genesis chronologies, Isaac was alive during the events of this chapter and would have been one hundred and sixty-eight. Jacob was one hundred and eight when Joseph was sold into slavery. See JPS Torah Commentary: *Genesis*, Nahum Sarna.

b 37:1–2 Although we are not told exactly what the "bad report" might have contained, his brothers saw him as a tattle-tale and trouble maker. He may have exaggerated or slandered his brothers to his father.

c 37:3 Jacob was ninety-one when Joseph was born. Joseph and his baby brother Benjamin were the only two sons Jacob had with his beloved Rachel.

d 37:3 Or "a coat of many colors" (LXX, Vulgate), a long-sleeved tunic that went down to his feet. Most tunics worn by men would only go down to the knees and were often made without sleeves. This "robe" would not be something one would wear at work, but was considered to be a robe of special significance for a prince. The same Hebrew word is found in 2 Sam. 13:18 referring to the robe of a princess. Fully aware of what happened with parental favoritism between him and his brother Esau, Jacob still lavished preference upon Joseph. It is possible that Jacob was designating Joseph as the royal priest of his family, thus bypassing Reuben, the firstborn, and planting seeds of angry jealousy in the hearts of all his half brothers.

e 37:4 Or possibly, "they pushed aside every attempt by Joseph to be friendly." See Shadal; cf. Tanh. B. Gen. 180.

f 37:9 The Septuagint adds, "and he shared it with his father."

me."[a] [10]When his father and brothers heard it, his father scolded him, "What kind of dream is that? Do you really think that I, and your mother, and your brothers are going to come and bow to the ground before you?" [11]So his brothers grew more jealous of him, but his father kept pondering Joseph's dream.[b]

Joseph Sold by His Brothers

[12]One day, when his brothers had gone to Shechem to care for their father's flock, [13]Israel called for Joseph and said to him, "Your brothers are grazing the flocks near Shechem. I want you to go join them."

"*Yes, Father*, I'll go." Joseph replied.

[14]Jacob added, "Go find out how your brothers are doing with the flocks and bring word back to me." So, his father sent him off from the valley of Hebron.[c]

When Joseph arrived at Shechem [15]and began to roam the countryside looking for his brothers, a man approached him and asked, "What are you looking for?"

[16]"I'm looking for my brothers, who are taking care of their flock," he answered. "Please tell me, do you know where they are?"

[17]The man replied,[d] "They've left here already. I overheard them mention that they were going to Dothan." So, Joseph took off to catch up with his brothers and found them at Dothan.[e]

---

a 37:9 These dreams had a major influence on Joseph's life from that day forward. If you had a dream about the stars of heaven bowing down to you, do you think it would not affect you? Joseph behaved with excellence because he saw himself as a "star." When you understand what controlled young Joseph, you will understand the true significance of the following chapters.

b 37:11 Even though the sheaves, stars, sun, and moon would all bow down to Joseph, his family missed it! They were "sheaves" and "stars" not thorns and snakes. Everyone in the family would be favored and anointed. The sheaves of wheat are Jacob's sons. They are God's crop on the earth, a ripened, harvested crop. They are stars, bright lights shining in the heavens. Instead of provoking his brothers to jealousy, this dream could have brought them joy over God's mercy to them as a family. The second dream speaks of government. God informed Joseph through the symbols of the sun, moon, and stars that the government would be given to Joseph one day. In Gen. 1:16–18 the lights of the sky were to "rule" the day and "rule" the night. These governing bodies bowing down to Joseph speak of the great authority he would one day be given over his brothers. This second dream is much like the vision in Rev. 12:1–2. The woman clothed with the sun signifies God's people (bride), with the moon under her feet and with the crown of twelve stars on her head. We must see God's church as ready to give birth to a corporate expression of Christ as his Body on the earth. From the standpoint of eternity, God sees us all as sheaves full of life and stars full of light. Although the sons of Jacob sinned, Christ still came through them (Matt. 1:1–3; Gen. 38:27–30). The jealous brothers would have no faith in his dreams, but Jacob, having been broken by God, kept the matter in his heart. For even Jacob had received messages from God in dreams.

c 37:14 Shechem is at least a four-day walk from the valley of Hebron. Joseph left Hebron (the place of "fellowship") to visit his brothers. Jesus left the fellowship of heaven to reveal his Father's love to those who killed him out of jealousy. Joseph's life story is a vivid preview of the life of Christ.

d 37:17 Dothan, the home of Elisha, means "two wells." Who was this man who directed Joseph to Dothan? Was it an angel? Perhaps. It was God's hand that led Joseph into this encounter with his angry brothers. God began the process of exalting Joseph by this encounter with his brothers. God would send him ahead of his brothers into Egypt (Ps. 105:16–23).

e 37:17 Dothan is about a day's walk from Shechem.

[18]As he was still a long distance away, the brothers recognized him *by his robe*, and by the time he reached them, they had plotted together to kill him. [19]They said to each other, "Here comes this dream expert.[a] [20]Let's kill him[b] and throw his body into one of these dry wells. We can say that a wild animal ate him. Then we'll see how his dreams turn out!"

[21]When Reuben heard of this, he tried to save Joseph's life. "Don't take his life," he said. [22]"No bloodshed! Let's throw him into this pit in the middle of nowhere, but don't hurt him." Reuben said these things because *he planned to return later* to rescue Joseph and take him back to his father.[c]

[23]When Joseph finally caught up with his brothers, they *seized him*, stripped him of his ornamented robe, his beautiful full-length robe, [24]and threw him into the dry, empty pit.[d]

[25]Afterward, the brothers sat down to eat their food.[e] When they looked up, they saw a caravan of Ishmaelite merchants coming from Gilead on their way to Egypt. They had *many* camels loaded with myrrh, spices, and perfumes. [26]Judah spoke up and said to his brothers, "What will we gain by murdering our brother and covering up his blood?[f] [27]*I have an idea!* Let's sell Joseph to these Ishmaelites and not lay a hand on him, for he is our brother, our own flesh and blood." His brothers agreed. [28]And when the Midianites *(also known as Ishmaelites)*[g] came by, Joseph's brothers lifted him out of the pit, and sold him to the Ishmaelites for twenty pieces of silver,[h] and the merchants took Joseph *far* away to Egypt.

[29]Later, Reuben went to the pit, and saw that Joseph was gone. *He was overcome with grief* and tore his

---

a 37:19 Or "lord dreamer" or "master dreamer."

b 37:20 His brothers scorned him for his gift and hated him for his dreams. They could not endure the thought of bowing down to a younger brother that was more favored than they were. Rather than bow down to Joseph, they sought to kill him. See Prov. 29:10.

c 37:22 Reuben was Jacob's firstborn and would have had the responsibility of representing his father's interests.

d 37:24 If we will remain faithful in a time of betrayal, we will be restored and wear the favor-garment once again. Joseph's life is really a series of three robes: the "robe of favor" given to him by Jacob and taken by his jealous brothers. The "stolen robe" that the false accusations of Potiphar's wife ripped from him, and the "royal robe" of reigning in Egypt as God's savior for Israel. That coat of many colors had to go before God could use young Joseph. What is there in your life that must be taken from you before you can be set free to be his instrument?

e 37:25 What callous indifference Joseph's brothers demonstrated as they sat near the well, eating a meal! No doubt they were within earshot of Joseph's cries, asking them for help.

f 37:26 See Job 16:18; Ezek. 24:7.

g 37:28 See Judg. 8:22–23; "Midianites" in *Harper's Bible Dictionary*, page 634.

h 37:28 In that day, twenty silver shekels was the going price to purchase a young male slave. See the Laws of Hammurabi, pars. 116, 214, 252; also Lev. 27:5. Isn't it amazing how the Lord sent the merchants from Midian at just the right time for Joseph? The Lord has ways to deliver us that are beyond our comprehension. You might say Joseph started at the bottom (of a pit). It is ridiculous to even try and figure out how God will pull it off—he just will! Judah sold Joseph for twenty pieces of silver; Judas (Judah) sold Jesus for thirty (Matt. 26:14–15). Whenever we de-value one another, we are selling them, "short changing them," failing to understand one's true value. How could a life be sold for mere silver? If Joseph's brothers had valued him as a sheaf or a star, they would not have sold him.

clothes. ³⁰He went to his brothers and said, "The boy is gone! What am I going to do now?"

³¹Then they took Joseph's colorful robe, killed a goat, and dipped the robe in its blood.ᵃ ³²They took the *blood-stained* robe back to their father and said, "We found this. Look it over—doesn't it belong to your son?"

³³Jacob recognized it *instantly* and cried out, "It's my son's robe! Some wild animal must have killed him. My son Joseph has been torn to pieces!"ᵇ ³⁴*Overcome with grief*, Jacob tore his clothes, put on sackcloth, and mourned for his son a long time. ³⁵All his sons and daughtersᶜ came and tried to comfort him, but he refused to be comforted. He told them, "No, I will mourn for him the rest of my life, until I join my son in the realm of the dead."ᵈ Joseph's father wept and wept for his son.

³⁶Meanwhile, the Midianites took Joseph to Egypt and sold him to Potiphar,ᵉ one of Pharaoh's officials, the captain of the guard.ᶠ

The Story of Judah and Tamar

38 Around that time, Judah left his brothers *at Hebron* and went to Adullamᵍ to stay with a man named Hirah.ʰ ²There he met and married a Canaanite girl, the daughter of Shua. He slept with her and ³she became pregnant and gave birth to a son, and Judahⁱ named him Er. ⁴She conceived again and gave birth to another son and named him Onan.ʲ ⁵While theyᵏ were staying in Chezib,ˡ she gave birth to a third son and named him Shelah.ᵐ

⁶*When their sons were grown*, Judah arranged for Er, his oldest son, to marry a girl named Tamar.ⁿ ⁷But Er had become so wicked in the sight of

---

a 37:31 This account contains significant irony, for it was "goat" hair that Jacob used to deceive his father Isaac. Now it is "goat" blood that is used to deceive the deceiver. See Gen. 27:9, 15–16.

b 37:33 The Hebrew text contains a powerful lament in these three words with alliteration: *tarof toraf yosef*.

c 37:35 "Daughters" would refer to Dinah and his daughters-in-law.

d 37:35 Or "Sheol" or "the underworld." This is the first reference of Sheol in the Bible and refers to a place believed to be beneath the earth where departed souls exist in the gloom of death, darkness, and silence.

e 37:36 Potiphar means "given by the sun-god Ra."

f 37:36 Or "the chief executioner." He was the warden over the Egyptian penal system and, perhaps, the chief steward over Pharaoh's affairs.

g 38:1 From Hebron to Adullam was a day's journey of about twelve miles.

h 38:1 Hirah means "fading" or "to turn pale."

i 38:3 Some Hebrew manuscripts, the Samaritan Pentateuch, and one ancient Targum has "she (Bath-Shua) named him."

j 38:4 Onan means "strong" or "vigorous."

k 38:5 Or "he" or "she" (LXX).

l 38:5 Chezib was a village about three miles south of Adullam and is likely the Achzib mentioned in Josh. 15:44. Chezib means "false."

m 38:5 Shelah means "a request" or "something asked for."

n 38:6 Tamar means "date palm." The *Midrash* states that Tamar was the daughter of Noah's son, Shem. See *Bereshit Rabbah* 85:10. This conjecture would mean that Tamar was not Canaanite (since Canaan was the cursed son of Ham), but was a descendant of Shem just as the sons of Israel.

Yahweh that Yahweh ended his life. [8]Then Judah said to Er's brother Onan, "Your duty[a] is to join yourself to her. Go perform your duty as a brother-in-law and provide an heir for your brother."

[9]Onan, however, did not want to produce a child that would not be his *own rightful heir*,[b] so whenever he and Tamar had intercourse, he purposely spilled his semen onto the ground to keep her from getting pregnant and having a child that would belong to his dead brother. [10]But what he did was wicked in Yahweh's sight, so he took Onan's life also.

[11]Then Judah said to his daughter-in-law Tamar, "Live as a widow in your father's house until my youngest son Shelah grows up." So Tamar went home to her parents, but Judah worried that Shelah would end up dead like his brothers.[c]

[12]After some time passed, Judah's wife, the daughter of Shua, died. When his time of mourning was over, he and his friend Hirah the Adullamite went to Timnah[d] *to enjoy the festivities* at the sheep-shearing.[e] [13-14]Meanwhile, Tamar had learned that Shelah had grown up, but Judah had still not given him to her to father a child *for her deceased husband*. So, when Tamar found out her father-in-law was coming to Timnah for the sheep-shearing, she removed her widow's clothes and covered herself with a veil to disguise herself. And she sat waiting at the crossroads[f] where Judah would have to pass by.

[15-16]When Judah saw her, she was wearing a veil over her face, so he thought she was a prostitute. He had no clue that she was his own daughter-in-law. So he approached her and said, "Come sleep with me."

"What will you give me if I do?" she answered.

[17]He responded, "I will send you a young goat from the flock."

"What guarantee can you give me that you will really send it?" She asked.

[18-19]"Well, what pledge do you want?" Judah asked.

Tamar answered, "Give me your necklace with your personal signet[g] and the staff[h] you're holding." So, he

---

a 38:8 This custom, called "levirate marriage," was later adopted into Hebrew law (Deut. 25:5–10). It was a disgrace for a dead man's living brothers to fail to have children with the widow of the deceased.

b 38:9 Since Onan's brother Er, the firstborn, died, Onan stood in line to receive a great inheritance from his father Judah. But if he fathered a child with Er's widow, that inheritance would be greatly diminished.

c 38:11 In other words, since Judah lost two of his sons already, he had no intention of ever giving Shelah to Tamar, fearing he would lose him too.

d 38:12 Timnah is about four miles northeast of Adullam.

e 38:12 The time of shearing the sheep was a time of celebration and festivities. See 1 Sam. 25:11, 36; 2 Sam. 13:23, 28.

f 38:13–14 Or "She sat at the entrance to Enaim." Enaim means "crossroads" or "intersection."

g 38:18–19 This *signet* refers to an engraved cylinder seal. "The center was hollowed out and a cord passed through so that the seal could be worn around the neck. When the cylinder was rolled over soft clay, the resultant impression served as a means of identifying personal possessions and of sealing and legitimating clay documents. It was a highly personal object that performed the function of the signature in modern society." See the JPS Torah Commentary: *Genesis*, Nahum M. Sarna.

h 38:18–19 Or "(tribal) scepter." The leaders of the twelve tribes of Israel each had scepters (Num. 24:17).

gave them to her, and he went and slept with her. When she got up and went home, she removed her veil and put her widow's garment back on. Later, she discovered she was pregnant.

²⁰Soon afterward, Judah sent the young goat by his friend *Hirah* the Adullamite to recover his items from the prostitute, but she was nowhere to be found. ²¹So he asked the townspeople, "Where is the temple prostitute that sits by the crossroads?"

They answered, "No prostitute has been there." ²²So he returned to Judah and informed him, "I couldn't find her, and besides that, the townspeople said that no prostitute has been there."

²³Judah replied, "Let her keep my pledge. *If we try to go get it now*, we'll become a laughingstock.ᵃ After all, I did send you with the payment I promised her, and you couldn't find her."

²⁴About three months later, Judah was told, "Your daughter-in-law Tamar has been promiscuous, and now she is pregnant!" Indignant, Judah said, "Bring her out, and let her be burned!"ᵇ ²⁵As she was being brought out, she sent word to her father-in-law, "Look,

the one who owns these things got me pregnant! See, whose signet and staff are these?" ²⁶Judah recognized them as his and said, "She is more righteous than I, for I never gave my son Shelah to marry her." And *he let her go free* and never slept with her again.ᶜ

²⁷When it was time for her to give birth, there were twins in her womb! ²⁸While she was in labor, one hand popped out, so the midwife wrapped a crimson thread around its wrist, saying, "This one came out first." ²⁹But immediately, he drew his hand back, and out came his brother; and she said, "Look how you have broken out of the womb!" So, he was named Perez, *the one who breaks through.*ᵈ ³⁰Afterward, his brother came out, the one with the crimson thread on his wrist. That's why they named him Zerah ("*the crimson one.*")ᵉ

Joseph Serves Potiphar

39 After the Ishmaelite traders brought Joseph down to Egypt, he was purchased by an Egyptian officerᶠ of Pharaoh, the captain of the guard, whose name was Potiphar.ᵍ ²Yahweh's *presence* was with Joseph

---

a 38:23 Or "we'll appear as contemptible (dishonest)."

b 38:24 See Lev. 21:9.

c 38:26 Or "he did not know her again." To *know her* is a Hebrew figure of speech for having sex with her. In Chapters 38 and 39 we have two contrasting accounts of lust and the evil it spawns. Why this abrupt interruption of the incredible story of Joseph? Why did God include this chapter in his inspired Word? One reason is that God wanted to paint a contrast between Judah's unwise choices and immorality and Joseph's righteous character, which is revealed in the following chapter.

d 38:29 Perez means "breach" or "breaking through." Perez was an ancestor of King David (Ruth 4:18–22; Matt. 1:3).

e 38:30 Zerah comes from a word that sounds like "(dawn's) crimson brightness." Or, it could be taken from an Aramaic root for "crimson (thread)." Achan (Josh. 7:1) was a descendant of Zerah (Num. 26:20).

f 39:1 This is actually the Hebrew word for eunuch. In Egyptian culture, the key officials surrounding the king were made eunuchs to prevent them from having sons that would compete for the throne. This may help the reader understand why Potiphar's wife chased after Joseph later in the chapter.

g 39:1 Potiphar means "one who belongs to the sun (god)."

and he became successful[a] while living in the house of his Egyptian master. [3]When his master realized that Yahweh's *presence* was with Joseph[b] and caused everything he did to prosper, [4]Joseph found favor with Potiphar. He was quickly promoted to become the overseer of Potiphar's house and was put in charge of all that he had. [5]From the moment Potiphar appointed Joseph over his household, Yahweh blessed the Egyptian's affairs for Joseph's sake. The blessing of Yahweh was upon everything Potiphar owned; his finances increased, his crops flourished, and his flocks and herds multiplied.[c] [6]So Potiphar placed all that he owned under Joseph's oversight. And with Joseph in charge, Potiphar had nothing to worry about, except deciding on what to eat![d]

Joseph and Potiphar's Wife

Now Joseph was *strikingly* handsome, very good-looking, and well-built.[e]

[7]It wasn't long before his master's wife noticed Joseph. She demanded: "Come make love to me."[f]

[8]"Never!" Joseph replied. "Don't you realize that my master has nothing to worry about with me in charge, for he has put everything he has under my care? [9]There is no one greater in his household than me,[g] nor has he kept anything back from me except you, because you're his wife. Why would I want to do such an immoral thing and sin against God?"

[10]Yet day after day, she was determined to seduce him. But Joseph continually refused her advances and would not even go near her. [11]Then one day, when he had to go into the house to do his work and no one else was there, [12]she grabbed him by his robe and said, "Come on, sleep with me!" But he abruptly ran out of the house leaving his robe in her hands![h] [13]Realizing he had fled, and she was

---

a 39:2 Or "prosperous." The implication is that Joseph excelled in everything. God's presence and favor do more for us than our skill, intelligence, and cleverness could achieve. God had his hand in everything that happened to Joseph and everything that happens to you (Rom. 8:28).

b 39:3 The Talmud teaches that the Hebrew text should be translated as "Yahweh was continually on Joseph's lips"; in other words, Potiphar noted that Joseph did everything as unto God and gave him the glory. There is something trustworthy about a person with no agenda other than to give God glory in everything.

c 39:5 Or "everything Potiphar owned, at home and in the field."

d 39:6 Or possibly a figure of speech for "his private affairs," or euphemistically for his "wife."

e 39:6 No other man is described in these terms in the Bible; however the Hebrew phrase is nearly identical to the description of Rachel (Gen. 29:17).

f 39:7 Although unnamed, Hebrew tradition identifies Potiphar's wife as Zuleika. As an Egyptian aristocrat, she was no doubt a beautiful woman.

g 39:9 Joseph understood the great favor shown to him and could not violate the trust of his master. He valued Potiphar's trust in him. Joseph knew that he was elevated to a place of honor; nothing was held back from him. Joseph had self-respect and respected Potiphar's wife. Though she was evil he was honorable toward her.

h 39:12 Interestingly, the triliteral Hebrew root for robe b-g-d is a homonym for "marital fidelity." There are times when running is a mark of a coward and there are times when running is the mark of courage. Joseph would rather run in embarrassment than linger, falling into the trap of sexual promiscuity (I Thess.4:3–8). Self-control is a true sign of integrity. It is better to lose a good coat than a good conscience! He may have lost his coat, but Joseph kept his character. If the Lord has destined you for greatness, if God has a work for you to do, there should be no surprise when this kind of temptation comes to you.

holding his robe in her hands, [14]she called for her household servants and said to them, "See! My husband brings this Hebrew foreigner here to make fools of us![a] He barged into my house and tried to have sex with me, and I screamed; [15]and when he heard me scream for help, he ran out of the house and left his robe!"

[16]She kept the robe beside her until his master came home [17]and she told him the same story: "This Hebrew foreigner you brought among us barged into the house and tried to violate me. [18]As soon as I screamed out for help, he ran outside and left his robe here beside me."

Joseph Goes to Prison

[19]When his master heard his wife's account about how his servant had treated her, he became furious.[b] [20]So Joseph's master took him and threw him into prison, the place where the king's prisoners are confined, and he was left there.[c] [21]But Yahweh was with Joseph and demonstrated to him his faithful love by giving him great favor in the sight of the warden. [22]The warden put all the prisoners under Joseph's care; he was placed in charge of all the prisoners and everything in the prison. [23]The warden had no worries about the prison with Joseph in charge, because Yahweh's presence was with Joseph and caused everything Joseph did to prosper.[d]

The Cupbearer and the Baker and Their Dreams

40 Some time later,[e] both Pharaoh's chief steward[f] and chief baker deeply offended their master,

---

a 39:14 Or "to play with us," a possible euphemism for having sex with them.

b 39:19 The text does not say with whom Potiphar was furious. Perhaps he knew his wife's promiscuous ways. He only had Joseph thrown into prison when a man with his authority could have had him killed. Perhaps he doubted the truth of her story, but to save face, he had Joseph imprisoned. According to the *Yalkut Shimoni*, Asenath, the daughter of Potiphar, did her best to convince her father of Joseph's innocence and what really happened. Later, when Joseph was freed from prison, Asenath became Joseph's wife.

c 39:20 In Psalm 105:17–18 we learn that Joseph's feet were in chains and an iron collar was placed on his neck (or "his soul"). It would be hard to imagine a lower point in Joseph's life. Betrayed by his brothers, sold as slave, and falsely accused, he suffered for a season until his time of deliverance arrived. As hard as it may seem, God may allow others to take advantage of us in order to carry out his secret will for our life. He will let us look like the fool in order to perfect our character. This is "the place where our King's prisoners" are confined (Eph.4:1)!

d 39:23 Joseph had a God-favored life. To study the life of Joseph is a study of the favor of God. He was faithful as a son, a shepherd, and a servant. He was diligent in all that he did. Wisdom guided him, even in a strange land, and everything he did prospered (Psalm 1:3)! He not only adjusted to living in Egypt but also flourished and became the personal attendant (administrator) of Potiphar's affairs and eventually the supervisor of the penal system. Joseph would never have been given such an honor if he had not demonstrated a high degree of integrity and faithfulness. Everyone could see that God was with Joseph. He that was faithful over a few things is now being made a ruler over much. See Matt. 25:21.

e 40:1 Eleven years passed since the time Joseph was sold into slavery. He was about twenty-eight at this time.

f 40:1 Or "cupbearer" (Lit. drink-giver). He was the king's trusted official who had a position to influence the king.

the king of Egypt.*ᵃ* ²Pharaoh was angry with his two officers, the chief steward and the chief baker, ³so he incarcerated them in the palace of Potiphar, the captain of the guard, in the same prison where Joseph was bound. ⁴The captain of the guard placed them under Joseph's charge, and they remained in custody for some time.*ᵇ*

⁵Then one night, they both dreamed—the steward and the baker, officials of the king of Egypt. They each had a *prophetic* dream with different interpretations.

⁶When Joseph came to them in the morning, he saw they looked miserable, ⁷so he asked Pharaoh's two officials who were under his custody, "*What's wrong?* Why the sad faces?"

⁸"We had dreams last night," they answered, "and we have no one to interpret them."

And Joseph said to them, "God can interpret your dreams! Please, tell them to me."

⁹⁻¹⁰So the chief steward shared his dream with Joseph first. He said, "In my dream, I saw a vine with three branches in front of me. I watched as it budded, then immediately it blossomed, and its clusters ripened into grapes. ¹¹I was holding Pharaoh's cup, so I took the grapes, squeezed them into his cup, and handed the cup to the king."

¹²Joseph said to him, "*God has given me* the interpretation of your dream: The three branches are three days. ¹³In three days, Pharaoh will pardon you and restore you to your post. You will once again hand Pharaoh's cup to him as you used to do as his steward. ¹⁴When things start to go well for you, remember me, and please be kind and mention me to Pharaoh so that he might release me from here.*ᶜ* ¹⁵For I was kidnapped from the land of the Hebrews, and I have done nothing here to deserve being thrown into this dungeon."*ᵈ*

---

a 40:1 Jewish tradition states that a fly had fallen into Pharaoh's cup of wine, and a pebble was found in his bread, thus causing this "offense." See *Midrash: Rashi.*

b 40:4 Jesus was falsely accused, maligned, and crucified between two thieves. At Calvary, the one next to Jesus was released (to enter Paradise), and the other killed. So it was with the two men imprisoned with Joseph, three days after they were released! Christ was rejected by his brothers (John 7:5), sold by one of his own (Matt. 26:14–15), eventually cast into the prison of death (1 Peter 3:18–19). Psalm 105:18 gives us additional information about Joseph's time in prison: *"His feet were bruised by strong shackles and his soul was held by iron."* The last phrase can be translated "his soul entered into iron." The inner strength of loving and serving in painful circumstances made Joseph's soul as strong as iron. He learned to serve and to rule over himself first, before God released him to rule over others.

c 40:14 Joseph could prophesy the release of another, but not himself. Often, prophetic gifts and words of revelation over other people simply do not come for the prophet. They are gifts to be used to bless others, not for self-consumption. We need others to come with a word for our need. This keeps us not only dependent upon God but upon others.

d 40:15 Joseph felt forgotten. He had been forgotten a long, long time. He became a slave when he was seventeen years old, and soon afterward, Potiphar cast him into prison. Not until he was thirty did Pharaoh release him from prison. Thirteen years is a long time to be forgotten. His faith in God and the fulfillment of his dreams kept Joseph faithfully waiting for his day of promotion. Perhaps, like Joseph, you have been let down by others who promised to be a help to you but did not follow through on their pledge. Don't despair, for God will never forget the dreams he has for his children (Jer. 29:11–13). Even if others let us down, God is always faithful and will bring his plans to pass at the appointed time.

[16]When the chief baker saw how favorably Joseph interpreted the dream, he said to him, "*Let me tell you my dream.* I saw three wicker breadbaskets stacked on my head *one above the other.* [17]In the top basket, I saw all kinds of bread and pastries for Pharaoh to enjoy, but the birds came and ate out of the basket above my head."

[18]Joseph said, "*God has given me* the interpretation of your dream: The three baskets are three days. [19]In three days, Pharaoh will behead you and impale you on a pole, and birds will eat the flesh off your corpse."

[20]Three days later, it was Pharaoh's birthday, and he threw a huge feast for all his household. He singled out among his servants the chief steward and the chief baker. [21]He pardoned the chief steward and restored him to his post, and the steward handed Pharaoh his drink. [22]But he had the chief baker *beheaded and* impaled on a pole. So, Joseph had accurately interpreted both their dreams, [23]but the chief steward completely forgot about Joseph and never remembered him.

From the Pit to the Palace

41 After two full years, Pharaoh dreamed that he was standing by the Nile, [2]and up from the river emerged seven healthy, fat cows, and they began grazing in the marshland. [3]Then he saw seven other cows come up out of the Nile right behind them. They were ugly and thin, and they stood beside the fat cows on the riverbank. [4]The seven ugly, thin cows ate up the seven healthy, fat cows.

After Pharaoh's dream he awoke [5]and fell back to sleep. He dreamed a second time. In his dream, he saw seven ears of grain, plump, ripe, and growing on a single stalk. [6]Close behind them sprouted seven ears of grain, thin and shriveled by the east wind. [7]And the seven thin ears swallowed up the seven plump and full ears. Then Pharaoh awoke from his *vivid and disturbing* dream!

[8]The next morning, his spirit was agitated, so he called for all the magicians[a] and wise men in Egypt. Pharaoh recounted his dreams to them, but no one could give him the interpretation.

[9]When the chief steward *heard about the dreams he remembered Joseph and* said to Pharaoh, "*Please*, your dream reminds me today of my failures. [10]Once, when Pharaoh was angry with his servants, he incarcerated me and the chief baker in the prison of Potiphar, the captain of the guard. [11]We both had dreams on the same night but with different meanings. [12]There was a young Hebrew man imprisoned with us who had been the personal servant to the captain of the guard. And when we told him our dreams, he interpreted them and told each of us their meaning. [13]And it happened just as he said. Pharaoh restored me to my post, but he had the baker impaled."

[14]After hearing this, Pharaoh immediately sent for Joseph. They rushed him out of the dungeon *to prepare him to meet with the king.*[b] When he had

a 41:8 The Hebrew word for magicians is *hartumim* and is used exclusively in connection with Egypt and Babylon.

b 41:14 Joseph's dreams landed him in a pit and later in a prison. It was Joseph's gift for interpreting dreams that brought him out from the prison to stand before Pharaoh (Prov. 22:29). When we are helpless to save ourselves, the Savior steps in (Rom. 5:6).

shaved and changed his clothes, he came and stood before Pharaoh.[a]

¹⁵Pharaoh said to Joseph, "I have had two dreams that no one can explain. I have heard that you are able to interpret a dream the moment you hear it."

¹⁶"I cannot do it alone," Joseph replied, "but God will help me to give Pharaoh the proper interpretation for Pharaoh's welfare."

¹⁷Then Pharaoh told Joseph, "In my dream I was standing on the bank of the Nile, ¹⁸and up from the river emerged seven healthy, fat cows, and they began to graze in the marshland. ¹⁹Right behind them followed seven other scrawny and emaciated cows. Never have I seen such ugly cows in all the land of Egypt! ²⁰The seven ugly, scrawny cows ate up the healthy, fat cows, ²¹but after consuming them, no one could tell that they had eaten them, for they looked just as bad as before. I awoke *with a start*, ²²*but immediately went back to sleep* and had another dream. I saw seven ears of grain, full and ripe, growing on a single stalk. ²³Right behind them sprouted seven thin, shriveled ears, scorched by the east wind. ²⁴The seven shriveled ears swallowed up the seven healthy ears. I have shared my dreams with my magicians, but no one can give me an interpretation."

Joseph Interprets Pharaoh's Dreams

²⁵Then Joseph said to Pharaoh, "Both your dreams tell the same story, for God has *prophetically* told Pharaoh what he is about to do. ²⁶Both the seven healthy cows and the seven healthy ears represent seven good years; it's the same dream. ²⁷The seven ugly and scrawny cows that followed and the seven shriveled ears scorched by the east wind are seven years also. They represent seven years of famine. ²⁸It is just as I have told Pharaoh; God has divinely revealed what he is about to do. ²⁹There will come seven years of great abundance throughout all the land of Egypt, ³⁰⁻³¹followed by seven years of intense famine. All of Egypt will forget the former abundance, for all the land will be ravaged by a famine, a very severe famine. They will not even remember their former abundance. ³²The reason that Pharaoh's dream was repeated is that God has determined that it will surely happen,[b] and that he will soon carry it out."

³³*Joseph continued*, "Let Pharaoh select a very wise and discerning man and set him over the land of Egypt. ³⁴Let Pharaoh appoint other officials throughout the land to collect one-fifth of all the crops each year during the seven plentiful years. ³⁵Have them gather all the food of these abundant years that are coming, and under Pharaoh's authority, have the grain stored in the cities for food. ³⁶Store it all as food reserve for the people during the seven years of famine coming upon Egypt, so that the land will survive the famine."

Joseph Promoted to Power

³⁷Joseph's proposal pleased Pharaoh and all his advisers. ³⁸He said to them, "Where can we find anyone else like this one, for he has the Spirit of God in

---

a 41:14 Joseph did not immediately beg to be released from prison. He approaches the mighty Pharaoh with dignity and respect. Joseph quickly acknowledged that only God has the power to interpret dreams, for he is the One who gives them. Like the Lord Jesus, Joseph did only what the Father revealed to him (John 5:19, 30).

b 41:32 See Deut. 13:1–5.

him!"*a* ³⁹So Pharaoh turned to Joseph and said, "Since God has divinely revealed this to you, there is no one as wise and full of insight as you. ⁴⁰I hereby place you in charge of all my affairs, and all my people will obey your commands.*b* Only I, the king,*c* will be greater than you! ⁴¹"Listen to me, Joseph," Pharaoh continued. "I am placing you in charge of all of Egypt." ⁴²Then he removed his signet ring,*d* placed it on Joseph's finger, and had him clothed with fine linen robes!*e* He adorned him with a golden collar around his neck. ⁴³Pharaoh had him ride in the chariot reserved for the second-in-command and sent runners going before him, crying out, "Kneel!"*f* In this way, Pharaoh placed Joseph over all the land of Egypt.

⁴⁴Pharaoh also said to Joseph, "I am Pharaoh. No one in all of Egypt will lift a finger*g* without your permission!"

A New Identity and a Bride
⁴⁵Pharaoh gave Joseph a new name: Revealer of Secrets.*h* He also arranged

---

a 41:38 How true this is of Jesus as well. There is simply no one like our Lord Jesus Christ. He walked in the fullness of the Spirit without limitation (John 3:34). Joseph was a forerunner of our Lord Jesus. His wisdom and understanding for interpreting dreams flowed out of a relationship with God's Spirit. True wisdom comes from the Spirit of Christ (Col. 2:3). This is the first time that Scripture mentions that someone has the Spirit of God in them. Later in the Old Testament, Bezalel, the craftsman of the Tabernacle, is similarly described (Ex. 31:3; 35:31) as well as Daniel 5:14.

b 41:40 The Hebrew text is literally "on your mouth all my people will kiss." See also Ps. 2:11–12, where a kiss demonstrates serving and worshipping God.

c 41:40 Or "only the throne," a metonymy for the king and his authority.

d 41:42 Pharaoh validated Joseph's authority by giving him his signet ring, which had the royal seal of Egypt engraved upon it.

e 41:42 Instead of prison garments, Joseph was given the finest of clothing (the linen garments of a priest!). Joseph lost a robe twice; now he receives a new one! He who had been dragging fetters of iron was now adorned with a chain of gold. Pharaoh gave Joseph an *usekh*, a broad collar made of gold. The Egyptians placed these collars on their deities or officials. Pharaoh recognized that God was with Joseph, and the Egyptians would recognize Joseph's authority. See Dan. 5:7; Est. 8:2. Instead of a dingy dungeon, Joseph was free. He was even given the keys to his own chariot! Joseph is now thirty years old (Gen. 41:46). This is the age at which Jewish men could enter priestly service at the Temple and the age at which Jesus began his earthly ministry. Nevertheless, it is a very young age to be awarded the highest governmental position in a powerful nation with the responsibility of running the affairs of the country. This testifies to Joseph's God-given wisdom and grace.

f 41:43 Joseph, once accused of rape, was now made Prime Minister, head of all the people, chief justice, and general of the armed forces in all of Egypt—all as a foreigner! From a prison to the highest office in the land in one day! Joseph had the strange experience of having what others dream about, but not what he dreamed about. His gifts were finally recognized, but not by his brothers. A million people shouting "Bow the knee" would not do for Joseph as much as eleven brothers doing the same. This exaltation, as glorious as it was, still fell short of what God promised Joseph in his dreams.

g 41:44 Or "no one will lift a hand or foot."

h 41:45 Or "Zaphenath-Paneah." The root word for Zaphenath is "to hide," and the root word for Paneah is "to disclose (explain)." The Greek of the Septuagint can be translated "savior of the world (sustainer of life)." Other scholars believe it could be translated, "God has said, 'he will live.'" Each of these possible translations can point us to Jesus Christ, the true Revealer of Mysteries, the Savior of the world, and the one God raised from the dead.

for him to marry the daughter of Poti-phera,[a] the priest of Heliopolis.[b] Her name was Asenath.[c] And Joseph took charge over all the land of Egypt.[d] [46]Joseph was thirty years old[e] when he entered the service of Pharaoh, king of Egypt.[f] Leaving Pharaoh's presence, Joseph traveled throughout the entire land of Egypt.[g]

Seven Years of Abundance
[47]During the seven years of abundance, the land produced bumper crops. [48]Joseph supervised the gathering up of all the great stores of food of the seven years of abundance and *strategically* placed them in various walled cities near where the harvest was gathered.[h] [49]He gathered such massive quantities of produce that he gave up trying to measure it all, for it was like counting the sand on the seashore.

Joseph's Two Sons
[50]Prior to the famine, Joseph and Asenath, daughter of Potiphera, priest of Heliopolis, had two sons. [51]Joseph named the firstborn Manasseh,[i] saying, "God has made me forget all my troubles and my parental home." [52]The second he named Ephraim,[j] saying, "God has made me fruitful in the land of my suffering."

[53]Eventually, Egypt's seven years of abundance came to an end. [54]Then began the seven years of famine, just as Joseph prophesied. Although there

---

a 41:45 Potiphera is the longer form of the name Potiphar. Some of oldest traditions of Rabbinical Judaism state that Potiphera was the same Potiphar that had Joseph imprisoned (see Rashi, Rashbam, Alshich). This would have been Joseph's final vindication of innocence, to marry the daughter of the one who accused him. However, more contemporary scholars believe Potiphera was a different individual than the captain of the guard.

b 41:45 Or "On (strength, vigor)" which is also recognized as Heliopolis, a modern suburb of Cairo. It was one of the most ancient Egyptian cities and was the seat of worship of the sun god "Re." Heliopolis is the home of the oldest obelisk on earth, the Obelisk of Sesostris I. Joseph was marrying the daughter of one of the most respected men in Egypt.

c 41:45 Asenath, the daughter of On the Egyptian priest, means "belonging to (the goddess) Neith." Joseph was given a bride while rejected by his brothers. Joseph is a type of Christ who finds a bride during this Church age. See 2 Cor. 11:2; Eph. 5:25–26.

d 41:45 Or "Joseph went out throughout the land of Egypt."

e 41:46 Jesus, too, was thirty when he began his public ministry. Ezekiel was thirty when he was visited by God. Thirty is the number of maturity and the priesthood, for a priest had to be thirty before they could serve in Temple worship.

f 41:46 Joseph had lived thirteen years in captivity.

g 41:46 Think of this as Joseph's royal tour, inspecting the kingdom he is to rule over.

h 41:48 One can see the wisdom of Joseph in storing the grain near where it would be needed, vs. keeping it all in one central storage place.

i 41:51 Manasseh sounds like the Hebrew words "he causes to forget."

j 41:52 Ephraim comes from the Hebrew word for "being fruitful," with an implication of "double fruitfulness." This is God's order: Manasseh, then Ephraim. God must cause us to forget our prisons of the past before we can become fruitful. The "King's prison" is the place to forget our pain so we can move on into the fruitfulness of becoming like Christ, one who forgives others. Instead of seeking revenge toward our brothers who have harmed us, we must give birth to a "Manasseh." To call your afflictions "blessings" is to become fruitful and give birth to an "Ephraim." In all of these things, we acknowledge that it is the glorious work of God (Phil. 4:8)!

was a severe famine everywhere else, food was available throughout the land of Egypt. ⁵⁵When the Egyptians grew hungry, the people cried out to Pharaoh for food. Then Pharaoh said to all his people, "Go to Joseph and do whatever he tells you."ᵃ

⁵⁶As the famine worsened over all the land, Joseph opened all the storehousesᵇ and sold grain to the Egyptians, for the famine was severe everywhere. ⁵⁷So because of the severity of the worldwide famine, people from all over the world had to come and buy grain from Joseph.

Joseph's Brothers Go to Egypt

42 When Jacob learned there was food in Egypt, he said to his sons, "Why are you standing around here staring at each other? ²I hear there is grain in Egypt; go there and buy some for us so we don't all starve to death." ³So Joseph's ten half brothers went down to buy grain in Egypt,

⁴but Jacob did not send Joseph's *full* brother Benjamin with them, because he feared something might happen to him. ⁵So Israel's sons were among those who went to Egypt to buy grain, for the famine in the land of Canaan was severe.ᶜ

⁶Now Joseph was the governor of the land of Egypt, which meant he supervised the sale of grain to all the people. *One day*, Joseph's *ten* brothers came and bowed down before him with their faces on the ground. ⁷As soon as Joseph saw them, he realized that they were his brothers! But he pretended he didn't know themᵈ and spoke to them harshly, "Where do you come from?"

"From the land of Canaan," they answered, "and we're here to buy food."

⁸Although Joseph recognized his brothers, they had no clue that it was Joseph speaking to them. ⁹Then at once, Joseph remembered the dreams

---

ᵃ 41:55 Joseph, in effect, became the Minister of Agriculture over the land. His first dream of bundles of wheat bowing before him was a prophetic hint of his future responsibilities.

ᵇ 41:56 As translated from the Septuagint, Vulgate, and Syriac. The Hebrew is "he opened all that was among them." Joseph opened the door for others to be fed. He was an exceptional administrator and a wise manager of Egypt's resources. Because he had passed each previous test and grew in character, he was ready when the Lord promoted him to such a place of power. He handled all this prestige without pride or arrogance. Joseph was a man prepared to rule in wisdom and to use his position of authority to provide for others. God now had a man he could use as a deliverer.

ᶜ 42:5 Joseph's ten brothers left for Egypt on a journey of eight to ten days to buy food for their very large families (Gen. 46:26).

ᵈ 42:7 Joseph was seventeen when he had his dreams. At the age of thirty, he was exalted over Egypt. About nine years later his brothers come to buy grain from him. After he had waited twenty-two years for the fulfillment of his prophetic dreams, here are his brothers bowing down before him. What a feeling that must have been! When his ten brothers came before him, he knew who they were, even though they didn't recognize him. His dream was being fulfilled right before his eyes—almost. As they were bowing down before him, he counted them; there were only ten, not eleven. Where was the eleventh? Joseph needed a plan.

he had about them *bowing down before him!*[a] *Pausing*, he said to them, "You are spies! You've come to see where our land is weak!"[b]

[10]His brothers replied, "No, master; we've come to buy food. [11]We, your servants, are honest men; we'd never think of spying! We're blood brothers, sons of one father."

[12]Joseph interrupted, "No! You are spies who have come here to find our weakness!"

[13]"We are your servants," they insisted. "We were twelve brothers, our youngest brother remained behind with our father, and one brother—well, he is no more."

[14]Joseph said to them, "It's just as I said; you are spies! [15]And here is how I'll test you: unless your younger brother comes and presents himself here *before me*, then as surely as Pharaoh lives, you shall not depart from here! [16]One of you must go and bring me your brother, while the rest of you will remain here in confinement. This way I will test your words to see if the story you have told me is true. If not, as surely as Pharaoh lives, you are spies!" [17]He placed them all in prison together for three days.[c]

Joseph Tests His Brothers

[18]On the third day, Joseph said to them, "Do as I say and you will live. I am a man who respects God. [19]If you are as honest as you say you are, then I will keep just one of your brothers here in confinement while the rest of you carry grain home for your starving families. [20]You must return with your youngest brother so that I may verify your story, and that you may not die." So they agreed to do so.

[21]*With Joseph standing there*, they began to speak among themselves, saying, "*Look what's happened to us!* We're being punished for what we did to Joseph long ago. We heard his cries of anguish and saw the agony of his soul when he begged us for mercy, but we turned a deaf ear. That's why all this trouble has come upon us!"

[22]Then Reuben spoke up, "Didn't I tell you not to sin against the boy? But you wouldn't listen! So now we're paying the price for his murder!"[d] [23]They had no clue that Joseph understood every word, for he had been speaking to them through an interpreter.

[24]*Deeply affected by what he heard*, Joseph began to weep and hurriedly left their presence. After *he*

---

a 42:9 At that moment, Joseph had the choice of revealing his identity to his brothers or remaining in disguise. He chose the latter, for the wisdom of God was in him. He wanted to test them to see if they were repentant of their betrayal. From a human standpoint, Joseph would have been happy for an instant reconciliation with them, but Joseph was a man broken by God and was now prepared to deliver others. Joseph spoke and acted in such a way that their hearts would be revealed and exposed. Did Joseph wonder if they had done to Benjamin what they had done to him? It was not a spirit of revenge driving Joseph, but a true love for his brothers and for the ways of God. The tests Joseph took them through were designed by God to see what they had done and come to repentance. See 2 Peter 3:9.

b 42:9 Or "to see the nakedness of the land."

c 42:17 He put them in confinement for three days, perhaps to let them know how he had suffered in prison for those many years; not to punish, but to prepare them. They could only conclude that God confined them because of what they had done to Joseph.

d 42:22 Or "Now comes the reckoning for his blood!"

had composed himself, he returned to them, and pointing to Simeon, said, "This one will remain here."ᵃ Then he had him tied and bound while they all watched. ²⁵Joseph then gave orders to have their bags filled with grain, to hide each man's money back inside his sack, and to give them provisions for their journey home. After this was done for them,ᵇ ²⁶they loaded their donkeys with the bags of grain and departed.

Joseph's Brothers Return to Canaan

²⁷Later, they camped for the night, and as one of themᶜ opened his sack of grain to feed his donkey, he discovered that his money was there right on top of the grain! ²⁸He shouted to his brothers, "My money! Look, someone put my money back in my sack!" ²⁹Troubled and trembling, they said to each other, "What in the world has God done to us?"

²⁹When they came to their father Jacob in Canaan, they told him the story of all that happened to them, saying, ³⁰"The governor of Egypt spoke harshly to us and accused us of being spies. ³¹We told him, 'We are not spies but honest men. ³²We're twelve brothers, sons of our father. Our youngest remained with our father in the land of Canaan, and one is no more.' ³³Then the man, the governor of Egypt, demanded, 'By this test, I will discern if you are honest men: Leave one of your brothers with me, take the grain you need for your families, and be on your way. ³⁴Return to me with your youngest brother, then I'll know you are not spies, but men of integrity. Then I'll release your brother back to you, and you'll be free to trade in the land.'"

³⁵As they each emptied their sacks of grain, each man found his money inside his sack! When they and their father saw their money returned to them, they were frightened. ³⁶Their father Jacob said to his sons, "You have taken away my children! First, Joseph is gone, and now, Simeon! And now, you want to take Benjamin from me! Everything is against me!"ᵈ

³⁷Then Reuben said, "Father, you may put my two sonsᵉ to death if I fail to bring Benjamin back to you! Trust me—I will bring him back!"

³⁸But Jacob replied, "I can't let my son Benjamin go with you. For his brother is dead, and of Rachel's sons,

---

a 42:24 Joseph wanted to be sure they would return to Egypt. Simeon's name means "he who hears." By keeping Simeon, Joseph is showing them that they "lost their hearing." Also, Joseph was testing them to see if they would abandon Simeon as they had done to him. While in prison, Simeon would have lots of time on his hands to listen—and discern. Simeon was known for his cruelty (Gen. 34:25; 49:5–7), and he possibly was the one that led the way in their persecution of Joseph.

b 42:25 As the nine brothers left for Canaan, Joseph gave them sacks of grain for their journey. At his orders, the brother's money was replaced in their sacks of grain. Joseph paid for the grain himself, for he loved his brothers. His secret love paid their debt (Isa. 55:1). They deserved no grain, they deserved no money, but mercy prevailed. The money in the sacks was also a part of Joseph's wise plan to test his brothers.

c 42:27 The Midrash identifies him with Levi. See Targum Jonathan.

d 42:36 And how many times have we said that everything is against us when, in fact, everything and every event is being woven together for our good because we love God (Rom. 8:28)? See also Ps. 34:19; Isa. 41:10, 13.

e 42:37 Reuben had four sons, so the Hebrew implies "two of my sons."

he alone is left.*a* If he were to meet with disaster on your journey, *I would die of grief*! You will send my white hair and broken heart sorrowing down to the grave!"*b*

Joseph's Brothers Return to Egypt with Benjamin

43 Now the famine in the land continued to grow more severe. ²When all the grain they had brought from Egypt was almost gone, their father said to them, "Go back and buy us more food."

³But Judah objected, "The Egyptian warned us repeatedly, 'You will not see my face again, unless Benjamin is with you!' ⁴We'll only go if you'll let our brother come with us. ⁵If you insist he remains here, we won't go, for the man solemnly told us, 'You will not see my face again, unless your brother is with you!'"*c*

⁶Israel*d* demanded, "Why did you make it so hard for me by telling the man you had another brother?"

⁷They answered him, "The man interrogated us about ourselves and our family, saying, 'Is your father still living? Do you have another brother?'

We had to answer his questions! We had no idea he would say, 'You must bring your brother here to me.'"

⁸⁻⁹Then Judah spoke up and said to Israel, "Father, I promise to guarantee his safety with my life.*e* You can hold me personally responsible if I don't return with him. I'll bear the blame before you for the rest of my life if I fail to bring him safely back to you! You have my promise. Entrust him to my care, and let us be on our way, so that we all don't die of starvation—we and you and all our children—we will live and not die! ¹⁰And besides, if we hadn't delayed so long, we could have gone and returned twice by now!"

¹¹*After considering their words*, their father Israel said to them, "If that's the way it has to be, then do this: Load your donkeys with the very best gifts you can find, choice products of the land, and offer them to the man. Take some balm and some honey, spices and myrrh,*f* pistachio nuts and almonds. ¹²Take double the money with you. Give him back the money that was returned in the top of your sacks, for it may have been a mistake. ¹³Take your brother, too, and be off!

---

a 42:38 Jacob could not see how insensitive his remarks were. Reuben was a son, Judah was a son, Levi was a son, and all the others. Jacob spoke as if the other sons did not matter; Jacob continued to show favoritism.

b 42:38 Or Hebrew Sheol.

c 43:5 Jacob's sons told him, essentially, "We won't see Joseph's face until he sees Benjamin." The name Benjamin means "son of my right hand." There is One greater than Joseph who is now waiting until he sees "the sons of his right hand," an overcoming company of sons and daughters who sit and reign with him in victory (Rev. 3:21). When the church matures into the full measure of sonship, we will see him whom our soul loves.

d 43:6 Israel is the name God gave to Jacob.

e 43:8–9 This was an amazing statement of sacrificial love from Judah. One day a son of Judah would come, a Lion from the tribe of Judah, Jesus, who would offer his life as a ransom for many. Only a father can understand the loss of two of his children, and Judah had experienced that loss. See Gen. 38:7, 10.

f 43:11 Ironically, these items were the same things carried in the caravan that took Joseph away as a slave (Gen. 37:25). Now they carry the same items to Joseph as tribute.

Go back to the man at once. [14]May the God who is more than enough[a] grant you mercy *and favor* before the man, so that he may send back both Simeon and Benjamin. As for me, if I suffer loss, then let it be so."

[15]So the brothers set off for Egypt and took double the money, the many gifts, and Benjamin. Once they arrived, they presented themselves before Joseph.

Joseph Prepares a Feast for His Brothers

[16]When Joseph saw his brother Benjamin with them, he said to his chief servant, "Bring the men to my house *and make them feel at home.* Butcher an animal and prepare a meal, for these men are to dine with me at noon." [17]Joseph's chief servant did as he was told and brought the men to Joseph's house.

[18]Now the brothers were very apprehensive as they were being led inside, and said to each other, "He brought us here because of the money that was put back in our sacks the first time we came to Egypt! He's looking for an opportunity to arrest us, turn us into his slaves, and take away our donkeys!" [19]So they approached the chief servant and spoke to him at the entrance of the house. [20]"If you please, my lord," they said, "we came here once before to buy food, [21-22]but *on our way home*, when we camped for the night and opened our sacks, we found each one's money in the top of his bag. All our money was there in our bags! We know it must have been an

oversight of some kind, and we have no clue who put it there, so we have brought it all back with us. Plus, we have additional money to buy more food."

[23]"Relax," he replied, "don't be afraid. Your God, the God of your father, must have been the one who put treasure in your bags. I have received your money; *it's all accounted for.*" Then the chief servant brought Simeon out to them. [24]Then he gave feed to their donkeys and brought the brothers into the house. He gave them water to drink and washed their feet. [25]The men laid out their gifts to present to Joseph, for they were told he would appear before them at noon and would dine with them.

[26]When Joseph came home, they presented to him the gifts they had brought with them into the house. They each bowed low before him with their faces to the ground. [27]He asked them how the family was doing, saying, "You mentioned your aging father; is he still alive? Is he doing well?"

[28]"Yes," they replied, "our father, your servant, is still alive and doing well." And they bowed low before Joseph in respect.

[29]Looking them over, he saw his brother Benjamin, his mother's son, and said to them, "So, I see you have returned with your youngest brother, of whom you spoke. God be gracious to you, my son." [30]Joseph hastily left the room, for he was overwhelmed with feelings of love[b] for his brother and on the verge of tears. He went into a private room and sobbed, as

---

a 43:14 Or "El Shaddai." See footnote for Gen. 17:1.

b 43:30 This is the Hebrew word *racham* and is used ninety times in the Bible and almost always refers to God's compassionate, merciful love for us. *Racham* is also the word for "womb." *Racham* is best described as nurturing love, the love a mother would have for her children.

tears ran down his cheeks.*[a]* *[31]*When he finally composed himself, he washed his face, reappeared, and ordered: "Serve the meal."

*[32]*First, they served Joseph who was seated apart from his brothers, then the brothers by themselves, and the Egyptians by themselves. (It would have been utterly offensive for the Egyptians to eat at the same table with the Hebrews.) *[33]*Now, the brothers had been seated before Joseph in their birth order,*[b]* from the firstborn at one end of the table to the youngest at the other end. They were all stunned when they realized the seating arrangement and looked at each other in astonishment. *[34]*Eleven plates of food were taken from Joseph's table and set in front of each of them, but Benjamin's portion was five times more than any of theirs!*[c]* They feasted and drank their fill with Joseph until they all became drunk.

Joseph Tests His Brothers

44 Joseph ordered his chief servant, "Fill the men's sacks with grain, with as much as they can hold, and put each one's money back in the mouth of his bag. *[2]*As for the youngest one, place my silver goblet in the mouth of his sack, along with the money he paid for his grain." And he did as Joseph said.

*[3]*At dawn, the men loaded their donkeys and set off for home. *[4]*They hadn't gone far outside of the city when Joseph said to his chief servant, "Now, go at once and pursue the men! And when you catch up to them, say to them, 'Why did you repay good with evil? *[5]*Why have you stolen the silver goblet*[d]* from which my master drinks, and the one he uses to discover secrets hidden from men!*[e]* You have done an evil thing!'"

*[6]*When the chief servant caught up with them, he repeated his master's

---

a 43:30 All of a sudden, this world leader, this captain over millions, collapsed inside. It was beginning to make sense to him—all the loneliness, those dark days in prison, the misunderstanding, and the pain of rejection. A family shattered for over two decades was being reunited. This took great discipline for Joseph to keep his secret from them. Joseph's heart moved him to tears—tears of tenderness and affection for his younger brother and his long-lost family. Like a little boy again, Joseph missed his daddy.

b 43:33 What a feast was before them! They had not eaten like this for months, maybe years. As they noticed the order of seating, the brothers were amazed but still had no clue. There are 39,916,800 different orders in which eleven individuals could be seated. Did they believe he had supernatural wisdom to know their birth order?

c 43:34 Joseph let them understand that Benjamin was his favorite, giving him a portion five times larger than the others. Five times more meat, five times more vegetables, five times more of everything! Why would Joseph have given more to Benjamin? Was he merely following the steps of his father's favoritism that brought all of this on? No. Joseph was testing them to see if they would be jealous again. Were they truly broken? Could they endure seeing one brother favored over the others and still rejoice? Or, would they get rid of Benjamin as they had him?

d 44:5 As translated from the Septuagint and Vulgate and implied in the Hebrew.

e 44:5 Or "for divination." Some historians tell of water being poured into a certain vessel, and then pieces of gold, silver, or precious stones were added, and then by the shape of designs that appeared at the surface of the water, the diviner could interpret events. Joseph did not say that he used the cup for divination but wants his brothers to think he does.

words to them. ⁷They answered him, "Why does my lord accuse us of such things? Far be it from your servants to do anything of the kind! ⁸Didn't we return from Canaan with the money we found in our grain sacks? Why then would we steal silver or gold from the house of your lord? ⁹Look for yourself. If any of your servants is found to have it, then he will die, and the rest of us will become our master's slaves!"

¹⁰"Very well then," Joseph's servant replied, "as you have said. *But I will show you leniency.* The one who has it will be my slave, but the rest of you will go free."

¹¹Each one quickly lowered his bag to the ground and opened it. ¹²Then the chief servant searched each bag, beginning with oldest and ending with the youngest—and he found the silver goblet in Benjamin's bag!ᵃ ¹³*Aghast,* the brothers ripped their clothes in despair. They all loaded their donkeys again and returned to the city.

¹⁴Joseph was waiting in his house when Judah and his brothers arrived. When they saw Joseph, they all fell to the ground before him.ᵇ ¹⁵Joseph said to them, "What have you done? Don't you know that divination would have given insight to a man like me?"

¹⁶Judah replied, "What can we say, my lord? How can we plead our case? How can we prove our innocence? God has revealed the guilt of your servants,ᶜ and here we are—our lord's slaves, both we and the one in whose sack the silver goblet was found."

¹⁷"No," Joseph commanded. "Only the one who stole my silver goblet will be my slave; the rest of you will go on home in peace to your father."

Judah Pleads for Benjamin

¹⁸Then Judah stepped forward and offered, "My lord, please, may I have a word with you? You are the equal of Pharaoh. Please don't be angry with me, your servant. ¹⁹My lord asked his servants, 'Do you have a father or another brother?' ²⁰We answered my lord, 'We have an aged father and our youngest brother, who is a child of his old age. The child's *full* brother is dead, so now he is the only child left of his mother, and his father loves him very much.' ²¹Then you said to your servants, 'Bring him here to me so that I might see him myself.' ²²We said to my lord, 'But he cannot leave his father; if he were to leave him, his father would die.' ²³Then you said to your servants, 'You will not see my

---

a 44:12 They had not stolen Joseph's silver cup, but they did steal Joseph's dignity and threw him into a pit. They were responsible for all of Joseph's afflictions. God was seeking to reveal their hearts through this false accusation they had to endure. Joseph's *silver* cup, hidden in Benjamin's bag, was a picture of the years of suffering Joseph went through as a slave sold for "silver." Joseph was *testing their loyalty.* Would they stand with Benjamin and love him, or would they sacrifice Benjamin as they had Joseph? Would they be loyal brothers now? Joseph gave them a chance to do away with Benjamin as they had done with him.

b 44:14 For the third time, Joseph's brothers bowed before him. What a sight for Joseph to see them all return. He had to know if they had really changed. Joseph was truly doing them a kindness. He was giving them a chance to pass a test they once had failed! Their guilt could be removed, not just by the mercy of Joseph, but they also had to "prove [their] repentance by a changed life." See Matt. 3:8.

c 44:16 Their long-suppressed feelings of guilt surfaced. God was awakening their conscience to what they had done to Joseph.

face again if I do not see your youngest brother.' ²⁴When we arrived home to your servant, my father, we told him every word you had spoken to us.

²⁵"Sometime later, our father said to us, 'Go back and buy some more food for us.' ²⁶We answered, 'We can only return to Egypt if we take our youngest brother with us. We won't see the man's face again, if he doesn't see our youngest brother.' ²⁷Then, your servant, my father, said to us, 'You know that my wife *Rachel* only gave me two sons. ²⁸One is gone from me—torn by a beast! I haven't seen him since. ²⁹If you take this one also from me, and something happens to him, you will send my gray hairs in grief down to the grave.'"

³⁰⁻³¹*Judah continued, "My lord*, if I went to your servant, my father, without the boy, and he saw that the boy was not with us, he would die! His very life is wrapped up with the life of the boy.ᵃ Now he is so old that the grief of his loss would kill him. ³²Furthermore, I, your servant, have guaranteed the boy's safety to my father. I told him, 'If I don't return the boy back to you, I will bear the blame before you, my father, for the rest of my life!'

³³⁻³⁴"So, please let me take the place of the boy, and I will remain here as a slave to you, my lord. Please let the boy go back with his brothers.ᵇ How could I return to my father without the boy? I don't want to witness the woe and grief that would overtake my father."

Joseph Reveals Himself to His Brothers

45 Joseph could no longer contain his pent-up feelings, so he cried out to his attendants, "Leave the room!" So no one was there when Joseph revealed his identity to his brothers.ᶜ ²He began to weep so loudly that the Egyptians heard it—even as far away as Pharaoh's house!ᵈ ³Joseph, *through his tears*, said to his brothers *in Hebrew*: "I am Joseph! Is father still alive?" His brothers stood there stunned, scared, and speechless.

⁴Joseph said to his brothers, "Please, come close to me." Inching forward, they came close to him. Then Joseph said, "It's me—your brother—whom you sold into slavery in Egypt. I am Joseph! ⁵Now don't be grieved. Don't blame yourselves because you sold me here. It was God who sent me ahead of you in order to save lives. ⁶The famine has now endured for two years, and the land will not bear fruit for five more years. ⁷God sent me ahead of you to ensure that

---

a 44:30–31 As father and son, the souls of Jacob and Benjamin were bound together in the bundle of life.

b 44:33–34 As Judah spoke for his brothers, he did not attempt to justify himself or pass the blame off onto Benjamin. Unlike the past, they did not turn on Benjamin as they had turned on Joseph. Judah stood as a savior for his brother. He had changed greatly from the one who conspired to sell his brother into slavery (Gen. 37:27) and now offers himself to be a slave as a substitute on behalf of his brother Benjamin. Jewish historians note that for many long years after this event, the tribe of Benjamin walked in faithful love toward the tribe of Judah even when the other ten tribes deserted them.

c 45:1 The family secret was a secret no more! Having held this secret for nearly a year, Joseph could contain himself no longer. He must reveal himself to those he loved. All the Egyptians and the interpreter were ordered to leave. Joseph waited for the last Egyptian to file out of the room, then his long-buried emotions surfaced.

d 45:2 Or "(word) reached Pharaoh's house."

you would live^a *and have descendants.* He has saved your lives through this marvelous act of deliverance. ⁸So it was God, not you, who sent me here.^b God has made me a father to Pharaoh, the master of his entire household, and the ruler over all of Egypt.

⁹"Hurry back to my father *and tell him that you have found me alive.* Tell him, 'This is what your son Joseph says, "God has made me ruler^c of all Egypt. Come to me without delay. ¹⁰You will settle in the land of Goshen,^d where you will be near me—you and all your children and your grandchildren, your flocks and herds and all that you possess. ¹¹For there will be five more years of famine, but I will provide all that you need to live in Goshen. You, your household, and all that you have will not live in poverty.'"

¹²"My brothers, you each can see for yourselves, and Benjamin can too, that I really am Joseph, for I'm speaking to you face-to-face in our own language.^e ¹³You must tell father everything you have seen here and how greatly I am honored in Egypt. But hurry and bring my father here to me."

¹⁴Then Joseph threw his arms around Benjamin's neck, sobbing, and Benjamin wept on Joseph's neck. ¹⁵With tears streaming down his face, Joseph kissed each brother, one by one. After *their tearful, emotional embrace,* they took time to speak brother-to-brother.^f

Pharaoh's Invitation

¹⁶The news reached Pharaoh's house: "Joseph's brothers have come." Pharaoh and his officials were greatly pleased when they heard it.

---

a 45:7 Or "to preserve you for a remnant on earth."

b 45:8 Joseph's compassion for his brothers ran deep. For the third time, he told them that it was God, not they, who orchestrated all the events to bring him to the throne. Once painfully betrayed by them, Joseph now began to encourage the brothers. His words flowed from a loving, forgiving heart as Joseph's kindness washed over them. Their guilt was overruled by Joseph's mercy. Through his tears, he convinced them not to dwell on their sin but on how God had worked through it all. Joseph had been sent by God ahead of them to preserve their lives. Though they did not realize it, Joseph's brothers were helping the Lord fulfill his promise to Abraham (Gen.12:1–3). Today, we must learn to see that even those who hurt us the most may be those who move us toward the throne. If you see yourself in the hands of a loving God, not others, you will not be offended. If Joseph's brothers had not sold him into slavery, how would his dreams have been fulfilled? Some of your dreams will never come true until you can handle both mistreatment and betrayal with forgiving love (Mark 11:25; Luke 23:34).

c 45:9 The brothers once asked in Genesis 37:8, "Do you actually think you're destined to rule over us?" Joseph's words, no doubt, would have reminded them of their question.

d 45:10 Goshen means "drawing near." It was a fertile area in the eastern part of the Nile delta that today is called Wadi Tumilat. It was known for grazing livestock (Gen. 46:32–34; 47:6, 11). Joseph's palace was apparently near Goshen.

e 45:12 Or "that it is my mouth that speaks with you."

f 45:15 All that transpired that amazing day was a prophetic portrayal of the glorious reconciliation that one day will occur between Jesus and his alienated Jewish brothers (Rom. 11:25; Eph. 4:18). Through the last two thousand years, he has been unrecognizable to the Jewish people in his "Gentile" garb, as it were. But one day the time will come when hearts will soften in repentance toward the Father, and Jesus will reveal his full identity as their long-lost Jewish brother and Messiah. See Rom. 9–11.

¹⁷Pharaoh said to Joseph, "Tell your brothers: 'Load your donkeys and return to Canaan. ¹⁸Get your father and your families and come back to me. I will give you the best of the land in Egypt, and you will enjoy the fat of the land.' ¹⁹Tell them also: 'Take Egyptian wagons with you for your wives and little ones and bring their father with them. ²⁰Give no thought to leaving your possessions behind; the best of all the land of Egypt will be yours.'"

²¹Israel's sons did as they were instructed. Joseph gave them wagons, as the king had ordered, and provided food for their journey. ²²He gave each of them a set of garments, and to Benjamin he also gave three hundred pieces of silver and five sets of garments. ²³He sent his father ten donkeys loaded with the best Egyptian goods and ten female donkeys loaded with grain, bread, and other provisions for the journey. ²⁴Then he sent his brothers off, admonishing them, "Don't quarrel*ᵃ* along the way." And they departed.

²⁵They left Egypt and went back home to their father Jacob in Canaan.

²⁶*When they arrived*, they *ran to their father and* announced, "Joseph is still alive! *Not only that*, he is the ruler of all Egypt!" The news so stunned Jacob that he nearly fainted.*ᵇ* He could not believe his ears! ²⁷But when they told him all that Joseph had said to them, and when he saw the wagons Joseph had sent to take him to Egypt, he recovered from the shock. ²⁸"My son Joseph is still alive!" Israel said. "Now I'm convinced! I must go to see him before I die."*ᶜ*

Israel and His Family Go to Egypt

46 Israel packed up all he had and went to Beersheba, where he offered sacrifices to the God of his father Isaac. ²God spoke to him in visions of the night, and called, "Jacob, Jacob!"*ᵈ*

"Yes, I'm here," he answered.

³"I am God, the God of your father. Do not be afraid to go to Egypt; for I will make your descendants a great nation there. ⁴I will go with you to Egypt, and I will bring your descendants back to this land. And the hand

---

a 45:24 Or "be trembling (with anxiety)."

b 45:26 Or "his heart was numb."

c 45:28 Why did Joseph wait for nine years before he sent for his father Jacob? He could have sent chariots to Canaan before now, bringing his father to Egypt to share his wealth and power. Why did he wait so many years until now? Was it because he did not care? No, Joseph cared deeply for his family; something else kept him back. Joseph was a man who chose to bear the pain of separation from his father, rather than run ahead of God. An enthroned prince, yet he placed God's interests over his. He knew that the plan of God must be fulfilled, not just the desires of Joseph. So, he waited and waited again. Instead of initiating contact with his father and brothers, he stayed within the timing of the Lord. Even when it was in his power, Joseph waited nine years before his loneliness was removed. The dreams of his youth included Jacob, his father, bowing before him also. More than anything else, Joseph longed to see his father, but for nine years he did nothing. Even when the time came, he himself did not go; he waited until the others brought Jacob back. He was restricted to the will of God. This is why Joseph was a ruler and a prince. If you are unable to rule yourself, you will not be a good ruler over others.

d 46:2 For the first time in twenty-two years, God appeared to Jacob. He was now one hundred and thirty years old. See Gen. 47:9.

of Joseph will be there to close your eyes when you die."[a]

⁵Then Jacob set out from Beersheba. His sons put him, their little ones, and their wives in the wagons that Pharaoh had sent. ⁶⁻⁷They took their livestock and the possessions they had acquired in Canaan and went to Egypt. Jacob took all his descendants with him: his sons, his grandsons, his daughters, his granddaughters.

The Family of Jacob

⁸Now these are the names of Jacob's descendants, the Israelites who went to Egypt with him:

Reuben, Jacob's firstborn, ⁹and his sons: Hanoch, Pallu, Hezron, and Carmi.

¹⁰Simeon and his sons: Jemuel, Jamin, Ohad, Jachin, Zohar, and Shaul (the son of a Canaanite woman).

¹¹Levi and his sons: Gershon, Kohath, and Merari.

¹²Judah and his sons: Shelah, Perez, and Zerah. (Judah's other sons, Er and Onan, had died in Canaan.) Perez' sons were Hezron and Hamul.

¹³Issachar and his sons: Tola, Puah,[b] Jashub,[c] and Shimron.

¹⁴Zebulun and his sons: Sered, Elon, and Jahleel.

¹⁵These thirty-three were the sons that Jacob and Leah had while in Paddan-Aram, besides his daughter Dinah.

¹⁶Gad and his sons: Zephon,[d] Haggi, Shuni, Ezbon, Eri, Arodi, and Areli.

¹⁷Asher and his sons: Imnah, Ishvah, Ishvi, Beriah, and their sister Serah. Beriah's sons were Heber and Malchiel.

¹⁸These sixteen were the descendants of Jacob and Zilpah (the slave woman whom Laban gave to his daughter Leah).

¹⁹Jacob's sons with Rachel were Joseph and Benjamin. ²⁰In Egypt, Joseph had two sons, Manasseh and Ephraim, by Asenath (the daughter of Potiphera, a priest of On). ²¹Benjamin's sons were Bela, Becher, Ashbel, Gera, Naaman, Ehi, Rosh, Muppim, Huppim, and Ard. ²²These fourteen were the descendants of Jacob by Rachel.

²³Dan and his son: Hushim.

²⁴Naphtali and his sons: Jahzeel, Guni, Jezer, and Shillem. ²⁵These seven are the descendants of Jacob and Bilhah (the slave woman Laban gave to his daughter Rachel).

²⁶The total number of the direct descendants of Jacob who went to Egypt was sixty-six, not including his sons' wives. ²⁷Two sons were born to Joseph in Egypt, bringing the total number of Jacob's family who went there to seventy.

Joseph and His Father Jacob

²⁸Jacob sent Judah ahead to ask Joseph to lead them in Goshen. When they arrived, ²⁹Joseph got in his chariot and rode to Goshen to meet his father, Israel. As soon as Joseph saw

---

a 46:4 Within Jewish culture, even to this day, the nearest relative or oldest son would gently close the eyes of a loved one at death. Indeed, Joseph did as God had promised Jacob. See Gen. 49:33; 50:1.

b 46:13 The Masoretic text reads "Puvah." This translation follows the Samaritan Pentateuch and Syriac (see 1 Chron. 7:1).

c 46:13 The Masoretic text reads "Job." This translation follows the Samaritan Pentateuch and some LXX manuscripts which read "Jashub" following Numbers 26:24 and 1 Chronicles 7:1.

d 46:16 The Masoretic text reads "Ziphion." This translation follows the Samaritan Pentateuch and the LXX which read "Zephon" as Numbers 26:15.

his father, he threw his arms around his *father's* neck and wept for a long time.[a] [30]Israel said to Joseph, "I am ready to die, now that I have seen you and know that you are still alive."

[31]Then Joseph said to his brothers and all his father's family, "I must go and tell the king that my brothers and all my father's family have come to me from Canaan. [32]I will tell him that you are shepherds and take care of livestock and that you have brought with you your flocks and herds and all you own. [33]When the king calls for you and asks what your occupation is, [34]be sure to tell him that you and your fathers before you have herded livestock all your lives. Then he will let you live in the region of Goshen." Joseph said this because Egyptians despise shepherds.

Jacob Blesses Pharaoh

47 [1-2]Joseph took five of his brothers with him to Pharaoh and presented them to the king. Joseph said to Pharaoh, "My father and my brothers have come from Canaan with their flocks, their herds, and all that they own. They have made their camp in the region of Goshen."

[3]Pharaoh asked the men, "What is your occupation?"

"We, your servants, are shepherds, just as our fathers were," they answered. [4]"We have come to stay as temporary residents in this country, because in the land of Canaan, the famine is so severe that there is no pasture for your servants' flocks. Please give us permission to settle in the land of Goshen."

[5]Pharaoh said to Joseph, "Now that your father and your brothers have arrived, [6]the land of Egypt is theirs. Let them settle in the best part of the land, in the region of Goshen. And if there are any competent men among them, put them in charge of my own livestock."[b]

[7]Later, Joseph brought Jacob into the house and presented him before Pharaoh. And Jacob gave Pharaoh a blessing.[c]

[8]Pharaoh asked Jacob, "How old are you?"

[9]Jacob answered, "My earthly journey has been one hundred and thirty years. My years have been few and hard, but it doesn't compare to the length of the earthly journeys of my fathers." [10]Then Jacob blessed Pharaoh again and departed.

[11]So Joseph settled his father and brothers in the choicest part of the land of Egypt, in the district of Rameses,[d] as Pharaoh had commanded. [12]Joseph also provided his father and brothers and their families, down to their little ones, with all the food they needed.

---

a 46:29 Words completely fail to describe the emotion of this scene as father and son embrace! The great Egyptian lord was once more only a boy needing his father. After two decades, Jacob saw the son he had given up for dead. The two men stood, staring into each other's eyes—weeping. What a family reunion this was!

b 47:6 Or "place them as princes over my livestock," thus making them officers of the crown and granting them legal protection. Ancient Egyptian inscriptions tell of the Pharaoh owning huge herds of royal livestock with superintendents watching over them.

c 47:7 Or "Jacob greeted Pharaoh with great respect." Jacob blessed Pharaoh, not Pharaoh blessing Jacob! Although he was the highest person on earth, Pharaoh came under the blessing of Jacob. A refugee from Canaan became the "blesser" of Pharaoh! With the authority of a prophet, Jacob blessed Egypt's ruler. The fact that Jacob blessed Pharaoh proves that he was greater than Pharaoh (Heb. 7:7).

d 47:11 Rameses was another name for Goshen.

¹³Now there was no food anywhere, for the famine was very severe. Both the land of Egypt and the land of Canaan languished because of the famine. ¹⁴And the people of Egypt and Canaan spent all their money to buy grain. Joseph gathered all the money from the sale of grain and deposited the wealth into Pharaoh's treasury. ¹⁵When the money ran out in Egypt and Canaan, all the Egyptians came to Joseph and pleaded with him, "All our money is gone; give us food! Why would you let us die in front of your eyes?"

¹⁶Joseph answered, "If your money is gone, then give me your livestock. I will give you food in exchange for your livestock." ¹⁷So in that year, they brought their livestock to Joseph—their horses, sheep, cattle, and donkeys—and he supplied them with food in exchange for their livestock. ¹⁸The next year, they came to him and said, "Master, it's no secret to you that we are broke. All our silver and livestock are now yours. We have nothing left but ourselves and our lands. ¹⁹Why would you let us die in front of your eyes, leaving all our lands uninhabited? Buy us and our lands in exchange for food. We'll become Pharaoh's slaves and give up our land. Only give us seed so that we may live and not die and so that the land will not become a desert."

²⁰So Joseph gained possession of all the farmland in Egypt for Pharaoh. Every Egyptian sold his land *in exchange for food*, for the famine was that severe. Eventually, the Egyptians had transferred all the land to Pharaoh.ᵃ ²¹Everyone became a slave to Pharaoh,ᵇ from one end of Egypt to the other. ²²However, he did not take over the land of the priests, for they received royal subsidies from Pharaoh. They lived on the food he provided for them, and that is why they did not have to sell their land.

²³Joseph said to the people, "Today I have acquired for Pharaoh you and all your land. Here is seed for you to sow in the land. ²⁴But when harvest comes, you must pay one-fifth to Pharaoh, and you may keep the rest for planting your fields and for food for yourselves and your families to nourish your household and your little ones."

²⁵"You have saved our lives!" they said. "May we find your favor, our lord, and we will be slaves to Pharaoh." ²⁶Thus, Joseph established the law of the land in Egypt, which is still in effect, "A fifth will go to Pharaoh." Only the land of the priests did not become Pharaoh's.

Jacob's Last Request

²⁷Israel and his descendants settled in Egypt in the land of Goshen. They had many children and multiplied, and they acquired property.

²⁸Jacob lived in Egypt for seventeen years and lived a total of one hundred and forty-seven years. ²⁹When the time of Israel's death was near, he summoned his *beloved* son Joseph and said to him, "*Son*, do me this favor

---

a 47:20 This was perhaps one of the greatest transferences of wealth in human history! This is important. For when the Israelites leave Egypt, this is the wealth they will take with them (Ex. 12:36). God used Joseph to make Egypt rich; in time, Egypt gave it back to God's people—with interest.

b 47:21 As translated from the Samaritan Pentateuch and the Septuagint. The Hebrew reads, "he removed the people to the cities."

before I die: Place your hand under my thigh as a pledge that you will show me kindness and loyal love. Do not bury me in Egypt, ³⁰but when I go to rest with my fathers, I want you to carry me out of Egypt and bury me where they are buried.ᵃ ³¹Swear that you will do this."

So Joseph took the oath and said, "I will do as you say."

Then Israel worshiped and leaned on the top of his staff.ᵇ

Jacob Blesses Joseph's Sons

48 Not long afterward, Joseph received the news that his father's health was failing, so he took his two sons Manasseh and Ephraim along with him. ²When Jacob heard that they had come to see him, Israel rallied his strength and sat up in bed.

³Jacob said to Joseph, "The God who is more than enough appeared to me at Bethelᶜ in the land of Canaan where he blessed me! ⁴He said to me, 'I will make you fruitful and multiply your descendants until I have made you a company of nations. And I will give this land to your descendants for an everlasting possession.' ⁵Furthermore, I will adopt as my very own your two sons who were born in the land of Egypt before I came here. *Yes*, I claim Ephraim and Manasseh as mine, no less than *my two oldest*,

Reuben and Simeon. ⁶As for any children born after them, they will be considered yours. They will receive their portion of the inheritance in the same territory as their brothers. ⁷For when I was returning from Paddan-Aram, *my beloved* Rachel died, to my sorrow, in the land of Canaan while we were still on our way, not far from Ephrath. So I buried her there beside the road to Ephrath (that is, Bethlehem)."

⁸When Israel noticed Joseph's two sons, he said, "Who are these?"

⁹"They are the sons that God has graciously given me here." Joseph said to his father.

"Please bring them closer," he said, "so that I may bless them."

¹⁰Now Israel could barely see, for his eyes were failing because of old age. So, Joseph brought his sons closer to him, and Joseph's father, *their grandfather*, hugged and kissed them.

¹¹*Tearfully*, Israel said to Joseph, "I never thought I'd see your face again, and now, God has let me see my grandchildren as well!"

Jacob Blesses His Grandchildren

¹²Joseph then removed them from his father's knees and bowed low in respect before his father with his face to the ground. ¹³And Joseph took his sons and had them stand facing their

---

a 47:30 This refers to the cave of Machpelah purchased by Abraham from the Hittites in chapter 23. Why did his burial place matter so much to Jacob? He was looking forward to the time of resurrection! Abraham, Isaac, and Jacob were all buried near the ancient site of Jerusalem, where many centuries later Jesus would be crucified, buried, and raised from the dead. On the day Jesus was nailed to the Cross, we are told that tombs nearby opened, and many holy people arose in resurrection life and were seen walking about the city (Matt. 27:52–53)! In faith, Jacob asked to be buried near the spot where the Messiah would be crucified! God honored that faith and raised many holy people to life in order to glimpse the city they had only dreamed of! Jacob knew the fulfillment of the promise would be in Canaan, not Egypt.

b 47:31 Or "by the head of his bed." See Heb. 11:21.

c 48:3 Or "Luz," the ancient name of Bethel. This appearance was with the heavenly stairway reaching into heaven. See Gen. 28:10–19.

grandfather Israel,[a] Ephraim at Israel's left hand, and Manasseh at Israel's right hand.[b] [14]But Israel crossed his arms, and stretched out his right hand on the head of the younger son, Ephraim, and his left hand on the head of the firstborn son, Manasseh. [15]He spoke this blessing over them:[c]

"May the God of my fathers,
    Abraham and Isaac, who lived
    devoted to him,
    the God who has been my Shepherd from my birth until this day,
    [16]the Angel who has delivered me
    from all harm,[d]
    may he bless these boys!
May their lives echo my name,
    and the names of my fathers
    Abraham and Isaac.
May they multiply into teeming
    multitudes throughout the earth!"

[17]When Joseph saw his father place his right hand on Ephraim's head, he was not happy, so he tried to move his father's hand from Ephraim to Manasseh's head. [18]"Not that way," Joseph said to his father, "Here, father, put your right hand on the firstborn's head." [19]But his father refused and said, "I know, my son, I know. Manasseh's descendants will also multiply and become a great people. His younger brother will become even greater than he, and his tribe will one day give rise to many nations."[e]
[20]So Jacob blessed them that day, saying,
"Israel will use your names when they pronounce blessings!
They will say, 'May God make you like Ephraim and like Manasseh!'"[f]

So *the crossing of his arms during* Jacob's blessing put Ephraim ahead of Manasseh. [21]Then Israel said to Joseph, "Son, I will die soon, but God's presence will go with you, and one day, he will take you back to the land of your

a 48:13 By placing them before him like this, Israel recognized Joseph's sons as his own by adoption. By adopting Joseph's sons, Jacob removed the firstborn blessing from Reuben and gave it to Joseph's sons.
b 48:13 Joseph positioned his sons so that Jacob's right hand would rest on the firstborn, Manasseh.
c 48:15 Or "Joseph." The Septuagint is "them."
d 48:16 The Lord had visited Jacob as an Angel, the Midnight Wrestling Man, his true Friend. At the end of Jacob's life, he could say that his Shepherd-Friend had delivered him from all harm. Instead of moaning and complaining about his hardships, this servant of God declared the mercy that had preserved him. Christ, the Angel of the Covenant, redeems us from all evil.
e 48:19 As the Spirit of Prophecy fell upon Jacob, he knew that it was God's will to bless and honor Ephraim above his brother Manasseh. Once again, the younger was set above the older and was given a greater blessing and a greater work. Maneuvering is our choosing, our selecting. Blessing is God's choice. It had taken Jacob a lifetime to learn this lesson: It is far better to wait until the blessing of God is seen and give up our maneuvering to have our own way.
f 48:20 Ephraim and Manasseh became strong leaders in Israel. Their descendants multiplied and grew mighty. Joshua was of the tribe of Ephraim, and so was Jeroboam. The tribe of Manasseh was divided after the conquest with one half on one side of the Jordan and the other half on the other side of the river. Jacob, foreseeing this division would weaken the tribe, "crossed" his arms! This blessing spoken by Jacob endured and still endures. When the Lord blesses, no one can turn it aside (Num. 23:8, 20). Jacob's hands that deceived and grasped what was not his have now become the hands that bless out of an overflow of life. The "heel-holder" became the "blessing-giver." The day will come when this transformation will take place in you as well.

ancestors. ²²I give you one mountain slope more than your brothers, the mountain slope of Shechem, *the fertile region* I took from the Amorites with my own sword and my own bow."ᵃ

Jacob's Last Words

4 9 Jacob called all his sons together and gathered them around his bedside. He said to them, "Let me prophesy to you about your future *destinies:*ᵇ

²"Come together and listen to me,
   O sons of Jacob
Listen to your father Israel.ᶜ

³"Reuben, my firstborn, you are my strength
and the firstfruits of my manhood.
You are preeminent in pride
and surpassing others in power.
⁴You are unstable—as turbulent as floodwaters;
you will no longer excel,
for you have slept with my concubineᵈ
and defiled yourself in your father's bed!ᵉ

⁵"Simeon and Levi, you are *two of a kind* and brothers *in crime,*

---

a 48:22 The Hebrew text is somewhat ambiguous, for the word for mountain slope can also mean "Shechem." The translator has chosen to leave both possibilities in the text. Additionally, it may be a reference to Mount Gerizim, which stands above Shechem. The implication is that because Joseph was raised up, he will inherit the higher ground.

b 49:1 The struggle between flesh and spirit had been fierce and protracted in Jacob, but as the end drew near, he ministered from a deep well as the Spirit of Prophecy fell upon him. Jacob became a shaper of destiny for his children as God revealed to him the future of his sons. His prophecies were based both on their character and on their actions. He spoke into their destinies and described God's plan for each one. Genesis 49 also prophesies to the day in which we live. The rest of the Old Testament and all the New Testament are the development of Genesis 49. These verses require the whole Bible for their understanding. How profound are the prophecies of Jacob!

c 49:2 The order of the blessings given by Jacob corresponds to the sons of Leah, then Bilhah, then Zilpah, two more sons of Leah, and finally the two sons of Rachel (Joseph and Benjamin). In the book of Numbers, the order of Jacob's sons is given by their encampment where they were situated in relation to the Tabernacle. In Exodus, they are the twelve gemstones on the breastplate of the High Priest. In Revelation, they are the twelve gates of the New Jerusalem. One of the surprising things in the Bible is that the names of Jacob's sons are inscribed on the gates of pearls through which God's people must pass. The names of the gates of pearls are Jacob's sons. This shows that God is the One who transforms the worst of us and makes us his pearls for eternity. All who enter the New Jerusalem will enter by the gates of the tribes. As Jacob's "spiritual sons," we can see our lives in the history and transformation of Jacob's sons.

d 49:4 Or "you went up to your father's bed," a euphemism for sleeping with his father's concubine.

e 49:4 See Gen. 35:22. Joseph received Reuben's birthright because he fled from the very defilement Reuben indulged in (Gen. 39:7–12). Joseph did not lie with Potiphar's wife, even though she begged him. Joseph gained by purity what Reuben lost by defilement. This birthright is not only the inheritance of a double portion of land and possessions but also to inherit the privileges of headship and priesthood. Reuben lost it all, even though he likely repented and was pardoned. You may be first in line for the blessing, but it is how you finish that counts. Sinful acts can disqualify you for spiritual privilege and leadership.

for your swords have committed
violent acts.
⁶O my soul, let me not join in their
secret plans.ᵃ
O my heart, never let me be
counted in their assembly,
for they killed men in fits of rage,
and for pleasure, they maimed
an ox.ᵇ
⁷Cursed be their anger, for it is
fierce,
and their wrath so relentless.
I will divide your descendants
throughout Jacob's *territory*

and scatter them throughout
Israel.ᶜ

⁸"O Judah, your brothers will praise
you.ᵈ
You will conquer your foes in
battle,ᵉ
And your father's sons will bow
down before you.
⁹Judah, you are like a young lion
who has devoured its prey, my
son, and departed.
Like a lion, he crouches and lies
down,

---

a 49:6 See Ps. 1:1.

b 49:6 Joseph was figuratively the ox they tried to hurt (Deut. 33:17).

c 49:7 Jacob chose neither Simeon nor Levi to replace Reuben as the firstborn, and they received no blessing because they were men of anarchy, not righteousness. Both Simeon and Levi had a disposition to kill others. Instead of using their swords for self-defense, they wielded their weapons in cruel rage to slaughter and plunder the city of Shechem (Gen. 34:25–30). Simeon and Levi themselves are not cursed, only their anger. By all accounts, Simeon became the fiercest tribe among all of Israel. When Ezekiel described the final division of the land, he included a portion for Simeon (Ezek. 48:24). They are one of the sealed tribes mentioned in Revelation 7:7. There is also a gate in the eternal city on which the name Simeon is inscribed (Rev. 21:12). In the New Testament another "Simeon" is named (*Simon* Peter), who once used a sword to cut off an ear. Even so, Simeon's destiny was to be "one who hears" from God and who blesses others with God's Word (1 & 2 Peter). Concerning Levi, because his natural ways were transformed, he was privileged to carry God's Urim and Thummim as a priest (Deut. 33:8). Levites had the wonderful privilege of serving God in his presence. Their inheritance was not a piece of land (Josh. 14:4), but the privilege of intimate worship. From the story of the Levites, we learn that God can redeem and transform us, even if we have lost our blessing because of past failures. Moses, the author of Genesis, was from the tribe of Levi!

d 49:8 Judah eventually became the source of leadership in Israel, the father of the Davidic dynasty, and ancestor of the Messiah, Jesus Christ. Even the word "Jew" derives from Yehudi (Judahite). In the Spirit, Jacob saw the blessing of honor and power descending upon his son, Judah. He would be a strong and courageous leader, with others showing him great honor. Remember, Judah became a changed man and displayed his true character by offering himself as a substitute for Benjamin (Gen. 44:33–34). The tribe of Judah produced many kings, and some were quite notable in their exploits for God. A conquering, ruling tribe, Judah remained somewhat faithful when the nation divided. Judah was to have the leadership among his brothers. See 1 Chron. 5:2.

e 49:8 Or "your hand will be upon the neck of your enemies."

and like a lioness—who dares to
awaken him?[a]
[10]The scepter of rulership will not
be taken from Judah,
nor the ruler's staff from his
descendants,
until the Shiloh comes[b]
and takes what is due him,
for the obedience of nations
belongs to him.

[11]He will tether his donkey to the
vine
and his purebred colt to the choicest branch.
He will wash his garments in wine
and his robe in the blood of
grapes.[c]
[12]His eyes are more exhilarating
than wine[d]
and his teeth whiter than milk.[e]

---

a 49:9 Judah is a wonderful picture of the One who is seen as the Mighty Lion of Judah. For Jesus Christ is the One who places his omnipotent hand on the neck of his enemies and delivers us. The lion, the king of beasts, terrifies its prey with his roar. When he seizes his prey, no one can resist him. After he has seized his prey, no one pursues him or seeks revenge, for the lion is a conqueror. Judah is compared to three kinds of lions: a young lion, a mature hunting lion, and a lioness. This is more than a prophecy of the tribe of Judah becoming strong and mighty; it is a prophecy of One who will come from Judah to devour his prey. Jesus is not a raging Lion; he is a resting Lion who has conquered every foe. He crouched and took his cross, but now lies down in perfect peace. His victory is total and secure. Who would dare rouse a lion when he is lying down after his kill, and who would rouse a lioness while she is guarding her cubs? These three phrases to describe the lion are truly descriptive of what our Savior-King has done for us! Jesus came as our Savior, "a young lion." He laid down his life on the cross to destroy the one who held us in fear of death. He was raised again to be seated at God's right hand, "like a lion, he crouches and lies down." Today, he guards us with tender love and compassion, "like a lioness."

b 49:10 Or "until he comes to Shiloh." The Messiah is the One given the name "Shiloh" or "the One whose right it is (to take the throne)" (Ezek. 21:27). When Jesus stood before Pilate, the people willingly allowed the scepter, or authority to rule, to depart from Judah (John 18:31). They gave up the power to rule and handed it over to a foreigner (Romans). The departing of the scepter was a sign that Shiloh, the One whose right it is to rule, had come! He has taken the scepter as the emblem of his authority to rule over nations. See Num. 24:17; Ps. 45:6.

c 49:11 In this poetic prophecy, we are given wonderful descriptions of the fruit of Christ's righteous rule over us. There will be great prosperity and fullness. He will impart his servant nature (donkey tethered to a vine, the church) and his purebred colt (display of his splendor, as Jesus rode into Jerusalem riding on a colt) to the choicest branch (we are the branches of his life, John 15). His garments (gifts) will be washed in wine (soaked in the anointing of the Holy Spirit), and his robes (righteous life) in the blood of grapes (in the power of the Spirit and the Blood). See Isa. 63:2.

d 49:12 As translated from the Septuagint. The Hebrew is "red with wine" or "darker than wine."

e 49:12 His dark eyes and white teeth point to the coming One, who will bring an abundance of wine and milk. His eyes are darker than wine, not by outward coloring, but from the inward, energizing wine of God's Spirit. The redness of his eyes speaks of the fires of holy passion, eyes of fire (Rev. 1:14). His white teeth speak of the vigor and healthy power of his person. He is rich in love and rich in power! He has drunk of the Holy Spirit deeply and without measure from the milk of God's loving heart.

¹³"Zebulunᵃ will settle along the
seashore
and become a safe harbor for ships,
and his borders will extend to
Sidon.ᵇ

¹⁴"Issachar is a strong donkeyᶜ
lying down between its
saddlebags.ᵈ
¹⁵When he sees that his resting
place is good,

and his portionᵉ is so pleasant,
then he will bend his shoulder to
the burden
and labor for his master.ᶠ

¹⁶"Dan will provide justiceᵍ for his
people
as one of the tribes of Israel.
¹⁷Dan will be a snake waiting by
the roadside,
like a snake in the grass.

---

a 49:13 Having spoken of the tribe from which Jesus was born (Judah), Jacob now prophesies of Zebulun, the tribe in whose territory he lived. Jesus began his ministry in the area settled by Zebulun. The people of Zebulun were the first to see this great Light dawning (Matt. 4:15–16). The disciples of Galilee were like a fleet of ships carrying the light of the gospel to the nations. It was from a mountain top in Galilee that Jesus sent out his disciples to the nations (Matt. 28:16–19) like ships of mercy. As the Galileans went out with the glad tidings, they became havens of refuge and a blessing to many. The tribe of Zebulun were known as merchants dwelling near the sea, who traded goods with others. Deborah praised their bravery for rallying to the cause and fighting against Sisera (Judg. 5:14–18). Elon, one of the mighty deliverers mentioned in Judges, was a valiant man from this tribe (Judg. 12:11–12). They were men of "undivided loyalty" to the king (1 Chron. 12:33).

b 49:13 Sidon is often a metonymy for Phoenicia, or southern Lebanon.

c 49:14 The Sons of Issachar are donkeys; they are meant to be burden bearers. A horse loves speed; a donkey is made for carrying burdens. A donkey is focused and sure-footed when it walks on mountain heights. A horse needs blinders or things will easily distract it; but a donkey keeps its attention on the trail ahead. A donkey can endure weeks of hard conditions with little rest, so true intercessors don't stop until they get their answer. The men of Issachar are noted in Scripture as those *"who understood the times and knew what Israel should do."* (1 Chron. 12:32). They become the counterpart of the intercessor of today.

d 49:14 The Hebrew *mishpetayim* is a homonym for "sheepfolds." Some scholars render it "campfires." It implies that the burdened donkey found a resting place near the sheep, near the campfire, and between saddlebags, ready to carry afresh the burden of the Lord.

e 49:15 Or "his land."

f 49:15 Issachar is truly a picture of the intercessor. There is an anointing of rest for those who give their lives in intercession. Nothing will shake their confidence, for they have entered his rest (Heb. 3:11). Issachar, the donkey, saw that rest was good. Nobody else did. He saw the anointing of rest. Burdens must be carried but carried within the pleasant land of resting in God's sweet presence. We must bow our shoulders to the burden of the Lord. God has a burden to share, but he waits for intercessors to find the resting place and to bow their shoulder to his burden. True Sons of Issachar will submit to voluntary labor and become slaves to prayer! Issachar bore it because he could see in the Spirit what God wanted to do in the land. God offers to his intercessors, his friends, the opportunity to partner with him to bring these things to pass. We must remember, it was a donkey that carried Jesus into Jerusalem. Could it be that intercessors are those whom God has chosen to "carry" his presence into the nations? We are to release them, for the Master needs his intercessors.

g 49:16 Or "judge." This is a wordplay on the name Dan. See Gen. 30:6 (and footnote).

He bites the horse's heels,
making its rider fall
backward.*

¹⁸"I wait in hope for your salvation,
O Yahweh!*

¹⁹"Gad will be raided by raiders,

but he will raid at their heels and
overcome them at last.*

²⁰"Asher's food will be rich,
and he will provide delicacies fit
for a king.*

²¹"Naphtali is a doe* set free,

---

a 49:17 The destiny of the tribe of Dan was to provide justice. As the conscience of the nation, they were to excel in helping against the suppression of an enemy. Just as a snake can strike at the legs of a horse and overthrow a mightier animal, so God would anoint Dan to administer justice when oppressed by others. Like a crafty serpent, this tribe would attack their enemies suddenly. Samson, one of the judges, was a Danite. Like a cunning serpent, Samson pulled down the house on the heads of the Philistines (Judg. 16:23–30); like a horse throwing off its rider so he tumbles backwards. Although Dan won the victory, it made him more independent and prouder. Soon, the tribe established a center of worship among them, with an idol erected by Micah there (Judg. 18:30). The idolatry of the tribe of Dan became one of the greatest stumbling blocks for the nation of Israel. Dan also bit the heels of God's people and made them stumble backwards! What potential we each have to bless or hinder God's people. The genealogies of 1 and 2 Chronicles omit the tribe of Dan altogether. During Joshua's conquest and allotment of the land, he gave the Danites no specific borders. Dan is not listed among the sealed tribes in Revelation 7.

b 49:18 Jacob interrupts his prophecy with a prayer. See Ps. 119:166. The Hebrew word for deliverance is similar to Yeshua, the Hebrew name for Jesus. Jacob, looking to the end of the ages, saw the coming of Jesus! Jesus is the true Judge of all the earth, who alone will provide justice for his people. Where Dan failed, Jesus will succeed in leading us into the salvation (deliverance) of the Lord.

c 49:19 Or literally, "A troop will troop upon Gad, but he will troop on their heels and overcome the troop at last." Gad symbolizes the beginning of the victorious life of an overcomer breaking forth. Throughout Israel's history, the Gadites were tremendous warriors. See Deut. 33:20–21; 1 Chron. 5:18–20; 12:8.

d 49:20 In Christ, you feast on food fit for kings, for you are in his royal family. Truly, we are blessed in grace—we have both a kingly family and royal dining! Rich food fit for a king. How would you like a prophetic word like this spoken over you? Asher's portion would be blessed with royal dainties. Out of the victory of Christ, Asher's portion is yours! Moses said of the tribe of Asher in Deut. 33:24–25 that their feet would be "bathed in oil." Oil soaked feet speaks of walking in the anointing and richness of the Holy Spirit. His footprints would be in oil. He will be anointed with the oil of gladness. Everywhere he walked he would leave the anointing and blessing of the Holy Spirit. The tribe of Asher settled in one of the most fertile places in Canaan and were exporters of oil and crops.

e 49:21 What a wonderful word picture this is. Psalm 22 has as its inscription, "To the tune of 'The Deer at the Dawning of the Day.'" Psalm 22 prophesied the death and resurrection of our Lord. Jesus is the Doe set free. With Naphtali, we see Christ not only as the victorious Lion but also as the resurrected Doe skipping on the mountaintops in freedom. He is the Resurrected Doe of the Morning Glory! The name *Naphtali* means "wrestling." What freedom we experience when we get up from our "wrestling match" a changed person and run to the mountains with him in victory (Song. 4:6–15). He has paid the price for our freedom; he has loosed us from our sins that we may run with him in resurrection life. We are his beautiful fawns. The Hebrew root word for "doe" can be translated "mighty man."

who bestows beauty on his
offspring.[a]

[22]"Joseph is a fruitful vine,
a fruitful vine growing by a
spring,[b]
whose branches[c] run over a wall.[d]
[23]Persecuters[e] fiercely attacked him;
they pursued him with their bow
and arrows.[f]
[24]But Joseph's bow remained
steady,
because the power of the Mighty
One of Jacob strengthened him,[g]

by the name of the *loving* Shepherd, the Rock[h] of Israel.
[25]The God of your father will help
and protect you;
the God who is more than enough
will bless you.
He will bless you with the blessings of heaven,
blessings of the deep that lie
beneath,
and blessings of the breast and
womb.
[26]The blessings of your father will
be greater

---

a 49:21 Or "speaks beautiful words" or "words that glisten." How lovely and powerful are the words of our resurrected Doe. This could refer to the Great Commission of Matthew 28 when Jesus gathered his disciples together on a mountaintop and sent them out with beautiful words, good news to preach to all peoples. When we have tasted the resurrection, we have beautiful words to give others.

b 49:22 He is called a "fruitful vine near a spring" or "by a fountain." Joseph, the clearest type of Christ in the Old Testament, is seen as a fruitful vine. The Lord Jesus called himself the fruitful vine and us his branches (John 15). When the Fruitful Vine lives through us, the fruit of the Spirit begins to be seen in our personality (Gal. 5:22–23). Jesus "branches out" through us, just as he branches out from the Father. Joseph, as a fruitful vine, dwelt near God. Joseph was God's "branching" out in a man (Zech. 3:8; 6:12). The "spring" or fountain is the life of the Father (Gen. 16:14; Ps. 68:26; John 4:14). The source of his life and purity was from the spring of eternal life dwelling in him (Ps. 1:3). All Joseph's fruitfulness came from the water of that Divine "spring."

c 49:22 Or "daughters."

d 49:22 Joseph, as a fruitful vine, has branches that run over the wall. The life of Christ in the believer will climb over a wall. Nothing will limit the branching forth of Christ in us when we walk in the Joseph anointing. Our Joseph has many branches that climb over our walls. No matter how high the wall, Joseph's branches will run over it. Even if you are taken into captivity to Egypt's dungeon, the springing well will cause your branch to climb over the walls. Nothing can hem you in if you dwell by the Fountain. We are his branches connected to a fruitful Tree who will bear his likeness and the fruit of his life in us. The enemy will always try to erect walls to restrict your fruitfulness, but his life will still climb over them all.

e 49:23 Or "Warriors (enemies)."

f 49:23 Arrows are often used metaphorically for slander and false accusation. Joseph was a victim of both. See Jer. 9:23, 7–8. The slander and abuse of others could not keep Joseph from his destined promotion, nor can the words of others hold you back when you set your heart on pleasing God.

g 49:24 The Hebrew text reads literally, "The arms of his hands were made strong by the hands of the mighty One of Jacob." God is pictured as putting his hands on Joseph's hands, placing his arms on Joseph's arms. The mighty God laid his hand upon Joseph's hand, stretched his arm upon the arm of Joseph, and strengthened him! And God will do this for you!

h 49:24 See Ps. 80:1; Isa. 30:29. The Hebrew is "the Stone of Israel," which may refer to the stone Jacob used as a pillow and while sleeping saw the stairway of the sky (Gen. 28:11–12, 18).

than the blessings of the eternal
mountains,
surpassing the blessings of my
ancestors![a]
May Joseph's blessings crown his
head
and rest on the brow of the one
set apart,[b]
prince among his brothers.

27"Benjamin is a ferocious wolf.[c]
In the morning, he devours his
prey;
in the evening, he divides the spoil."[d]

28All these men became the twelve
tribes of Israel.[e] These were prophetic
words their father spoke to them when
he blessed them, blessing each son
with a parting word appropriate to him.

The Death of Jacob
29Afterward, Jacob *sat on the side of his
bed* and instructed his sons with these
words: "I am about to join my people
in death. Bury me with my ancestors
in the cave of the field of Ephron
the Hittite—30the cave in the field of
Machpelah, near Mamre, in the land
of Canaan. My grandfather Abraham
purchased that field as a burial site
from Ephron the Hittite. 31*My grandfather* Abraham and *my grandmother*
Sarah are buried there. *My father* Isaac
and *my mother* Rebekah were buried

there also. And it is the place I buried
my wife Leah. 32So, *bury me there*, in
that cave, in the field that was purchased from the Hittites."

33When Jacob finished his final words
of instruction to his sons, he lifted his
feet onto the bed, breathed his last,
and was gathered to his people.

Jacob's Funeral
50 Joseph flung himself over
Jacob, kissing him and weep-
ing. And his tears fell on his father's
face. 2-3*When he was able to compose
himself,* he ordered the royal physi-
cians to embalm his father. So, they
began the required forty-day process.
The Egyptians mourned for Israel for
seventy days, 4and when the weeping
period was over, Joseph approached
Pharaoh's officials and said to them,
"Please, may I ask a personal favor?
Bring my appeal before Pharaoh and
tell him:[f] 5"My dying father made me
promise that I would bury him in the
land of Canaan—in a tomb he had
hewn with his own hands. Please give
me permission to go and bury my
father; then I will return.'"

6Pharaoh said to Joseph, "Go to
Canaan, bury your father, and keep
your promise to him."

7So Joseph went to Canaan to bury
his father, and all the officials of Pharaoh, the elite members of his court,

---

a 49:26 The Hebrew is uncertain.

b 49:26 The Hebrew implies Joseph was "separated like a Nazarite (for God)." It looked as if
Joseph had been in exile for thirteen years when, in fact, he was being prepared by God and
set apart for his true destiny.

c 49:27 Or possibly, "Benjamin shall tear a wolf in pieces."

d 49:27 The tribe of Benjamin was war-like and known as fearless soldiers. See Ehud (Judg.
3:15), and Judg. 5:14; 20:15–16, 21, 25; 1 Chron. 12:2. King Saul was a Benjamite. In the New
Testament, Saul of Tarsus, a Benjamite, became the Apostle Paul, who fought the excellent
fight of faith (Phil. 3:5).

e 49:28 This is the first of many biblical references to the "twelve tribes of Israel."

f 50:4 A mourner was considered unclean and unable to come directly to Pharaoh, so Joseph
made his appeal to Pharaoh's officials. See Est. 4:2.

and all of Egypt's dignitaries accompanied him. [8]All of Joseph's household and all his brothers and their father's household went, too. Only the children and livestock remained behind in Goshen. [9]Many chariots and horsemen—a huge entourage—accompanied Joseph *to Canaan* in a grand procession!

[10]When they arrived at the threshing floor of Atad[a] on the other side of the Jordan,[b] they mourned loudly with bitter sorrow for a long time. And Joseph spent seven days there in ceremonial mourning for his father.[c] [11]When the people of Canaan saw the depth of mourning at the threshing floor of Atad, they said, "This is a solemn occasion of grief for the Egyptians," and named the place near the Jordan, The Mourning of the Egyptians.[d]

[12]So Jacob's sons did as they were instructed [13]and carried his body to the land of Canaan. They buried him there in the cave in the field of Machpelah near Mamre, where Abraham had purchased a burial place from Ephron the Hittite. [14]After burying his father, Joseph returned to Egypt with his brothers and all who had gone with him to bury his father.

Joseph Comforts His Brothers

[15]When the brothers realized they were now without their father, they said, "What if Joseph still bears a grudge against us and decides to pay us back for all the trouble we brought on him?" [16]So they sent this message to Joseph: "Before he died, your father left us this instruction: [17]'Tell Joseph that I beg him to completely forgive the sin of his brothers who treated him so harshly.' Now, please forgive us, servants of the God of your father, of the horrible wrong we did to you." Joseph cried and wept as they read this message to him.[e]

[18]Then his brothers came and threw themselves down before Joseph's feet, saying, "We are here as your slaves!"

[19]But Joseph *dried his tears* and said, "Don't be afraid. How could I ever take the place of God?[f] [20]Even though you intended to hurt me, God intended it for good. *It was his plan all along,*[g] to ensure the survival of many people. So, don't worry. I myself will provide for you all that you need, both for you and your little ones." [21]Then with *more* kind, reassuring words, Joseph comforted his brothers.

---

a 50:10 Atad means "brambles."

b 50:10 The phrase "the other side of the Jordan" usually refers to Transjordan. It is possible that the funeral procession crossed over the Jordan near Jericho, the place where Joshua would later cross with Israel to take possession of Canaan.

c 50:10 A strict custom of a seven-day period of mourning remains in Judaism even to this day. See 1 Sam. 31:13; Job 2:13. For the first time, Joseph returned to what had been his boyhood home for thirty-nine years, sadly, for his father's funeral.

d 50:11 Or in Hebrew, *Abel Mizraim*.

e 50:17 Their shame brought him to tears. Without hesitation, he offered them reassurance and forgiveness. Joseph spoke kindly to those who hurt him, and he comforted their hearts. He refused to harbor a grudge or treat them differently for what they had done.

f 50:19 Only God can judge, for he has perfect love and knows all things. Since we are not in his place, we have only the right to forgive. Many assume the role of a judge when they have someone cornered and vulnerable, but Joseph refused. He understood that God turned the evil intentions of others into something good. God has power to transform pain into blessing when we love him through it all.

g 50:20 See Prov. 16:9; 20:24; Rom. 8:28.

Joseph Dies in Egypt

²²Joseph lived in Egypt along with his father's family and lived to be one hundred and ten years old.ᵃ ²³He lived to see the third generation of Ephraim's children. Joseph also lived to see the children of Makir, son of Manasseh; and Joseph gave Makir's children inheritance rights.ᵇ

²⁴Then Joseph declared to his brothers, "I will die one day, but God will certainly come to youᶜ and fulfill his promises to bring you *and your descendants* from this land and lead you to the land he promised to Abraham, Isaac, and Jacob." ²⁵So Joseph had his brothers, the sons of Israel, make a solemn oath, saying, "When God comes to you, you will carry my bones up from Egypt."ᵈ

²⁶Joseph died at the age of one hundred and ten. He was embalmed and placed in a coffin in Egypt.ᵉ

---

a 50:22 From ancient Egyptian writings we learn that Egyptians considered the age of one hundred and ten to be the ideal life span.

b 50:23 Or "Makir's children were born on Joseph's knees," a figure of speech for being given inheritance rights.

c 50:24 Or "visit you."

d 50:25 Even in death, Joseph fixed his eyes on eternity. Joseph foresaw life beyond the grave. By his astonishing declaration about his bones, Joseph proclaimed he lived for the promises, rather than temporal concerns; he refused to be identified with his successes, accomplishments, or the blessings on his life, but only with the promises. He proclaimed that his home was not Egypt but the promised land. See Heb. 11:22.

e 50:26 Genesis began with God and ends with a coffin in Egypt. It begins with God's command for light to sparkle, thrusting its way throughout the universe, and it ends here with this sad moment as a family grieves over a loved one who passes away. Genesis ends with the reader longing for the curse of sin and death to be broken. Exodus will bring us closer to seeing the Passover Lamb (1 Cor. 5:8) who will one day be born to take away the sin of the world.

YOUR PERSONAL INVITATION
TO FOLLOW JESUS

We can all find ourselves in dark places, needing some light—light that brings direction, healing, vision, warmth, and hope. Jesus said, "I am light to the world and those who embrace me will experience life-giving light, and they will never walk in darkness" (John 8:12). Without the light and love of Jesus, this world is truly a dark place and we are lost forever.

Love unlocks mysteries. As we love Jesus, our hearts are unlocked to see more of his beauty and glory. When we stop defining ourselves by our failures, but rather as the ones whom Jesus loves, our hearts begin to open to the breathtaking discovery of the wonder of Jesus Christ.

All that is recorded in the Scriptures is there so that you will fully believe that Jesus is the Son of God, and that through your faith in him you will experience eternal life by the power of his name (see John 20:31).

If you want this light and love in your life, say a prayer like this—whether for the first time or to express again your passionate desire to follow Jesus:

Jesus, you are the light of the world. I want to follow you, passionately and wholeheartedly. But my sins have separated me from you. Thank you for your love for me. Thank you for paying the price for my sins, and I trust your finished work on the cross for my rescue. I turn away from the thoughts and deeds that have separated me from you. Forgive me and awaken me to love you with all my heart, mind, soul, and strength. I believe God raised you from the dead, and I want that new life to flow through me each day and for eternity. God, I give you my life. Now fill me with your Spirit so that my life will honor you and I can fulfill your purpose for me. Amen.

You can be assured that what Jesus said about those who choose to follow him is true: "If you embrace my message and believe in the One who sent me, you will never face condemnation, for in me, you have already passed from the realm of death into the realm of eternal life!" (John 5:24). But there's more! Not only are you declared "not guilty" by God because of Jesus, you are also considered his most intimate friend (John 15:15).

As you grow in your relationship with Jesus, continue to read the Bible, communicate with God through prayer, spend time with others who follow Jesus, and live out your faith daily and passionately. God bless you!